Spirit-led
Days

Day by Day with the Holy Spirit

Rev. Gordon Williams

with
Diane Roblin Lee

Spirit-led Days: Day by Day with the Holy Spirit
Copyright © 2003 Rev. Gordon Williams
All rights reserved
Printed in Canada
International Standard Book Number: 1-894860-26-8

Published by:
Castle Quay Books
1740 Pilgrims Way, Oakville, Ontario, L6M 1S5
Tel: (800) 265-6397 Fax: (519) 748-9835
E-mail: info@castlequaybooks.com
www.castlequaybooks.com

Copy Editing: Janet Dimond
Cover, Book Design and Layout: Diane Roblin Lee
Photo of Margaret Williams: Geoffrey Williams
Background Photography: Warren Lee
Logo Design: Rick and Sharon Janzen

Scripture quotations, unless otherwise indicated, are from the Revised Standard
Version of the Bible, Zondervan Bible Publishers, Grand Rapids, Michigan: fourteenth printing © 1981

National Library of Canada Cataloguing in Publication

Williams, Gordon, 1937
        Spirit-led days : day by day with the Holy Spirit / Gordon Williams ;
with Diane Roblin Lee.

Includes bibliographical references.
ISBN 1-894860-26-8

    1. Bible--Devotional use. I. Roblin Lee, Diane II. Title.

BV4811.W4493 2003   242'.5   C2003-904828-4

Dedication

Margaret Francis Williams

This devotional book is dedicated to my daily Counselor, the Holy Spirit, and to my daughter, Margaret Francis Williams.

Besides being our only daughter, and working closely with me in ministry, Margaret was a Christian songwriter and singer, whose music ministry, Life Line, produced two C.D. recordings entitled *The Answer* and *Fire and Water*. With the special friendship of her guide dog, Darcy, she learned to walk, day by day with the Holy Spirit, through her diabetes and blindness. Margaret never allowed her disabilities to prevent her from serving Jesus Christ, who promised to never fail her or forsake her (Hebrews 13:5). She was escorted by Him into His presence on November 25, 2000 (2 Corinthians 5:8).

3

Foreword

I first met my friend, Gordon Williams, when he joined the staff of Canada's first national Christian television ministry, 100 Huntley Street, hosted by our friend Rev. David Mainse. I know Gordon's wonderful family well: his wife Ruth, his daughter Margie and his three sons, Geoff, Karl and Doug.

Gordon was one of the five on-air clergy (representing Pentecostal, Anglican, Free Methodist, United Church and Roman Catholic faiths), their unity being part of the miracle of 100 Huntley Street.

Gordon and I shared an office and secretary for many years, giving me the opportunity to get to know him better than most, as a friend and colleague.

We have ministered together to many thousands of people over the years. We travelled across Canada and into the United States doing meetings, rallies, church services and television programs together. We hopscotched across Canada holding rallies and doing ministry during 100 Huntley Street's "Salute to Canada," which was a month of daily television programs originating in a different city each day; starting in Victoria, British Columbia, and ending in St. John's, Newfoundland.

Gordon is a person who loves Jesus and seeks the guidance of the Holy Spirit every day. This daily devotional book reflects his devotion to Jesus Christ. I recommend it to you because I know Jesus and I know Gordon. It is the result of many years of learning to develop ears that listen to the Holy Spirit.

Father Bob MacDougall, S.J.

Getting Acquainted
with the Holy Spirit

*T*rue understanding of the function of the Holy Spirit is the greatest secret in Christian circles today. It is a secret which prevents believers from living the balanced, normal Christian life Jesus came to bring – a secret that can be unlocked only through recognizing and receiving the daily ministry of the Holy Spirit. This daily guide has been designed as your key.

Of the three *real Persons* of the Trinity, the Holy Spirit is generally ignored as the greatest stranger. Jesus Christ came not only to provide salvation – *"For God so loved the world that He gave His only Son, that whoever believes in Him should not perish, but have eternal life"* (John 3:16) – but also to introduce the Holy Spirit to those who believe in Him.

John the Baptist explained this profound mystery, saying, *"I indeed baptize you with water for repentance, but He who is coming after me is mightier than I, whose sandals I am not worthy to carry; He will baptize you with the Holy Spirit and with fire"* (Matthew 3:11).

It is one thing to talk about God as being "triune" – a "Trinity" or "three Persons in One" – but it can be difficult to relate to Him in terms of the Holy Spirit. God the Father and God the Son seem acceptable, while an encounter with the Holy Spirit is often dismissed as an emotional experience or imagined enlightenment. The fact that He cannot be seen and dwells inside believers does not negate His existence. That is simply the nature of His being. He is never received naturally – only as a result of being supernaturally sent by Jesus to live or abide inside our bodies. Through His Holy Spirit, God is omnipresent.

The Holy Spirit is the Spirit of Jesus Christ (Romans 8:9), without whom we cannot belong to Jesus. He brings us under the Lordship of Jesus Christ (1 Corinthians 12:3b) and gives us power (Acts 1:8) to be able to witness about the things that Jesus has done in our lives and throughout history.

Jesus described the Holy Spirit as a Person. He called Him the "Counselor" or "Comforter." The Greek word means "defense lawyer." Because very few of us are fully acquainted with God's law, He knew we needed a "Counselor" who would be with us constantly; Somebody who not only knew God's law, but knew how to live by the *Spirit* of the Law so that we would not fall into the trap of legalism into which so many religious people fall. *"But the Comforter, which is the Holy Ghost, whom the Father will send in My Name, He shall teach you all things, and bring all things to your remembrance, whatsoever I have said unto you"* (John 14:26).

The Holy Spirit enables us to gain great rewards as we overcome our problems through Him (Revelation 2:7,11,17,26,29; Revelation 3:5,6,12-13,21-22). Having Him within makes us more *normal* – more like Jesus. He does not come to make us weird or strange, but to help us become *"conformed to the image of His Son"* (Romans 8:29).

The Holy Spirit is the One who gives us the power to *"present our bodies a living sacrifice, holy and acceptable to God which is our spiritual worship"* – not to be *"conformed to this world,"* but to be *"transformed by the renewal of our minds, that we may prove what is the will of God, what is good and acceptable and perfect"* (Romans 12:1,2).

He comes to do a work of "justification" by declaring us forgiven and clean before God. It is He who initiates the process of "sanctification" or "holy-ization" or "making saved people holy and keeping them holy" (1 Peter 1:2). It is only after a person has experienced what Jesus calls being "born anew" (John 3:3) and being baptized with the Holy Spirit (Acts 1:8) that he or she can then *"worship the Father in spirit and in truth"* (John 4:23). In other words, He prepares us for acceptable worship.

The Holy Spirit comes to equip us for ministry by distributing the gifts of the Holy Spirit (Romans 12:6–8; 1 Corinthians 12:1–11). These powerful gifts allow us to meet other people's needs as we serve Jesus Christ in the Church. While many have little understanding of the gifts and have preferred to discredit their use in the present age than risk any perceived confusion, we do not have to be afraid of what the Holy Spirit will do in our lives. Kathryn Kuhlman said many times, "The Holy Spirit is a Gentleman. He will never do anything to embarrass or hurt you." While He will come into our lives to empower us to carry out God's will and plan for our lives and our Church, He will never force Himself upon us. Never.

As one of my seminary professors at Princeton Theological Seminary, Dr. George F. Hendry, used to remind us over and over again, "The Heavenly Father is God over us. Jesus Christ is God who walks alongside of us. The Holy Spirit is God who comes and dwells inside of us." The Holy Spirit is God's Spirit and Jesus' Spirit. How unfortunate that He is a stranger to most Christians.

We need to take the time to get to know Him. He is a wonderful Person and desires to know us intimately – but He will come into our lives only upon invitation.

As a real Person, the Holy Spirit has a personality. He has a great sense of humour, is entirely reliable and will never let us down or disappoint us. Hebrews 13:5 assures us that He will never leave us nor forsake us. He comes in and brings the agape love (1 Corinthians 13:4–8) of God; to support us, strengthen us, encourage us and direct us.

The Holy Spirit protects us from deception. There are many spirits in this world of ours who are not from God, but there is only one Holy Spirit. By getting to know Him personally, we have protection from being led astray by evil or unclean spirits.

Jesus commands us – His Church – seven times in Revelation 2–3: "*He who has an ear, let him hear what the Spirit says to the Churches.*" The Holy Spirit is available as God's primary facilitator of communication through what is called "prayer." However, most people never hear Him because of the following:

1) They have never received Him on their own "Days of Pentecost." Too many have mistaken the experience of forgiveness and salvation, for the baptism of the Holy Spirit. (See my book, *Like a Rushing, Mighty Wind* for further explanation of this.)

2) They have never learned how to recognize the Holy Spirit's voice as He tries to communicate with them from the inside rather than the outside.

According to these commands of Jesus, we are supposed to be actively seeking the Holy Spirit's advice every day – hearing from Him regularly.

Because we have not learned this lesson and because of rampantly sinful, selfish feelings toward God, some church leaders regularly warn people not to be preoccupied with the Holy Spirit. One writer says, "Unfortunately, too many become so infatuated with the Holy Spirit and some of the tinglies that are associated with His presence that they marginalize Jesus Christ the Redeemer." **The reality is that we are supposed to be infatuated with the Holy Spirit because He makes us infatuated with the Father and with Jesus Christ.**

Another writer said, "Once we have put the three persons next to each other, almost like 'three gods,' we are not far away from allowing people to select their 'favorite god' out of this pantheon." What nonsense! Such thinking betrays what I call "spiritually Gentile thinking" by which sinful people discover excuses for jealousy because they want honour which is not theirs. God is not in competition with Himself. He is in *cooperation* with Himself. He *complements* Himself. The "Trinity," as explained as Father, Son and Holy Spirit is the only safe "pantheon" to choose from, because this so-called "pantheon" is the same One God.

Although God makes it very clear that He is a jealous God (Exodus 20:5; Deuteronomy 4:24), that jealousy does not extend to Himself or His Self-revelation of Himself as Father, Son and Holy Spirit. He is jealous only with regard to people worshiping and serving other gods in His place. No – God is not in competition with Himself. To honour any one of the Trinitarian revealed Persons of God is to honour them all.

When John the Baptist's disciples complained that Jesus was attracting more people than he, he replied, *"He must increase, but I must decrease"* (John 3:30). As we receive the baptism of the Holy Spirit, the self decreases as God increases within us, in order that we can be rightfully preoccupied with the Father, Son and Holy Spirit.

Having experienced the presence of the Holy Spirit in my own life, and knowing His transforming power, it is my desire that every person should have the experience that Jesus meant for us all – the baptism in the Holy Spirit. He provided it to accompany our salvation (Acts 19:2), so that we can have what I call "the *normal* Christian life."

Because most Christians do not know how to cooperate with the Holy Spirit as described in the New Testament, I was led to write a book, *Like A Rushing, Mighty Wind*, a couple of years ago. The response to that book has been tremendous. However, understanding must be followed by daily listening and hearing the voice of the Holy Spirit.

That is the reason for this daily devotional book. It has been designed as a tool to assist Christians in becoming acquainted with the Person and work of the Holy Spirit. Through daily prayer and meditation in the Scriptures, the ways of the Holy Spirit will become more familiar. His hand of guidance will become recognized so that God's plan for our lives can be accomplished through His power.

Welcome to the exciting work and ministry of the Holy Spirit. He will draw you closer to your Heavenly Father and help you to experience more of Jesus. Your eyes and ears will be opened to see and hear Him. Through the Holy Spirit, you will experience the love of God more perfectly. He will empower you to serve Jesus Christ faithfully with a new confidence. As you commune with Him daily, He will be your constant companion – sent special delivery from Jesus!

The Spirit in Creation

"and the Spirit of God was moving over the face of the waters" (Genesis 1:1–2:7).

The Holy Spirit was at work in the creation of the world, creating each element out of nothing. Jesus directed every detail (John 1:1–3), and wrought it into existence through the power of His Holy Spirit. Many people have a problem believing in the Biblical "Creation story." Paul tells us that, *"The unspiritual man does not receive the gifts of the Spirit of God, for they are folly to him, and he is not able to understand them because they are spiritually discerned"* (1 Corinthians 2:14).

I spoke once with a scientist in charge of the largest radio telescope in the world. He said that before he became a Christian, there were all sorts of things in the Bible's account of Creation that didn't fit together. It just didn't make sense. However, as soon as he invited Jesus Christ to come into his life and received the Holy Spirit, everything came together and made sense. Karl Barth, the theologian, once said, "As soon as we experience God's 'new creation' we can then understand God's first Creation." Creation can be understood only through faith in Jesus Christ.

Prayer

Holy Spirit, please recreate me out of the nothingness of sin so that I can see and understand things through faith.

Notes: _____

_____

_____

The Spirit Who Abides – for a Lifetime

"My Spirit shall not abide in man for ever, for he is flesh, but his days shall be a hundred and twenty years" (Genesis 6:1–8).

In the beginning, God gave His Spirit to His people. However, because of mankind's sin, He could not fulfill His original plan to allow people to live forever. *"You may freely eat of every tree in the garden; but of the tree of the knowledge of good and evil you shall not eat, for in the day that you eat of it you shall surely die"* (Genesis 2:16,17). Because of sin, Adam and Eve and all of their descendants were limited to 120 years, and later to 70 years (Psalms 90:10).

"Sin" is what God calls our actions when we break His laws and do not keep His commandments. It shortens our lives. God's justice demanded that people who cared to do what was right only in their own eyes would have to pay the consequences of their actions. His first consequence was to withdraw the Holy Spirit from them (1 Samuel 16:14); although today, once received, He never leaves us (Hebrews 13:5). The second consequence was to limit their life-span. *"For the wages of sin is death, but the free gift of God is eternal life in Christ Jesus our Lord"* (Romans 6:23).

Prayer

Holy Spirit, thank You for showing me the way out of sin, that I may live forever with You.

Notes: _____

_____

_____

Spirit-Led Days

The Spirit
Who Gives Favour

"Can we find such a man as this, in whom is the Spirit of God?" (Genesis 41:33–41).

*B*elieve it or not, non-believers can recognize the presence of the Holy Spirit in the lives of believers. Pharaoh saw God's favour resting on Joseph. Pharaoh had a dream that not even his wisest counselors could interpret – yet Joseph explained it. Egypt was about to face a period of seven years of unprecedented plenty, followed by seven years of total famine. Pharaoh's dream was a warning from God so that Egypt would not perish.

God still speaks in dreams to people today. In the *Book of Job*, we learn that, *"God speaks...in a dream, in a vision of the night"* (Job 33:14–18). The Holy Spirit still gives us the interpretation of dreams, sometimes to warn others, so they can be saved from impending disaster.

The wise person seeks the Holy Spirit so that he or she can serve God faithfully without complaining. God ministered through Joseph in a way he would not have chosen, yet in the most effective way, considering the big picture. Like Paul, we must learn to say, *"Not that I complain of want; for I have learned, in whatever state I am, to be content"* (Philippians 4:11).

Prayer

Holy Spirit, help me to be a person like Joseph, who serves You faithfully...wherever and however You lead me.

Notes: _____

_____

_____

The Spirit of Specialized Abilities

"See, I have called by name Bezalel...and I have filled him with the Spirit of God..." (Exodus 31:1–5).

The Holy Spirit still equips individuals whom God has chosen to be gifted supernaturally with various skills, abilities and gifts. Like Bezalel, we can be given *"ability and intelligence, with knowledge and all craftsmanship, to devise artistic designs...for work in every craft"* (Exodus 31:1–5). The Holy Spirit was the creative arm of God in Creation. No two people or creatures are identical. Every mountain, every river, every cloud, every snowflake is created to be unique. Is it so strange to understand that the Creator Holy Spirit can add to, and improve, His creative work in each one of us? He can increase our intelligence, give us knowledge that we have not acquired, and give us craftsmanship and artistry that will honour God. It is awesome to recognize that the Tabernacle was built and furnished with instruments of worship according to the specific instructions that God gave Moses to build – by ordinary people gifted to do extraordinary things through supernatural design.

Prayer

Holy Spirit, please give me special gifts and abilities so that I can be a faithful instrument of worship.

Notes:
_____

_____

The Spirit Shared

"I will take some of the Spirit which is upon you and put it upon them..." (Numbers 11:14–25).

*T*he spirit is willing but the flesh is weak. Everyone who wants to serve God has physical limitations. Moses was no exception. He became exhausted. *"I am not able to carry all this people alone; the burden is too heavy for me"* (Numbers 11:14). There comes a time when all of us have to recognize that we cannot serve God without the help of others. That is why God chooses elders to help the leadership in His Church. No pastor, minister or priest can do *all* the work alone.

A good leader, like Moses, recognizes his own limitations. They are not news to God. When Moses asked for help, God already had a plan, as He does for each of us. He told Moses to call together 70 of the elders and officials of Israel with whom He would share the Holy Spirit given to Moses. In those days of the First Covenant, God was very selective about who was given the Holy Spirit. This was a special group of men and women.

Today, it is different. It is His desire to pour out the Holy Spirit upon all flesh.

Prayer

Lord Jesus Christ, please pour out Your Holy Spirit upon me so You can use me in Your work and ministry of saving others.

Notes: _____

_____

_____

The Spirit of the Prophets

"Are you jealous for my sake? Would that all the Lord's people were prophets, that the Lord would put His Spirit upon them!" (Numbers 11:26–30).

For some, it is very upsetting that God sometimes uses people they do not think He should be using. Such was the case of Eldad and Medad. They were not amongst the 70 chosen leaders to whom the Lord initially gave the Holy Spirit. Nevertheless, when the Spirit came upon them, they began to prophesy. How could this be? They were not approved by the leadership. Joshua was upset. He told Moses to stop these men from giving their prophecies. Joshua had a lot in common with Jesus' disciples who forbade a man from casting out demons in Jesus' Name. But Jesus said, *"Do not forbid him; for no one who does a mighty work in My Name will be able soon after to speak evil of Me"* (Mark 9:39). Fortunately, Moses was not a man who got jealous when God used other people to serve Him. He recognized that their prophecies were from God. He was excited about it. Just think of what would happen if all the Lord's people were prophets. Wouldn't that be exciting! God's people need to have the attitude of Moses and Jesus.

Prayer

Holy Spirit, help me to rejoice like Moses when I see You use unexpected people to serve Jesus Christ. Please, equip me and let me be such a person.

Notes:

_____

_____

_____

The Spirit of Blessing

"And the Spirit of God came upon him, and he took up his discourse..." (Numbers 24:1–13).

The prophet Balaam was commanded by Balak, the king of Moab, to curse Israel as they travelled on their way to the Promised Land. God sent an angel to warn Balaam not to do it. Blind to the presence of the angel who stood in his way, Balaam tried to force his donkey to keep going. The donkey could see what he couldn't. Much to Balaam's shock, God caused the donkey to speak. Then, God opened Balaam's eyes so he could see the angel of the Lord standing in his way. Suddenly, it was clear to him that he had sinned against God and he was not to curse God's people for all the wealth in the world. He learned that we are not *"to go beyond the Word of the Lord..."* but when speaking, *"what the Lord speaks, that will I speak"* (Numbers 24:1–13).

If we want to serve Jesus Christ, we must not sinfully use the gifts of the Holy Spirit to make money for ourselves. We are not to curse anyone, especially God's people. Jesus said, *"...bless those who curse you ..."* (Luke 6:28).

Prayer

Holy Spirit, please guard my way, that I may give blessings and not curses.

Notes:

_____

_____

_____

The Spirit in Leadership

"Take Joshua, the son of Nun, a man in whom is the Spirit...and you shall commission him" (Numbers 27:15–23).

When God chooses new leadership, He does not take a popularity vote. He hand-picks His person for whatever job needs doing. When the time came for Moses to retire, out of all those in Israel to whom God had given the Holy Spirit, Joshua was God's choice. He had demonstrated his faithfulness to God and to the vision God had given Israel to enter the Promised Land. Only he and Caleb had voted to proceed despite the challenges ahead. They were the only two, besides Moses, who remained steadfast (Numbers 26:65). The rest had lost their courage, as people do when they take their eyes off God's call and vision. After 40 years in the wilderness, the time had come to go into the Promised Land. Joshua was ready to go again.

In order to fulfill God's plan for our lives, we, too, must learn to be faithful even when nobody else is. Unlike Peter, who sank into the water when he took his eyes off Jesus (Matthew 14:30), we must stay above our circumstances by keeping our eyes firmly fixed on Him. This is possible only through the help of the Holy Spirit. When, like Joshua, we receive Him, God can use us and keep us steadfast.

Prayer

Holy Spirit, please fill me, and help me to be faithful so that Jesus can use me to fulfill His plans.

Notes: _____

_____

_____

The Spirit of Obedience

"And Joshua, the son of Nun, was full of the Spirit of wisdom, for Moses had laid his hands upon him; so the people of Israel obeyed him, and did as the Lord had commanded Moses" (Deuteronomy 34:9–12).

A Spirit-filled man or woman of God cannot command obedience and respect from other people unless he or she has demonstrated obedience both to God and to those whom God has placed in authority over him or her. Even Joshua had to prove himself. There are not many people who will be faithful for more than 40 years, and do what they are asked to do by both God and their Church leadership – but Joshua was such a man. He listened to the Holy Spirit who gave him wisdom from above. People who use God's wisdom over many years develop a reputation for faithfulness and obedience. In order to be a person in authority, one must have been a person *under* authority.

Jesus was amazed by the faith of the centurion who asked Him to heal his servant. This was a man who understood how authority operated: *"but say the word, and let my servant be healed. For I am a man set under authority"* (Luke 7:7,8).

Prayer

Holy Spirit, help me to be a faithful person who will go and do whatever Jesus asks me to do, as I live by faith under God's authority.

Notes: _____

_____

_____

The Spirit of Judging

"The Spirit of the Lord came upon him, and he judged Israel" (Judges 3:10,11).

*W*henever any nation stops following the God of Israel and worships other gods, they do evil in His sight and make Him angry. The result is slavery to sin and control by other nations.

This happened to Israel. When the Israelites finally turned back to God and asked Him to save them, He picked a faithful man named Othniel to be their judge and deliverer. Under the guidance of the Holy Spirit, Othniel led Israel to fight against the king of Mesopotamia and the Israelites were set free. He gave leadership for 40 years and there was peace in Israel.

Today, the Holy Spirit still equips people to lead others back to God. He wants us to take His direction so that we can be set free from sin and slavery. With His help we are free to no longer *"judge by appearances, but judge with right judgment"* (John 7:24). God changes people when they respond as we tell them about Jesus. When they ask, *"Brethren, what shall we do?"* we know to say, *"Repent and be baptized every one of you...and you shall receive the gift of the Holy Spirit"* (Acts 2:38).

Prayer

Holy Spirit, please use me to be the right kind of judge, one who helps people find freedom as they turn back to God.

Notes: _____

_____

_____

The Spirit of Valour

"But the Spirit of the Lord took possession of Gideon, and he sounded the trumpet, and the Abiezrites were called out to follow him" (Judges 6:34–7:9).

Gideon did not see himself as a *"mighty man of valour."* He saw himself as a failure and thought God had abandoned His people. Not surprisingly, when God called him to save Israel, he wanted to be sure that it was God.

First, he prepared an offering. Although it was burned up with fire, he remained unconvinced that it was God's plan to use him. Thus, he laid out a fleece before God again – just to make sure that God really wanted to use him. Of course, God fulfilled the request. When the Holy Spirit came upon Gideon, he discovered a new boldness that propelled him to move forward, serving God. Under God's direction, with only 300 men, Gideon destroyed the Midianite army of over 120,000 soldiers and set Israel free, doing the impossible under the power of the Holy Spirit.

When we allow ourselves to be baptized with the Holy Spirit today, we too can do the impossible for God.

Prayer

Holy Spirit, please empower me to be a mighty man or woman of valour doing what is naturally impossible, so that Jesus can use me effectively to set people free from sin's slavery.

Notes: _____

_____

_____

The Spirit of "Yes" and "No"

"Then the Spirit of the Lord came upon Jephthah, and he passed through...on to the Ammonites" (Judges 11:4–40).

God chose Jephthah, an outcast, to save Israel from the Ammonites who had invaded Israel. His great reputation as a warrior gave the elders confidence in asking him to lead them. He agreed, on the condition that he would be their leader after he defeated their enemies.

Jephthah knew he needed God's help, but his tragic undoing came when he tried to impress God by making an unnecessary vow to Him. He vowed that whoever came to greet him when he returned victorious, would be offered up for a burnt offering to God. Imagine his horror when, after victory, the first person to greet him was his beloved daughter! When she heard about the vow, she insisted that he keep his promise to God.

If Jephthah had listened to the Holy Spirit, he would never have made such a foolish vow (promise). *"When you vow a vow to God, do not delay paying it; for he has no pleasure in fools"* (Ecclesiastes 5:4–6). Jesus said, *"Let what you say be simply 'Yes' or 'No'; anything more than this comes from evil"* (Matthew 5:37).

Prayer

Holy Spirit, please save me from speaking foolish vows (promises), and give me the wisdom to obey Your voice.

Notes: _____

_____

The Spirit Who Stirs

"And the Spirit of the Lord began to stir him...And the Spirit of the Lord came mightily upon him" (Judges 13:24–25; 14:1–9; 15:14–16,20).

Samson was the strongest man in the Bible. His strength came from God and was dependant on his faithfulness to Him. Unfortunately, he made the mistake of thinking that, as a chosen man of God, empowered with the Holy Spirit, he could sin with immunity. He believed his own press, revelling so brazenly in the praise of sinful people that he broke every one of his Nazirite vows and *"he did not know that the Lord had left him"* (Judges 16:20). His disobedience and disregard of God's law resulted in his fall as a blinded prisoner of his enemies. Thankfully, he repented and God let him serve Him one last time before he died.

Spiritual pride can blind any of us from the realization that we have left the Lord. Like Samson, we can lose everything Jesus has given us by committing *"apostasy"* (Hebrews 6:4–6) or *"blasphemy against the Holy Spirit"* (Mark 3:29). Like Samson, we need to be stirred to serve God in humility and Holy Spirit power.

Prayer

Holy Spirit, please keep me close to Jesus, serving Him without complaining, in humility and thankfulness, that I shall never lose God's favour.

Notes: _____

_____

_____

The Spirit Who Anoints

*"Then the Spirit of the Lord will come mightily upon you,
and you shall prophesy with them..."* (1 Samuel 10:1–13).

*B*efore God can fully use a person, He gives that person a
new heart and fills him or her with the Holy Spirit. This anointing
with the Holy Spirit allows God to communicate directly with
that person.

God did this for Saul, just as Samuel had prophesied. Saul
was chosen by God to be the first king of Israel and was anointed
with oil by Samuel to make it official. In addition, God gave Saul
the blessing of the gift of prophecy, so that he could speak a
genuine word from the Lord with true authority.
It surprised the people that God would give them a man who was
both a king and a prophet. *"Is Saul also among the prophets?"*
(1 Samuel 10:11). This confirmed that Saul was God's choice.

To this day, God adds blessing upon blessing and gift upon
gift to confirm to those who have discernment that He has chosen
certain people for ministry. They are not always the people we
think should be chosen. But they are the right choice. The same
is true for each one of us. When God calls us to give leadership,
we are most often the ones who cannot understand it. The only
convincing we need is the Holy Spirit.

Prayer

*Holy Spirit, please help me to accept God's call to serve Him
even when I can't understand it.*

Notes: _____

_____

_____

The Spirit of Might

"and the Spirit of the Lord came mightily upon David from that day forward" (1 Samuel 16:1–13).

$\mathcal{S}$aul refused to give God unquestioned obedience and so lost favour with Him. God decided to choose a new king. He sent Samuel to Jesse's home where Samuel met seven of Jesse's sons, all of whom looked like possible choices for the next king. But God rejected them all, *"for the Lord sees not as a man sees; man looks on the outward appearance, but the Lord looks on the heart"* (1 Samuel 16:1–13). It was the eighth son God wanted. As Samuel anointed David with oil, the Holy Spirit came upon him and confirmed God's choice.

The same is true today. God anoints those He chooses with the Holy Spirit. God still looks at people's hearts in order to see whether or not He can use them. We can't make ourselves acceptable to God. This is the work of Jesus Christ. *"For there is no distinction; since all have sinned and fall short of the glory of God, they are justified by His grace as a gift through the redemption which is in Christ Jesus"* (Romans 3:22–24). *"Create in me a clean heart, O God, and put a new and right spirit within me"* (Psalm 51:10).

Prayer

Holy Spirit, please remind me often to be faithful so that I shall not disqualify myself from serving God.

Notes: _____

_____

_____

The Spirit Who Departed

"The Spirit of the Lord departed from Saul, and an evil spirit from the Lord tormented him" (1 Samuel 16:14–23).

When the Holy Spirit leaves, all Hell breaks loose. This is what Saul experienced. Not only did the Holy Spirit leave, but God sent an evil spirit as a replacement. The result was that Saul was tormented. He could find peace only in praise music. Thus, he sent for David, who played and sang for him, causing the evil spirit to flee.

There is nothing more terrifying than the thought that the Holy Spirit would leave us and be replaced by an evil spirit. Thankfully, under the New Covenant (contained in the New Testament), God does not leave us anymore. *"For the gifts and the call of God are irrevocable"* (Romans 11:29).

However, we must understand that if we ignore the Holy Spirit and the Scriptures, it may *seem* as though He has left us. *"For rebellion is as the sin of divination, and stubbornness is as iniquity and idolatry. Because you have rejected the Word of the Lord, He has also rejected you from being king"* (1 Samuel 15:23). When we rebel against God, we act like people who follow an evil spirit. We need to study God's Word so that with the Holy Spirit's help we can remain faithful to Jesus Christ.

Prayer

Holy Spirit, please help me to always respond to Your truth, that I shall never become rebellious and reject God's Word.

Notes: _____

_____

The Spirit of Spiritual Warfare

"Then the Spirit came upon Amasai, chief of the thirty, and he said, 'We are yours David; and with you...for your God helps you'" (1 Chronicles 12:16–19).

War against a common enemy makes for strange allies. It was the fight against the Philistines that led Amasai and his men to join David. But David had to be sure that they would not betray him, so he looked for a sign from God. The Holy Spirit confirmed that they were trustworthy friends in war by causing Amasai to confess that he saw that God was on David's side – for it is in worship and prayer that we see what people are really like. The Holy Spirit shows those with spiritual eyes and ears who is a friend and who is an enemy.

Today, as we do warfare against the devil and his forces, the Holy Spirit will show us who is on God's side and who is not. We use different weapons. *"For the weapons of our warfare are not worldly, but have divine power to destroy strongholds"* (2 Corinthians 10:4). God reveals the sheep, the wolves, and the angel of light through His Word and the Holy Spirit.

Prayer

Holy Spirit, as my Protector, please show me who is on Your side and who is not, so that I can do battle with the enemy through Your divine power, and win the victory for Jesus Christ.

Notes: _____

_____

_____

The Spirit of Full Portion

"And Elisha said, 'I pray you, let me inherit a double share of your spirit'" (2 Kings 2:9–18).

 $\mathcal{E}$ lisha was the prophet Elijah's assistant. Elisha learned how to be a prophet from Elijah. Like him, he was ambitious for God – but he wanted to do *more* for God than Elijah. Thus, when Elijah said to him, *"What shall I do for you before I am taken from you?"* He answered, *"I pray you, let me inherit a double share of your spirit"* (2 Kings 2:9). He wanted twice the power of the Holy Spirit so that He could do twice as much ministry as Elijah. His prayer was answered as he picked up Elijah's mantle. Elijah worked eight miracles in his ministry while Elisha worked 16...a double share.

Today, many people pray for a double portion of the Holy Spirit and somebody else's mantle. The Holy Spirit doesn't give out portions like He used to. He gives us full power. *"...for it is not by measure that He gives the Spirit"* (John 3:34). Jesus said, *"He who believes in Me...out of his heart shall flow rivers of living water"* (John 7:38).

Let's not limit ourselves. Today we can see more than 16 miracles in one meeting as we are empowered by the Holy Spirit.

Prayer

Holy Spirit, I come to You to receive Your full power and my mantle. I place no limits on serving Jesus Christ through You.

Notes: _____

_____

_____

The Good Spirit

"Thou gavest Thy good Spirit to instruct them...Many years Thou didst bear with them and didst warn them by Thy Spirit through the prophets; yet they would not give ear"
(Nehemiah 9:20–25; 29–31).

Ezra brought Israel together in order to pray for a renewal of Israel's covenant with God. He recognized that the Holy Spirit is *"good"* and taught Israel how to serve God. Besides responding to their spiritual needs, He fed them and clothed them, to the extent that they lacked nothing.

In spite of all of the blessings, they acted presumptuously, stiffened their necks, did not obey God's commandments, ignored God's wonders and miracles, worshipped idols instead of God, tried to go back to Egypt, and were disobedient and rebellious.

Nevertheless, God, through the Holy Spirit, looked after them. Even when Israel wouldn't listen to His warnings by the Holy Spirit through the prophets, the Lord did not reject His people. He does not break His covenant. His Word is His bond. God is faithful even when people are not. He is the *"good"* Spirit.

Prayer

Good Holy Spirit, please be my *"Instructor," "Teacher,"* and *"Supplier"* of all my needs according to Your riches in glory in Christ Jesus. Thank You for everything.

Notes: _____

_____

_____

The Spirit Who Gives Understanding

"But it is the Spirit in a man, the breath of the Almighty, that makes him understand" (Job 32:1–8).

The Holy Spirit is different and separate from the human spirit. God's Spirit is eternal. Our spirit is temporal. God's Spirit is holy. Ours is sinful.

We are not born with God's Spirit in us. We have to receive Him. The Holy Spirit is never to be confused with the spirit with which we are created. That is why Elihu pointed out that the Holy Spirit is *"the breath of the Almighty."* He is distinct and different from us. In the Old Testament, very few men and women were given the Holy Spirit. Under the New Covenant in the New Testament, God makes His Holy Spirit available to all who will receive Him (John 3:5, Acts 1:8), so they can know Him intimately.

When the Holy Spirit comes into a person, He brings understanding and discernment (1 Corinthians 12:14). *Suddenly*, the things of God become clear to us. *Suddenly,* we can understand the Scriptures. *Suddenly*, God's actions make sense. *Suddenly*, our eyes are opened and we can see as God sees.

Prayer

Holy Spirit, please breathe Your *"Breath of the Almighty"* on me. Refresh me. Give me *"understanding,"* so I can serve Jesus Christ faithfully, with joy and excitement.

Notes: _____

_____

_____

The Maintaining Spirit

"If He should take back His Spirit to Himself, and gather to Himself His breath, all flesh would perish together, and man would return to dust" (Job 34:10–20).

*M*ost people take life for granted – thinking that God set this world of ours in motion like a clock that will run without any assistance from Him. Few see any role for the Holy Spirit except, of course, that He was involved in Creation.

But Elihu saw things differently. He saw that the Holy Spirit holds this world together – more importantly, that the Holy Spirit keeps *"all flesh,"* meaning all people, alive. He knew that if God should ever withdraw His Spirit from the world, every living creature, including people, would die and return to dust.

This active participation of the Holy Spirit in maintaining our existence is necessary because of sin and the constant destruction it causes, both in nature and to us physically. Every sin does the same amount of damage throughout the world that Adam and Eve's first sin caused. We have forgotten about the sinfulness of sin. We don't understand the depths of its ravages. The Holy Spirit is God's "Maintenance Man" who keeps us alive.

Prayer

Thank You, Holy Spirit, for keeping me alive in order to "live and move and have my being" in God.

Notes: _____

_____

_____

The Upholding Spirit

"...and take not Thy Holy Spirit from me. Restore to me the joy of Thy salvation, and uphold me with a willing spirit"
(Psalm 51:1–12).

The greatest fear that King David and many Christians have, is that if they sin, God will remove the Holy Spirit from their lives. David sinned greatly. He committed adultery with his neighbor's wife and had him killed. He thought he had committed the perfect crime, but forgot that *God was watching*. When faced with that reality, the terror of sin struck the greatest fear in him that any person could experience – fear of the removal of the Holy Spirit from his life, and fear of losing both salvation and the upholding encouragement that comes from God's presence.

Under the Old Covenant, God did take His Holy Spirit away from people who went too far in their arrogant sinning. Today, under the New Covenant, God does not take away the Holy Spirit. *"I will never fail you nor forsake you"* (Hebrews 13:4).

That is both a promise and a warning. The promise is that He will always be there to help and guide us. The warning is that He will always be there to convict us of sin. The encouragement is that He will restore the joy of our salvation.

Prayer

Holy Spirit, thank You for not giving up on me. Uphold me as You restore the joy of my salvation.

Notes: _____

_____

_____

Spirit-Led Days

The Renewing Spirit

"When thou sendest forth Thy Spirit, they are created, and Thou renewest the face of the ground" (Psalm 104:24–30).

*E*veryone expects God to supply everything. If people don't get what they need, they blame God. Natural disasters are called "acts of God" and insurance companies refuse to pay.

But, when we actually do look to God, He really *does* provide food and all the good things that we need. David once remarked, *"I have been young, and now am old; yet I have not seen the righteous forsaken, or his children begging bread"* (Psalm 37:25). God renews us as He supplies our needs.

Beyond our basic *needs*, God wants to give us the desires of our hearts. For those of us who truly love Him, our greatest desire is to see His face. There is nothing in the world more refreshing than knowing we are in His presence – and nothing that brings more insecurity than sensing His presence to be hidden from us. We lose confidence and become fearful. *"When thou hidest Thy face, they are dismayed"* (Psalm 104:29).

We forget that God became flesh and lived among us as Jesus, *"the visible image of the invisible God"* (Colossians 1:15). Jesus said, *"He who has seen Me has seen the Father"* (John 14:9). As we allow God's Holy Spirit to point us to Jesus, we are renewed.

*P*rayer
Holy Spirit, please show me Jesus so that I can see God. Renew me as You fill my hands and heart with good things.

Notes: _____

_____

_____

The Inescapable Spirit

"Whither shall I go from Thy Spirit?" (Psalm 139:7–18).

How many times have we tried to escape from God? No matter how far or how long we run away from Him, He is always there waiting for us. He is "the Hound of Heaven." When He calls us into any ministry, business or work, He does not take "no" for an answer. He waits patiently and persistently for our eventual "yes."

I know this is true from personal experience. I tried to escape from God and said "no" to ministry for several years. But wherever I went, God was always waiting for me. Finally, I decided He must know what is best for me.

It doesn't matter where we run, the Holy Spirit will be there. If we could go to Heaven, the Holy Spirit would be there. If we could go to Hell, He would be there. If we could go to the furthest part of the Earth, or to the bottom of the sea, the Holy Spirit would be there (Psalm 139:8,9).

Why won't He leave us alone? Because He loves us. Only when we finally stop running and submit to His love, form a close relationship with Him and live His plan for our lives, can we find the *"peace of God that passes all understanding"* (Philippians 4:7).

Prayer

Holy Spirit, thank You for Your persistence and the assurance that I can't ever escape from You.

Notes: _____

_____

_____

The Spirit of Wisdom

"...behold, I will pour out My thoughts to you. I will make My words known to you" (Proverbs 1:20–33).

*T*here are two kinds of wisdom. First, there is earthly wisdom; which is sensual, devilish, causes envy (jealousy), strife (selfish ambition), confusion (disorder), and every kind of evil work (vile practice). Secondly, there is wisdom from above; which is pure, peaceable, gentle, easy to be entreated (open to reason), full of mercy and good fruits, without partiality (without favouritism), and without hypocrisy (without insincerity).

Anyone who depends on earthly wisdom, or who will not follow God's wisdom, will get increasingly frustrated with life as his or her dilemma worsens. We need God's wisdom in order to make right decisions and solve our problems with good judgment. Then we can be successful in every area of life. James tells us, *"If any of you lacks wisdom, let him ask God, who gives to all men generously and without reproaching, and it will be given to him"* (James 1:5). Thus, we know we can receive God's wisdom through prayer. Further, the Holy Spirit may give us the *gift* of the *"word of wisdom"* (I Corinthians 12:8), another means through which God provides His problem-solving wisdom.

Prayer
Holy Spirit, please give me Your wisdom from above, so I can live confidently, knowing I will have good judgment.

Notes: _____

_____

_____

The Spirit Who Rests upon Us

"And the Spirit of the Lord shall rest upon him..."

(Isaiah 11:1–9).

The coming of Jesus to be the Saviour of the world was carefully planned by God. Even the family into which He would be born was carefully chosen. The Holy Spirit was to be with Him continually. Take a look at the Holy Spirit's résumé: wisdom and understanding, counsel and might, knowledge and the fear of the Lord. It is no wonder that when Jesus was just 12 years old he amazed the teachers in the temple in Jerusalem with His understanding and his answers. The Holy Spirit had made him wise beyond his age and any natural abilities. *"And the child grew and became strong, filled with wisdom; and the favour of God was upon Him"* (Luke 2:40). Jesus' delight was in the fear of God. He came to save the world through the power of the Holy Spirit.

Like Jesus, we can accomplish God's plan only through the power of the Holy Spirit. *"But you shall receive power when the Holy Spirit has come upon you"* (Acts 1:8). When He comes upon us, like Jesus, we will appear to be wiser than our age, education, or experience, bringing honour to Jesus Christ.

Prayer

Holy Spirit, please come freshly upon me and prepare me for all of God's plans for my life, and for that of my church, so that Jesus can be honoured and our Heavenly Father worshipped.

Notes: _____

_____

_____

The Spirit from On High

"...until the Spirit is poured upon us from on high"
(Isaiah 32:14–18).

*S*cripture tells us that after the Messiah comes and has completed His work of salvation, the Holy Spirit will be poured upon us from above. When this occurs, we will see the results everywhere we look. The wilderness will become a fruitful field and the fruitful field will become a dense forest. Justice will be seen in the most remote areas of the world as people live according to God's law and treat each other with impartiality. Righteousness (a right relationship with God) will be experienced in the workplace. The result will be peace, quietness, and trust – the components of God's security system – finally allowing us to live without distress.

This Messiah, Jesus Christ, has come and has done His work. Many of us have experienced salvation and the baptism of the Holy Spirit as described by the prophet, Isaiah. God has installed His security system in us. We can now do what Paul told us: *"...and let the peace of Christ rule in your hearts"* (Colossians 3:15). Isaiah's prophecy has come true.

Prayer

Holy Spirit, please make me a fruitful field, a righteous worker treating all with impartiality, and living in right relationship with God, enjoying His peace wherever I go.

Notes: _____

_____

_____

The Spirit Who Directs Us

"Who has directed the Spirit of the Lord, or as His counselor has instructed Him?" (Isaiah 40:10–14).

There is nothing funnier than to hear people try to tell the Holy Spirit how He should go about His business. The one thing I have learned over the years, is that if we make suggestions to the Holy Spirit about how He can solve a problem, He will never use them! He answers prayer according to God's will. Our Heavenly Father is His only counselor. Jesus Christ is His only director. God is His only source of enlightenment. Our Heavenly Father is His only path of justice and knowledge. Jesus Christ is His only source of understanding. The Holy Spirit is sent to be *our* guide, teacher and counselor.

"There is a way which seems right to a man, but its end is the way to death" (Proverbs 14:12). In our sinful arrogance, we often try to tell the Holy Spirit how to carry out His work; but God's ways are not our ways. His thinking has not been affected and warped by sin. So – when we don't understand what God is doing, we must remember: *"We know that in everything God works for good with those who love Him, who are called according to his purpose"* (Romans 8:28).

Prayer

Holy Spirit, I am so grateful that I can count on Your direction coming straight from our Heavenly Father and Jesus. Please remind me to seek Your counsel on every matter.

Notes: _____

_____

_____

The Spirit of the Chosen

"Behold My servant, whom I uphold, My chosen in whom My soul delights; I have put My Spirit upon Him..."

(Isaiah 42:1–9).

*T*he prophets gave specific indicators that would identify God's servant and our Saviour: the Holy Spirit would be upon Him. He would bring God's justice to all the nations by calmly and quietly sharing the Gospel. When bruised, persecuted or crucified, he would not break. He would accomplish His purpose: *"For God so loved the world that He gave His only Son that whoever believes in Him should not perish but have eternal life"* (John 3:16). Jesus fulfilled the whole profile outlined in Isaiah 42:1–9.

The same standards apply today. As God's servants, these qualities must be seen in us (Mark 16:17,18). The Holy Spirit must be visible in us doing the things that Jesus did (John 14:12). Without the Holy Spirit, we break. With Him, we succeed.

I met a Ukrainian Christian who spent 30 years in a Communist prison. Tortured almost every day, he could have been released by simply denying Jesus Christ. However, he wouldn't even consider it, because of all that Jesus did for him. The Holy Spirit allowed him to be bruised without breaking.

Prayer

Holy Spirit, please empower me to do what Jesus did, so that others can receive His ministry as they see I am His faithful servant.

Notes: _____

_____

_____

The Spirit for our Descendants

"I will pour My Spirit upon your descendants..."

(Isaiah 44:1–8).

*W*hat a wonderful promise! God wishes not only to save us and all our descendants, but to give us all the Holy Spirit, whether we are children, adults or elderly. *"Repent, and be baptized every one of you in the Name of Jesus Christ for the forgiveness of your sins; and you shall receive the gift of the Holy Spirit"* (Acts 2:38). *"Let the children come to Me, and do not hinder them; for to such belongs the Kingdom of God"* (Mark 10:14).

It is entirely natural for a child to receive the baptism of the Holy Spirit and speak in tongues – like seven-year-old Alyssa, who, after receiving the Holy Spirit with the evidence of tongues (Mark 16:17, 1 Corinthians 12:10), said, "I feel stuffed with the Holy Spirit!"

Many of our children will go far beyond us in serving the Lord. Some may name their children after God's great people, such as "Jacob." They may even embarrass us with their zeal – like those coming out of gangs who choose to be tattooed with the Name of the Lord. Others, like many in South and Central America, will add God's Name to their family name. What boldness the Holy Spirit will give them as they declare, "I am the Lord's," in their own way!

Prayer

Holy Spirit, please give me a new freedom and boldness to witness for Jesus Christ.

Notes: _____

_____

_____

The Permanent Spirit

"My Spirit which is upon you, and My words which I have put in your mouth, shall not depart..." (Isaiah 59:16–21).

What a relief to read this! Spirit-filled Christians often feel, for various reasons, that the Holy Spirit has left them. They may have believed a lie of the devil, absorbed discouragement from other Christians, felt guilty because of their own sins and failures, been ignorant of the promises of the Bible, lacked prayer time, or lacked Godly fellowship. Sometimes, it's because of unfaithfulness in various areas of their Christian walk.

When we receive the Holy Spirit, He is with us *forever*. He will not leave us: *"I will never fail you or forsake you"* (Hebrews 13:5), regardless of our feelings. We need to learn to live in the security of God's promise. It's interesting that the promise of the Holy Spirit's presence is connected to the words which God says He will put in our mouths by the normal experience of speaking in tongues (Mark 16:17, Acts 2:4). This is called the "initial evidence" of the baptism of the Holy Spirit. So, whenever we "feel" that the Holy Spirit has left us, all we have to do is begin to speak or pray in tongues and we'll know that the Holy Spirit has not left us.

Prayer

Holy Spirit, please remind me to pray using my spiritual language of tongues so I can be edified and encouraged, secure in the knowledge that You are always with me.

Notes: _____

_____

_____

The Anointing Spirit

"The Spirit of the Lord God is upon Me, because the Lord has anointed Me..." (Isaiah 61:1–6).

The Holy Spirit is the One who anoints people whom God calls to be set aside for ministry. Originally, sacred oil was poured over, or rubbed on, a person's head to consecrate him or her for ministry. Today, the Holy Spirit anoints people through His presence and power in their lives, thus preparing them for the ministry to which God has called them. Jesus Christ is the promised and anointed Messiah. "Jesus" is His Name which means, "Yahweh is salvation." "Christ" is His title, which means "Anointed One."

Isaiah 61 outlines the Anointed One's "job description." He will preach good tidings to the poor, heal the brokenhearted, proclaim liberty to the captives, set free those who are bound in their prisons, proclaim the Lord's coming, comfort all who mourn, give hope and joy, set people free to praise God as His righteous people, and baptize them with the Holy Spirit (Matthew 3:11). Just as the Holy Spirit equipped Jesus for such a wonderful ministry, He wants to anoint us as "trees of righteousness," called by Jesus to share in the same ministry.

Prayer

Holy Spirit, please anoint me for sevice and prepare me to share Jesus' ministry as a servant of our God.

Notes: _____

_____

_____

The Grieving Spirit

"But they rebelled and grieved His Holy Spirit; therefore..."
(Isaiah 63:10–14).

Talk about ungrateful people! God had delivered His people from slavery in Egypt. The Holy Spirit had worked in saving them, guiding them, and giving them rest. Not only had He looked after all their needs, He had ministered to them with astounding miracles. And yet – they rebelled against God. How the Holy Spirit must have grieved!

We all need to be appreciated and thanked when we have gone out of our way to help people. It is no different with the Holy Spirit. It may be difficult to understand, but He is a Person with feelings. He can be grieved or hurt, made to feel sad, suffer pain, and feel hatred. He experiences love, joy, peace, patience, kindness, goodness, faithfulness, gentleness and self-control. Because He has never sinned, He is even more sensitive than we.

"Where is He who put in the midst of them His Holy Spirit?" (Isaiah 63:11) the Israelites complained. Because the Holy Spirit is "God in us," He was there all the time, right in front of them in a pillar of cloud and fire (Exodus 13:21). Sadly, they ignored Him – just as many of us ignore Him today. It is not surprising that the only unforgivable sin is blasphemy against Him (Matthew 12:31).

Prayer

Holy Spirit, I appreciate You and thank You for all You have done for me as my Friend and Guide.

Notes: _____

_____

_____

The Lifting-up Spirit

"And when He spoke to me, the Spirit entered into me and set me upon my feet; and I heard Him speaking to me"

(Ezekiel 1:28–2:8).

God's glory caused Ezekiel to fall upon his face. When God told him to stand up, he couldn't do it, so the Holy Spirit entered him and lifted him up on his feet. Then God spoke to him. Ezekiel got the message – loud and clear. God was sending him on a "mission impossible" to be a prophet to Israel, a rebellious nation which had proven they would not listen to Him. He had God's permission to say: *"Thus says the Lord God"* (Ezekiel 2:4). Today, the Holy Spirit gives people the gift of prophecy to call people to repent.

The Holy Spirit is the One who catches our attention so that we can hear what God wants us to do. The Spirit *"will not speak on His own authority, but whatever He hears He will speak; and He will tell declare to you the things that are to come"* (John 16:13). He cooperates with God our Father who sits on His throne. As "God inside us," the Holy Spirit stirs us to get our full attention, lifting us to hear His clear communications to us.

Prayer

Holy Spirit, please lift me up and empower me to complete the "mission impossible" that God is calling me to do.

Notes: _____

_____

_____

The Taking-Away Spirit

"The Spirit lifted me up and took me away, and I went in bitterness in the heat of my spirit" (Ezekiel 3:12–17).

Ezekiel was an unwilling volunteer when God called Him to be a prophet – so unwilling that the Holy Spirit had to literally pick him up and carry him to the exiles at Telabib. He was burning with bitterness because he didn't want to be a prophet. After God ministered to him with a strong hand, however, Ezekiel cooled off and became willing to listen to reason. God said, *"Son of man, I have made you a watchman for the house of Israel"* (Ezekiel 3:17). A watchman is a prophet with the responsibility of listening to God and then giving God's people His warning so that they can repent and be saved from their sin.

Today, God has many "unwilling volunteers" in the Church. Many are willing to serve God on their own terms, but have difficulty with the terms of Jesus' invitation: *"If any man would come after me let him deny himself and take up his cross and follow me"* (Matthew 16:24). People still do not want to hear God's call to repentance. After spending time with Jesus, however, like Ezekiel, they eventually come into agreement, become overwhelmed by the Holy Spirit, and get excited about God's call.

Prayer

Holy Spirit, please transform me into a willing volunteer for Jesus Christ.

Notes: _____

_____

_____

The Continuously Helpful Spirit

"But the Spirit entered into me, and set me upon my feet; and He spoke with me: 'Go, shut yourself within your house'"

(Ezekiel 3:22–27).

God deals with us in different, and sometimes strange, ways. Ezekiel was so sensitive to the "glory" or the presence of the Lord, that every time he experienced it, he fell on his face. Today, we call this "being slain in the Spirit" or "falling under the power of the Holy Spirit." Because Ezekiel just couldn't stand up when in the presence of God, the Holy Spirit had to stand him up so that God could talk to him. He told Ezekiel to go into his house where He would tie him up so that he couldn't go out among the people. God was also going to "glue" his tongue to the roof of his mouth so that he wouldn't be able to talk. Only after God spoke to him would he be able to rebuke the people. When Ezekiel did speak, he was to say, *"Thus says the Lord."*

God often calls us to a particular place where He can prepare us for ministry. It could be to a church, a prayer closet, a retreat, a seminary, a Bible school, or any place where He can teach us obedience.

Prayer

Holy Spirit, please lead me to that place of preparation and obedience so that I, too, can say, "Thus says the Lord."

Notes: _____

_____

_____

Spirit-Led Days

The Spirit Who Restores Us and Helps Us to Witness

"And the Spirit of the Lord fell upon me, and He said to me, 'Say: thus says the Lord...'" (Ezekiel 11:1,5,16,17,19–20).

The Holy Spirit showed Ezekiel the people who were plotting evil things. We sometimes forget that *"the eyes of the Lord run to and fro throughout the whole Earth, to show his might strong in behalf of those whose heart is blameless toward Him"* (2 Chronicles 16:9). Nothing escapes God's attention. That is why He provided a New Covenant for us through which we can be restored to Him. He said to Ezekiel, *"I will give them one heart, and put a new Spirit within them; I will take the stony heart out of their flesh, that they may walk in my statutes and keep my ordinances and obey them; and they shall be my people, and I will be their God"* (Ezekiel 11:19). Jesus Christ accomplished this through His ministry, His death on the Cross, His resurrection, and through putting a new Spirit, His Holy Spirit, into us.

The ministry continues today. Once we have had a Heavenly "heart-transplant" and been baptized in the Holy Spirit, we are called by God to be witnesses to other people so that they, too, can be restored to Him. Like Ezekiel, we have the Holy Spirit to help us.

Prayer

Holy Spirit, please give me Your boldness to bring others back to God.

Notes: _____

_____

_____

The Holy Spirit Within Us

"A new heart I will give you, and a new Spirit I will put within you" (Ezekiel 36:22–32).

God was frustrated with Israel. Having profaned His great Name among the nations and led people to laugh at the Lord God of Israel, they had ruined His reputation.

Israel had become a defiled people no longer fit for holy use. What would God do? Because He still loved His people, He provided a means for their return to Him: He would give them new hearts. He would forgive them and replace their hearts of stone with new hearts of flesh – hearts that were flexible, teachable, and uninfected by the sin of rebellion. But that was not enough. He would give them a new Spirit – His Holy Spirit – whom He would put within them. The Holy Spirit could then guide them to walk in His statutes and observe His ordinances.

The "them," of course, includes us. Despite the intervening 6000 years, we are no less frustrating a people than the Israelites were. Rebels by nature, we need His life within to overcome sin.

God's solution is exactly what Jesus called being *"born again of water and the Spirit"* (John 3:5). This experience is necessary in order to make us right with God, place us in His Kingdom, and give us eternal life. And it doesn't hurt at all.

Prayer

Holy Spirit you are welcome in my heart. Please guide me so that I can contribute to Jesus' good reputation.

Notes: _____

_____

_____

The Bone-Connecting Spirit

"And I will put my Spirit within you, and you shall live, and I will place you in your own land; then you shall know that...I have done it, says the Lord" (Ezekiel 37:1–14).

The Holy Spirit took Ezekiel out to a valley filled with the skeletal remains of thousands of people – the Valley of Dry Bones! *"Son of man, can these bones live?"* God asked Ezekiel. Ezekiel really had no idea. *"O Lord God, Thou knowest."*

God told the prophet to do something strange. *"Prophesy to these bones, and say to them, O dry bones, hear the word of the Lord."* As Ezekiel prophesied, an amazing thing happened: the Holy Spirit moved over the bones and they came together and were covered with flesh. God placed the Holy Spirit within them, and the people were resurrected and given new life.

The same thing will happen on the Day of Resurrection. The dead will be raised to life and we who are left shall be changed (Matthew 24:29; 1 Corinthians 15:51–54). Thanks to Jesus, we do not have to wait for the Resurrection to be made new and receive the Holy Spirit. The Holy Spirit is the life-giving Spirit of both Creation and Re-creation.

God often asks us to do things that may appear foolish to us because we do not understand the power of the Word of God.

Prayer

Holy Spirit, please make me living proof of the life-giving power of the Word of God.

Notes: _____

_____

_____

The Poured-Out Spirit

"and I will not hide My face any more from them, when I pour out my Spirit upon the house of Israel, says the Lord God" (Ezekiel 39:21–29).

Because God could no longer tolerate their sin and iniquity, He sent Israel into exile and scattered His people throughout the different nations to teach them to be faithful to Him. He turned His back on them so that even when they called on Him, He ignored them until all those who had been unfaithful had died. This was a repeat of the 40 years in the wilderness. At the point of this Scripture, He had promised to return them from exile and restore their fortunes – which He has done for the earthly Israel. Israel, as we know it today, has gone back to their land.

But, there is something more here. The majority of Jews have not experienced the final part of this promise. First, God showed mankind His face: *"He who has seen Me has seen the Father"* (John 14:9). Jesus is God's face: *"He is the image of the invisible God"* (Colossians 1:15). Then, on the Day of Pentecost, He fulfilled the second part of his promise when 120 people received the pouring out of His Spirit (Acts 2:4), which continues today. However, only those Jews and Gentiles who have received the Holy Spirit are fully restored to God. The great remainder have yet to enter in.

Prayer

Holy Spirit, thank You for residing in me as proof of my restoration.

Notes: _____

_____

_____

The Temple-Filling Spirit

"The Spirit lifted me up, and brought me into the inner court; and behold, the glory of the Lord filled the temple"
(Ezekiel 43:1–13).

Once again, the Holy Spirit lifted Ezekiel up and carried him into the inner court of God's temple which was filled with God's glory (or presence). There, He showed Ezekiel a temple that was even more magnificent than the one in which Israel worshipped. It was more impressive than any man-made church. *"Son of Man, this is the place of My throne and the place of the soles of My feet, where I dwell in the midst of the people of Israel forever"* (Ezekiel 43:7).

While the Bible tells us that the New Jerusalem has no temple (Revelation 21:22), Paul tells us where we can locate the temple that God showed to Ezekiel. *"Do you not know that you are God's temple?...For God's temple is holy, and that temple you are"* (1 Corinthians 3:16–17). When we receive Jesus Christ as Saviour and Lord and are baptized in the Holy Spirit, we become an integral part of God's temple, His dwelling place. He arranges us into inner and outer courts. Our hearts are His throne room. The whole territory upon which we stand is holy. Jesus is the temple's cornerstone – our High Priest and sacrificial Lamb.

Prayer

Holy Spirit, please keep me holy as God's temple, clean and fit for worshipping Him.

Notes: _____

_____

_____

The Spirit of the Holy God

"At last Daniel came in before me...in whom is the Spirit of the Holy God..." (Daniel 4:1–37).

God gave Nebuchadnezzar, king of Babylon, a dream that troubled him. He called in all of his wise men: magicians, enchanters, the Chaldeans, and astrologers – to interpret his dream, but none could do it. Finally, Daniel arrived. Four times Nebuchadnezzar described him as the one *"in whom is the Spirit of the Holy God."* The king had great confidence in Daniel. He was different from all of the other wise men because he served the God of Israel. Of course, Daniel was able to interpret the king's dream – a call to the king to repent, turn to God, worship Him and serve Him – which he did.

Like Daniel, whether we like it or not, we cannot hide the presence of the Holy Spirit in us. He can be seen in everything we do. The Holy Spirit is our Counselor who continues to interpret the dreams God gives us (Job 33:15,16) and give us advice through them (Acts 2:17) as He did for Daniel.

Prayer

Holy Spirit, please use me so that other people will be able to see You in me and be encouraged to repent and follow Jesus Christ.

Notes: _____

_____

_____

The Outpouring of the Spirit

"And it shall come to pass afterward, that I will pour My Spirit on all flesh..." (Joel 2:21–32).

Here is the promise of the New Covenant. Under the Old Covenant, *"all flesh"* did not have the opportunity to receive the Holy Spirit. Only specially chosen men and a very few women were filled with the Holy Spirit in order to give leadership to God's people. But the New Covenant held a new promise. We entered into "afterward" or "the last days" on the Day of Pentecost when the Holy Spirit was poured out into the 120 believers who waited in the Upper Room. Both men and women were baptized with the Holy Spirit. All flesh – men and women, young and old – can now receive the Holy Spirit. Both sons and daughters can now prophesy. God will give the elderly dreams and young people visions. Everyone can now serve God in the power of the Holy Spirit.

There will be great signs in the Heavens and on the Earth before the *"Day of the Lord"* comes, but *"whoever calls on the Name of the Lord shall be delivered* (saved)" (Acts 2:16–21). Today, Jesus is still pouring out the Holy Spirit upon whomever will call on His Name. Welcome to the *"last days"* and the exciting ministry that God promised!

Prayer
   Holy Spirit, please be freshly poured out into my flesh so I can do all that God promised.

Notes: _____

_____

_____

The Spirit of the Prophet

"But as for me, I am filled with power, with the Spirit of the Lord..." (Micah 3:8–12).

Micah outlined the credentials of a real prophet of God: he is filled with the power of the Holy Spirit, justice and might. With his authority to expose and preach against the sin of God's people and to call those who are sinning to repent and serve God, no one is exempt from his finger of reproof – from the king to the poorest person. The Holy Spirit directs the prophet and the prophet gives the prophecy. Sadly, there were too many bad prophets in those days just as there are too many today.

Although God still calls men and women to be prophets, He now gives them the *"gift of prophecy"* (1 Corinthians 12:10) so that the prophets are triply accountable to God, the Church, and the Scriptures.

Prophets are responsible to *speak* the *"word of prophecy"* that God gives them. They are not supposed to *explain* it: *"no prophecy of Scripture is a matter of one's own interpretation"* (2 Peter 1:20). They are simply to give it, trusting the Holy Spirit to explain it and convict the guilty person.

Prayer

Holy Spirit, please empower me with the gift of prophecy. Keep me in a repentant attitude, flexible and obedient, ready to deliver "the word of prophecy" to your people and your Church.

Notes: _____

_____

_____

The Abiding Spirit

"My Spirit abides among you; fear not"
(Haggai 1:13,14; 2:1–9).

"*W*ithout a vision the people perish" (Proverbs 29:18, KJV). Even with a vision, however, many people become fearful. There is always somebody who does not want it. Such was the case in the story of Haggai. Haggai had to remind the governor of Judah that God did not operate by means of an opinion poll. The poll had determined: *"The time has not yet come to rebuild the house of the Lord"* (Haggai 1:2). God, however, differed from the results of the poll: *"This is the time to rebuild My house."* The polls still say that places of worship are not a priority; but God continues to differ. While it's true that we, individually, are the "temple" of God, nice places for corporate worship are important to Him.

As with any church building project, the people complained, asking where all the money was coming from. "We can't afford it," they whined. God's answer is always the same, *"I will provide,"* so that *"the splendor of this house shall be greater than the former."* When we take our eyes off God, fear floods in. When we keep our eyes fixed on Jesus our Provider, however, the money comes (Genesis 22:14; Philippians 4:19). Fortunately, the Israelites listened to the Holy Spirit and rebuilt God's house.

Prayer

Holy Spirit, You are a Spirit of power, love, and a sound mind. Abide in me, setting me free to receive your provision as I build according to Your direction.

Notes: _____

_____

_____

The Accomplishing Spirit

"Not by might, nor by power, but by my Spirit, says the Lord of hosts" (Zechariah 4:6–10).

When God accomplishes anything, He does not like to share the credit with others. During the rebuilding of the temple of the Lord, it seemed as though it would never be finished. Even Governor Zerubbabel was getting discouraged. Mercifully, God gave Zechariah a word of encouragement for him. He said that the rebuilding of His house would not be a military project (might), nor would it be completed by human resources (power). It would be accomplished through the ministry of the Holy Spirit, who would remove every obstacle that stood against the completion of God's temple. And that's exactly what happened.

We all need to learn the lesson of the temple. We must keep our attention glued on the ministry that God has given us. We simply need to minister as God directs, and then He will supply the money, people, and resources to get the practical things done. Whenever we start a new ministry, there are people who despise *"the time of small things."* They're interested only in supporting a big ministry. God, however, sends the Holy Spirit to bless His new ministry.

Prayer

Holy Spirit, please remind me that You often start small, but You complete what You have begun, and bring glory to Jesus.

Notes: _____

_____

_____

The Spirit of Grace and Supplication

And I will pour out on the house of David and the inhabitants of Jerusalem a Spirit of compassion and supplication..."

(Zechariah 12:10–13; 14:8,9).

What an awesome thing! This is a prophecy of what was going to happen on the day of which God said *"they will look on Him whom they pierced."* People would mourn for Him as one mourns for an only son, and grieve for Him as one grieves for a firstborn. That occurred on the day that the only begotten Son of God, Jesus, was crucified (John 19:37). This is a picture of the mourning among God's people for piercing God Himself, when Jesus paid for all the sin of the world. He paid for Israel's sin and for our sin. The Holy Spirit moved over the hearts of the people in Jerusalem, as He moves over hearts today, to break through any hostility towards the Messiah, preparing people to receive Him.

The Holy Spirit brings God's grace – **G**od's **R**edemption **A**t **C**hrist's **E**xpense – (undeserved love) into our lives, and intercedes in prayer for those for whom Jesus died. Non-Christians miss knowing the tender, caring, interceding Holy Spirit who brings living water to restore us (John 7:38).

Prayer

Holy Spirit, thank You for bringing God's grace to me and interceding for me so that, through my mourning, I found my Saviour Jesus and His living water.

Notes: _____

_____

_____

The Spirit Who Prepares

"and he will be filled with the Holy Spirit, even from his mother's womb" (Luke 1:5–17).

John the Baptist was conceived under very unusual circumstances. Although his parents were aged beyond what was normal for having a baby, his father Zechariah prayed for a son. As he served in the temple, the angel Gabriel appeared to him and told him that his wife Elizabeth was about to bear a son. The baby was to be named "John" and would be prepared for a special ministry, beginning even in his mother's womb, where he would be filled with the Holy Spirit. John was to prepare the way for the Messiah, calling people to repentance. Imagine that! – a baby filled with the Holy Spirit in his mother's womb!

Most people do not understand that they, too, are specially chosen and created for a particular ministry. This is true for all of us. Every one of us can say to God with David, *"For Thou didst form my inward parts, Thou didst knit me together in my mother's womb"* (Psalm 139:13). None of us were accidents. God has a plan similar to John the Baptist's (to prepare the way for the Lord Jesus) for every person. After we have been filled with the Holy Spirit (at our request), we can begin to see His purpose unfold.

Prayer

Holy Spirit, please fill me, and prepare me for the ministry for which I was conceived and born.

Notes: _____

_____

_____

The Spirit of the Most High

"The Holy Spirit will come upon you, and the power of the Most High will overshadow you; therefore the Child to be born will be called holy, the Son of God" (Luke 1:26–38).

Mary was a virgin and not married when she was told that she was going to be the mother of the only begotten Son of God. *"How shall this be?"* she puzzled.

Jesus was conceived through the Holy Spirit. This should not surprise us when we remember that the Holy Spirit was involved in the creation of the world. *"With God all things are possible"* (Matthew 19:26). Jesus was being born in order to fulfill God's plan to save our world from sin. He was the Lamb of God who would take away the sin of the world by dying on the Cross of Calvary. This plan was conceived in the Garden of Eden and implemented beginning with a young woman who loved God.

Jesus was born to save you and me, but also to send the Holy Spirit into our lives so that He could be not only our Saviour, but also our Lord. When we respond to His provision, we can join in His ministry and know the joy of seeing other people saved, baptized with the Holy Spirit, healed, delivered of demons, and set free to take their place in Jesus' Church.

Prayer

Thank you, Holy Spirit, for conceiving Jesus to be my Saviour and Lord, and for filling me with Your power to minister to other people.

Notes: _____

_____

_____

The Recognizing Spirit

"And when Elizabeth heard the greeting of Mary, the babe leaped in her womb; and Elizabeth was filled with the Holy Spirit" (Luke 1:39–56).

Baby John leaped in his mother's womb at the sound of Mary's voice. At the meeting between Mary and Elizabeth, the Holy Spirit ministered and Elizabeth was filled with the Holy Spirit.

Just as He did at the meeting of Mary and Elizabeth, the Holy Spirit moves inside us when we meet fellow Spirit-filled Christians. One good example of this would be my experience with a Christian man I once met at a retreat. At the moment of introduction, something leaped within both of us. Recognition occurred. Intrigued, we sat down and tried to ascertain where we might have met before. Finally concluding that our paths had never before crossed, we suddenly realized that our common denominator, the Holy Spirit, had sparked the feeling of recognition, as He regularly does, between fellow believers who meet for the first time.

The Holy Spirit knows when a person is ready and needs to receive Him. This was the case with Elizabeth. He put her on the same spiritual wavelength with Mary so they could have fellowship in their time of pregnancy.

Prayer

Holy Spirit, thank You for recognizing my need for You and meeting it.

Notes: _____

_____

_____

The Understanding Spirit

"And his father Zechariah was filled with the Holy Spirit, and prophesied..." (Luke 1:18–23; 57–80).

There are two equally remarkable, but opposite types of miracles in this Scripture. First, Zechariah was struck dumb because of his unbelief and was unable to speak until his son was born. Then, after his son was born and he named him John to prove his faith, his speech was restored.

It is one thing to say that we believe the Bible and that God works miracles; but it is another thing to respond with unbelief, when God sends an angel to say that He's going to do a miracle, as Zechariah did. This happens often with believers who have never been filled with the Holy Spirit. We all need Him to fill us, reassuring us that *"with God all things are possible"* (Matthew 19:26). Zechariah needed to be filled with the Holy Spirit to enable him to believe the amazing things that God was doing in fulfillment of Scripture.

After obediently writing the name "John," Zechariah's voice was restored. He was filled with the Holy Spirit and prophesied. Quiet obedience and a right attitude prepared him to be the father of the man of whom Jesus said, *"no one greater has arisen."*

Prayer

Holy Spirit, please fill me and give me Your understanding and Your eyes of faith so I can be used by Jesus to serve God.

Notes: _____

_____

_____

The Prophecy Fulfilling Spirit

"Joseph, son of David, do not fear to take Mary your wife, for that which is conceived in her is of the Holy Spirit..." (Matthew 1:18–25).

God joined with mankind in history, as baby Jesus, in order to fulfill prophecy. He was "the Word" who *"became flesh and dwelt amongst us, full of grace and truth"* (John 1:14). Using the creative power of the Holy Spirit, he was conceived as Jesus and entered the world through a human birth channel so that He could live like us. As our High Priest, He was tempted in every way that we are – yet did not sin. To save His people – us – from evil, He came as "Emmanuel," meaning "God with us." He came to be our High Priest in a way that He could empathize with us. In the power of the Holy Spirit He, as our Saviour and Lord, is able to minister to our *real* needs, which are to be reconciled to God through salvation, and to find the key to staying faithful to Him.

The "key," or staying power, is the Holy Spirit who gives us the ability to conquer the accuser through the blood of the Lamb and the word of our testimony (Revelation 12:11).

Prayer

Holy Spirit, please work through me in the fulfillment of prophecy so that, like Joseph and Mary, I can cooperate with You in the realization of Your plan.

Notes: _____

_____

_____

The Inspiring Spirit

"And it was revealed to him by the Holy Spirit that he should not see death before he had seen the Lord's Christ. And inspired by the Spirit he came into the temple" (Luke 2:22–35).

Those who are led by the Holy Spirit learn very quickly to follow His inspiration or nudges without question. They know that failing to do so will result in missing out on receiving ministry or being used by God.

Simeon was a righteous man who prayed for the Messiah to come and save Israel. He was getting very old. The Holy Spirit revealed to him that *"he should not see death before he had seen the Lord's Christ"* (Luke 2:26). I suspect that if he had told anybody else that the Holy Spirit had told him this, he would have been laughed off as a crazy old man. When the Holy Spirit said to *"Go to the Temple,"* he went in obedience.

If Simeon had not gone, he would have missed out on the greatest day of his life. He saw Jesus. As soon as he saw Him, he knew that He was the Christ and he blessed Him and prophesied over Him. How many of us miss seeing Jesus do great things because we ignore the inspiration of the Holy Spirit?

Prayer

Holy Spirit, please give me a prophecy and teach me obedience to Your inspiration.

Notes: _____

_____

_____

The Spirit of Repentance

"I baptize you with water for repentance, but He who is coming after me is mightier than I, whose sandals I am not worthy to carry; He will baptize you with the Holy Spirit and with fire" (Matthew 3:1–12; Mark 1:1–8; Luke 3:15–18).

John the Baptist and Jesus were a ministry team. John preached repentance and baptized with water. Jesus preached the Kingdom of Heaven and prepared people to be baptized with the Holy Spirit.

There are two steps involved in our relationship with God:

1. Repentance opens the door for Jesus to become our Saviour, forgiving us of our sin and giving us salvation.
2. The baptism of the Holy Spirit allows Jesus to become our Lord and direct our lives.

To serve Jesus Christ fully and faithfully, we must experience both. For some people, these are two separate experiences occurring at different times. For others, the two are experienced at the same time. It really doesn't matter as long as both happen.

Without the filling of the Holy Spirit we have no power to be faithful after repentance. We wonder why we keep sinning and repenting, yet failing over and over again. With the power of the Holy Spirit we can have power to be faithful witnesses.

Prayer

Holy Spirit, I want all that Jesus has for me. Please, baptize and fill me now.

Notes:

The Identifying Spirit

"and he saw the Spirit of God descending like a dove, and alighting on Him..." (Matthew 3:13–17; Mark 1:9–11; Luke 3:21,22; John 1:29–34).

John the Baptist knew that he was looking for the Messiah, but he didn't know who He was. Thus, when Jesus went to be baptized by John, the Holy Spirit had to identify Him. Even so, John didn't want to baptize Jesus because he knew that He was not a sinner. Baptism was for sinners who repented. However, Jesus told him to go ahead, *"for thus it is fitting for us to fulfill all righteousness"* (Matthew 3:15). Jesus, instead of getting rid of sin, took on the sins of the world. *"For our sake He made Him to be sin who knew no sin, so that in Him we might know the righteousness of God"* (2 Corinthians 5:21). He paid for the sin he took on the Cross of Calvary.

Just as the Holy Spirit identified Jesus for John, He still identifies believers for other believers today. That identification enables us to do ministry together, pray together, worship together, and have fellowship like that of John and Jesus. This proof of identity protects us because there are those who would like to counterfeit the work of the Holy Spirit and lead us astray. The mutual witness of the Holy Spirit, however, allows us to trust.

Prayer

Holy Spirit, help me to become so familiar with You that I will sense it immediately when You identify fellow believers to me.

Notes: _____

_____

_____

The Spirit Who Leads into the Wilderness

"Then Jesus was led up by the Spirit into the wilderness to be tempted by the devil" (Matthew 4:1–11; Mark 1:12,13; Luke 4:1–13).

It is incredible to understand that the Holy Spirit was responsible for leading Jesus to the place of temptation.

Before God can use any of us, we have to be tested to see if we are ready to serve God faithfully. The Greek word for "temptation" means to test the quality of a person or the temper of metal to see if it can do what it has been made to do. The Holy Spirit cannot lead us into great exploits if we cannot be counted on to be faithful to do what God wants. God has to know what it would take to tempt us to stay away from worship, prayer meetings, or going on a mission.

We need to study how Jesus dealt with temptation. Under the guidance of the Holy Spirit, He successfully used Scripture to pass the test. At the conclusion, the devil was under no illusion that He had dealt with anyone but the Son of God. Defeated, he left. If we want to serve Jesus, we too must be led by the Holy Spirit into our own wildernesses to be tempted by the devil. As we use the tools Jesus used, we will emerge triumphantly.

Prayer

Holy Spirit, please guide me through my temptation in my wilderness so I can serve Jesus faithfully.

Notes: _____

_____

_____

The Spirit in Opportunity

"And Jesus returned in the power of the Holy Spirit..."
(Luke 4:14,15).

After successfully defeating the devil, Jesus headed home to start His ministry. He was returning to Galilee like a one-man army, ready to claim victory after victory. Everybody seemed to be excited as He taught in the synagogues in the surrounding towns. Wherever he preached the Gospel, people were saved and healed of various diseases. Blind eyes were opened, the lame walked, and demons were cast out of people!

Everything was going exactly the way that we would have imagined. Having overcome temptation, he had defeated the devil. He was now dealing with the works of the devil and the effects of sin. Every time He taught in a synagogue, He was well received. He was glorified by everyone who experienced His ministry.

In Christian circles, Jesus was a "10" on the star ratings. His ministry left the kingdom of darkness reeling like a losing boxer. In the "honeymoon" phase of His ministry, He took full advantage of the doors open to the influence of His Holy Spirit. Like Jesus, we have to take advantage of every opportunity to preach the Gospel because we may never "pass that way again."

Prayer

Holy Spirit, please don't let me miss the many opportunities to exercise ministry and set captives free.

Notes: _____

_____

_____

The Upon-me Spirit

"The Spirit of the Lord is upon me..." (Luke 4:16–28).

What a reaction Jesus received to His first sermon in His home church / synagogue! His reputation had preceded Him and *"all spoke well of Him."* Initially, every eye was upon Him as He opened the Book of Isaiah and read the prophecy which described the expected Saviour. When He said, *"Today, this Scripture has been fulfilled in your hearing,"* people reacted. *"Is this not Joseph's son?"* they queried. How could the expected Saviour be a local boy they were accustomed to seeing in ordinary circumstances? Challenging Him to perform the miracles in Nazareth that He did in Capernaum, they were *"filled with wrath"* at His illustration of the inability of any prophet to do much for the conditions of his own land. Determining to kill Him, they endeavoured to throw him off a cliff. The honeymoon was over!

Religious people usually react with anger in the presence of Jesus and the Holy Spirit. The pure Gospel message will produce a negative reaction. No one could preach the Gospel better than Jesus did – yet He allowed Himself to be led by the Holy Spirit to the Cross. We too, must take up our own cross to follow Him (Matthew 16:24). The cross for many of us is that negative reaction of sin in other people to the Gospel and the Holy Spirit upon us.

Prayer

Holy Spirit, please be upon me at all times so I can fulfill Scripture and take the criticism.

Notes: _____

_____

_____

Spirit-Led Days

The Rejoicing Spirit

"In that same hour he rejoiced in the Holy Spirit..."
(Luke 10:21–24).

Jesus taught that real joy comes from having our names written in the Book of Life in Heaven.

Joy also comes as the result of serving Him and doing ministry. Luke describes a situation where the disciples were excited. They had just come back with a good report, having seen many people enter the Kingdom of Heaven. Not only were the sick healed, but the demons were even subject to their authority!

Joy comes on hearing a good report about the defeat of Satan. *"I saw Satan fall like lightning from Heaven"* (Luke 10:18). Jesus demonstrated what we all need to do after we have been doing ministry and have seen the Holy Spirit move with His authority and power through us. He rejoiced and then went to prayer. He thanked our Heavenly Father, Lord of Heaven, for revealing the truth of Who He was. He thanked Him for revealing the things of the Kingdom to His disciples – including all of His followers, who are really like children when it comes to understanding the things of the Kingdom. Like the disciples, we have seen what many prophets and kings desired to see: Jesus, the Son of God – the ultimate reason to rejoice!

Prayer

Holy Spirit, thank you for the joy of knowing my name is in Your Book, knowing and serving Jesus, and getting good reports.

Notes: _____

_____

_____

The "Good Things" Spirit

"How much more will the Heavenly Father give the Holy Spirit to those who ask Him!" (Luke 11:1–13; Matthew 6:6–13; 7:7–12).

*J*esus taught that prayer is important so that we can know God as our Heavenly Father, acknowledge His Kingdom, seek His will, have our physical needs met, find daily forgiveness, and receive help in dealing with the evil one. It is important to know that God wants to meet all of our needs. *"He satisfies him who is thirsty, and the hungry He fills with good things"* (Psalm 107:9).

Jesus tells us in the Gospels that we have another critically important need: our need for the Holy Spirit. We need to know Him so that we can have a very intimate, personal relationship with the God who comes inside us. As Toyohiko Kagawa, the great Japanese Christian experienced, "Those who have received the Holy Spirit come to have the feelings of God." With such a heart, allowing Jesus to exercise His Lordship over our lives feels like a great privilege – a welcome release.

Jesus wants us to understand that, although He has come to save the world and baptize with the Holy Spirit, it is the Heavenly Father who sends Him to us.

Prayer

Heavenly Father, please let me know You intimately through the filling of the Holy Spirit, as Jesus said. Make me hungry and fill me with good things. Come, Holy Spirit. Come and fill me with Your power so that I can know God's feelings.

Notes: _____

_____

_____

The Spirit Upon Us

"I will put My Spirit upon Him, and He shall proclaim justice to the Gentiles" (Matthew 12:9–21).

Here is the fulfillment of Isaiah's prophesy (Isaiah 42:1–4). Jesus healed a man's withered hand on the Sabbath. As usual, a few Pharisees were there to criticize Him, saying that He wasn't supposed to work on the Sabbath. Healing a man was work in their eyes, because they couldn't understand healing, let alone heal anybody themselves. Because they couldn't control Him, they conceived a plan to kill Jesus. That's probably why Jesus ordered those who had been healed not to talk about Him.

No matter whether it is Jesus or someone upon whom God has put His Spirit, today's Pharisees will react badly when people are healed in a meeting. However, they are reacting negatively to the Holy Spirit and not to us who minister healing. We have to be careful not to take the criticism personally. Whenever God puts His Spirit on or in anybody, the Gospel will be preached and people will be healed. Sin always reacts against the Holy Spirit. People can't hurt God so they attack His messengers: Jesus or us.

Prayer

Holy Spirit, please strengthen me and remind me to rejoice when I am criticized after praying for the sick and seeing Jesus heal them. Thank You, Holy Spirit.

Notes: _____

_____

_____

The Exorcising Spirit

"But if it is by the Spirit of God that I cast out demons, then the Kingdom of God has come upon you" (Matthew 12:22–32).

Demons or evil spirits are always a real problem – especially for people who are not Christians. It seems that people either get too preoccupied with them, or don't want to acknowledge they exist. Unfortunately, they do. They attempt to possess, harass, torment and kill people. Fortunately, they cannot possess Spirit-filled Christians – although they can harass us. What a wonderful thing that Jesus gave us authority to cast them out of people and to set them free! (Luke 9:1; 10:17; Mark 16:17).

The possessed man in this particular account had been made blind and deaf by the demon that possessed him. Jesus set him completely free. He did so to show people that the Kingdom of God had come upon them. We know they recognized it, because they asked, *"Can this be the son of David?"*

The good news is that demons are more afraid of us than we are of them. To cast them out, we simply have to firmly command them to leave in the Name of Jesus Christ. Despite any screaming, roaring, yelling, swearing, threatening, lying or arguing they may do, they will leave. The person who was being harassed will return to his or her right mind.

Prayer

Holy Spirit, give me Christ-confidence and show me how to use my power and authority over demons to set people free.

Notes: _____

_____

_____

The Dangerous Spirit

"...but whoever blasphemes against the Holy Spirit never has forgiveness, but is guilty of eternal sin" (Mark 3:20–30).

The only unforgivable sin, Jesus says, is *"blasphemy against the Holy Spirit."* Jesus gave this severe warning just after He had cast a demon out of a man. Those watching on looked at Jesus and, instead of seeing the Holy Spirit in Him, they misidentified the Holy Spirit as Beelzebub or Satan, accusing Jesus of having an evil spirit.

Jesus tried to get them to understand. *"How can Satan cast out Satan? If a kingdom is divided against itself, that kingdom cannot stand."* These were people who were supposed to be able to tell the difference between the work of the Holy Spirit and Satan.

We can be in great danger if we mistake the counterfeit work of Satan for the work of the Holy Spirit. Conversely, the danger can come from not recognizing the work of the Holy Spirit.

Our protection against the "unforgivable sin" is the Bible. In it, God shows us the difference between the works of the Holy Spirit and Satan. To ignore the Bible is to place ourselves in danger of blaspheming against the Holy Spirit in two ways: by either calling the work of the Holy Spirit the work of Satan, or to call the work of Satan the work of the Holy Spirit.

Prayer

Holy Spirit, help me to recognize Your works according to Scripture so I won't be misled by my feelings, experience or Satan.

Notes: _____

_____

_____

The Speaking Spirit

"...for it is not you who speak, but the Spirit of your Father speaking through you" (Matthew 10:16–20).

We are Jesus' sheep. We don't look very dangerous. We usually look more like victims. The wolves like to attack and kill us – but, we are a new kind of hybrid "attack-sheep," extremely dangerous to all "sinner-wolves." Jesus sends his attack-sheep (us) out to attack these sinner-wolves and change them into sheep. It's miraculous the tactics we sheep use to subdue our victims! When the wolves attack us, we don't resist. We attack-sheep are most dangerous after we have been arrested, taken into court, beaten, or dragged before governors and kings. For it is then that the Holy Spirit begins to speak through us. Before they know it, the wolves are talked to death – or rather into life through Jesus Christ!

Every situation, good or bad, is an opportunity to witness to the people involved. King Agrippa thought Paul was standing trial for his life; but when the Holy Spirit started speaking through Paul, bearing witness to Christ, the king realized that he, himself, was on trial for his soul. He said to Paul, *"In a short time you think to make me a Christian!"* You want to believe it!

Prayer

Holy Spirit, please speak through me so that I can be free to witness to anybody, anywhere.

Notes: _____

_____

_____

The Defensive-Coordinator Spirit

"...for it is not you who speak, but the Holy Spirit"
(Mark 13:9–13).

*J*esus was always honest with us. He warned us that following Him would not make us popular. In fact, He said that many people would hate us for following Him. He told us we would be persecuted, arrested, tried before church councils and political authorities. Our families would turn against us and try to kill us. We'll never be able to say, "But, Jesus you never told us." He made it abundantly clear that following Him would never be dull – either because we would live a supernatural lifestyle, or because people might hate us and try to kill us. Whatever happens, according to these Scripture verses, it is all planned as part of the "end-times" preparation for Jesus' return.

Mercifully, we are not left alone when we serve Jesus. The Holy Spirit remains as our Comforter. He will coordinate our defense. We don't have to get uptight or anxious, because He will give us what to say *at the time* and not before. If we listen, He will have something fresh to say to us every day. We need to spend time getting familiar with His voice by talking to Him everyday.

Prayer

Holy Spirit, help me to listen to what You want me to say in every situation. Help me to trust that You will coordinate my defense and that I don't have to worry. I just need to listen.

Notes: _____

_____

The Teaching Spirit

"...for the Holy Spirit will teach in that very hour what you ought to say" (Luke 12:8–12).

The Holy Spirit is a flexible and accurate teacher. He knows the mind of Jesus and how to minister in every situation. Because each opportunity for us to witness has its own unique challenges, the Holy Spirit doesn't teach us what to say before the very hour. We'd probably forget what He said, anyway. He does not give us previously prepared speeches that fit any and every occasion. He teaches us what to include in our personal testimony as we witness to different kinds of people, and He prepares us to handle vicious attacks against Jesus and us. The good news is that no matter how difficult acknowledging Jesus before men might be, Jesus will acknowledge us before the angels. Imagine that! – Jesus talks about us!

We need to develop an "up close and personal" relationship with the Holy Spirit. Getting in the habit of consulting Him before we have to speak for Jesus is critical. We need to become so teachable, dependable, and dependent on Him, that the Holy Spirit will have no problem getting us to cooperate.

Prayer

Holy Spirit, please teach me to recognize Your voice so that I'll be ready, with Your help to represent Jesus in every situation.

Notes: _____

_____

_____

The Spirit of David's Son

"How is it then that David, inspired by the Spirit, calls Him Lord..." (Matthew 22:41–46).

Paul told us that *"the unspiritual* (natural) *man does not receive the gifts of the Spirit of God: for they are folly* (foolishness) *to him: and he is not able to understand them because they are spiritually discerned"* (1 Corinthians 2:14).

This is why the Pharisees thought Jesus was crazy. They did not understand God's logic. The "natural" person is one who has not received the Holy Spirit into his or her life. We need Him to teach us so we can understand the things of God. Religious people, like the Pharisees, may claim to know God, but view true matters of the Spirit as foolishness. Their lack of spiritual understanding blocks them from accepting Jesus as their Saviour. For instance, in this passage, it didn't make sense to the religious people that Jesus was called the Son of David, while David referred to the Messiah as "my Lord." When we receive the Holy Spirit, we understand that Jesus lived before He came to Earth in human flesh.

It is only after we ourselves experience salvation and the Holy Spirit comes into our lives that we can understand the "mysteries" of God – and how precious they are.

Prayer

Holy Spirit, show me more of the things of God so that I can receive *"the things of the Spirit"* and honour my Lord Jesus.

Notes: _____

_____

_____

The Spirit of " My Lord"

"David himself, inspired by the Holy Spirit, declared, 'the Lord said to my Lord...'" (Mark 12:35–40).

*J*ust because somebody can quote the Bible doesn't mean they understand it or know the Author. The Sadducees were blind to spiritual things, as are many who fill church pews today. Those who know Jesus as their Lord have no problem understanding David's statement that Jehovah God, *"the Lord,"* spoke to *"my Lord,"* meaning Jesus. However, it's impossible for anybody who does not know Jesus as Saviour and Lord to comprehend spiritual truths. This is why the Sadducees – then and now – couldn't accept His teachings. For instance, they did not believe in the resurrection of the dead, which Jesus both taught and demonstrated by raising the dead – as He will do on the Last Day. Jesus said of them, *"You are wrong, because you know neither the Scriptures nor the power of God"* (Matthew 22:29). What an insult to people who prided themselves on those very things! But true.

After we are baptized with the Holy Spirit and receive Jesus as "my Lord," the Scriptures become clear and we stand in awe at the power of God.

Prayer

Holy Spirit, help me know "my Lord" Jesus intimately so that I can understand the Scriptures and the power of God.

Notes: _____

_____

_____

The Comforter Spirit

"Blessed are those who mourn, for they shall be comforted"
(Matthew 5:1–13).

This verse should be translated: *"Blessed are those who mourn, for they shall receive the Comforter."* Here, Jesus is not talking about people who mourn the death of loved ones. He is teaching us that the nine Beatitudes are all necessary elements in becoming mature Christians. In the first Beatitude, He is talking about people who recognize they are *"poor"* – in abject poverty with regard to the Holy Spirit – and become born-again so they can enter the Kingdom of Heaven. The second Beatitude teaches that when we are sorry for our sins and *"mourn"* because of our sinful, Godless life, Jesus will send the Comforter, the Heavenly Defense Lawyer, the Holy Spirit, into our lives. With the help of the Comforter, we become *"the meek"* – those who are under the control of the Holy Spirit, teachable in all things, and ready to act on God's command. Each "Beatitude-step" is necessary to become the *"light of the world"* and the *"salt of the Earth."*

The Holy Spirit begins to accomplish this work in us when we are ready to cooperate.

Prayer

Holy Spirit, please be my Comforter as I grow to maturity in Jesus Christ, my Lord.

Notes: _____

_____

_____

The Spirit Who Brings New Birth

"Truly, truly I say to you, unless one is born anew, he cannot see the Kingdom of God" (John 3:1–8).

Jesus teaches that there are two essential components for seeing and entering the Kingdom of God. He calls the process being *"born again"* or *"born from above."* This is a supernatural work of God accomplished through Jesus Christ in the power of the Holy Spirit. The first component is that of being born *"of water,"* (Matthew 3:11) which is symbolic of repentance or turning away from the sin we confess. The second component is being born of the *"Spirit"* (John 3:5) meaning the "Holy Spirit," who cleanses us of our sin and fills us with His power.

Many people object to hearing that it is necessary to be *"born again."* However, it is so simple that even little children can experience it. The new birth was designed for everyone and doesn't hurt a bit. If you haven't experienced it, you can. All you have to do is to call upon the Name of Jesus. Even though you cannot see Him, He'll be there. Ask Jesus to please forgive you for any sin or wrong you have done. Then, invite Him to come into your life and your heart. Try it and your place will be reserved in Heaven.

Prayer
Thank You, Jesus, for bringing salvation and eternal life to me.

Notes: _____

_____

_____

The Measureless Spirit

"...for it is not by measure that He gives the Spirit"
(John 3: 31–36).

*A*gain we are reminded that when Jesus sends the Holy Spirit, He does not give anyone bigger or smaller portions, or double portions. Each person gets the full portion of the Holy Spirit. He shows no favouritism. The original Greek says that He *"gives the Holy Spirit without measure or degree."* That means that we don't get a part or portion of Him. It's not as though each person gets a little chunk of the Holy Spirit according to their worthiness and is accorded ten minutes a day of His time. No. Amazingly, we each get the whole of Him with His full attention so that He can have a full relationship with each of us all the time!

God's plan is that the Holy Spirit is given to be our Heaven-appointed, God-sent, resident Lawyer, Comforter, Teacher, on 24/7 availability; because our ministry and battle against the enemy goes on around the clock. Just as the Father gives all things to the Son, the Son, Jesus, gives the whole of the Holy Spirit to us so He can continuously give us the *"good things"* (Matthew 7:11) and let us know that *"God is true."*

Prayer

Holy Spirit, thank You for coming into my life in Your full measure and giving me Your full attention. Help me to give Jesus my full attention. Thank You for being with me all the time.

Notes: _____

_____

_____

The Living Water Spirit

"...you would have asked Him and He would have given you living water" (John 4:4–15).

There is a thirst that plagues every human being which can't be satisfied by any amount of water. Within each person is a void reserved for the living water of the Holy Spirit. Only He can fill it, quenching the thirst created by the emptiness.

Those who don't know God usually can't understand why they feel so empty inside. In an attempt to quench the thirst, one person will become an alcoholic; another will go from partner to partner, inside and outside of marriage, trying to satisfy the deep longing of the heart; another will become a workaholic, stuffing the raging thirst as far below the conscious mind as possible. Predictably, all human attempts fail because nothing can replace the desire for relationship with God that lies within every human.

Jesus met a woman at a well outside a Samaritan village. He engaged her in conversation as she drew her water. Touching the nerve of her inner thirst, His startling knowledge of her elicited a response that connected her to the source of her thirst. She needed forgiveness and the living water that only Jesus could supply. As she responded, the Holy Spirit filled her with *"power, love, and self-control"* (2 Timothy 1:7). He wants to do the same for us.

Prayer

Thank you Holy Spirit, for becoming a spring of "living water" inside me. I will never thirst again.

Notes: _____

_____

_____

The Spirit in Worship

"God is Spirit, and those who worship Him must worship in Spirit and in Truth" (John 4:16–26).

The Samaritan woman tried to start a religious argument with Jesus in order to block Him from touching her heart and her unhappy life with her need to know and worship God. He didn't allow her to sidestep His love any more than He allows it of us.

Today, there are many people and religions with their own opinions about how to worship God. The only problem is that God has His own opinion about what is acceptable worship! Jesus represents that opinion.

God is a Spirit. In Greek, there are two words for spirit – one refers to God's Spirit (pneuma), and the other to the human spirit or soul (psyche). The only worship acceptable to God is that which flows out of the psyche in unity with the pneuma (Holy Spirit). Unacceptable worship is performed unilaterally through our human spirit. Thus, Jesus tells us that only those people who are born again and filled with the Holy Spirit can worship God the Father in Spirit (Holy Spirit) and in Truth (Jesus Christ). Without these conditions being met, worship goes no higher than the roof.

Prayer

   Holy Spirit, please teach me how to worship the Father in Spirit and in Truth so You and I can both be satisfied.

Notes: _____

_____

_____

The Spirit of Words

"It is the Spirit that gives life, the flesh is of no avail; the words that I have spoken to you are Spirit and Life"

(John 6:52–69).

*J*esus told us that *"The gate is narrow and the way is hard that leads to life, and those who find it are few"* (Matthew 7:14). Following Jesus is not easy when we try to do it in our own strength (flesh). We fail. We find ourselves in constant conflict with Jesus' teaching and in a continuous struggle with the Holy Spirit as He gradually tries to transform us to be like Jesus.

We still have people today who want to make following Jesus into a popularity contest and who try to turn Christian ministry into unoffensive entertainment that will make the Gospel acceptable. Many television and radio ministries have made their hosts and preachers into popular personalities – like movie stars – whose goal is to keep their ratings up and attract people by conforming to this world.

There is a built-in offense to the Gospel of Jesus Christ. Jesus lost much of His following because He said, *"He who eats My flesh and drinks My blood abides in Me, and I in him"* (John 6:56). In other words, if we want to follow Him, we have to walk the walk and suffer the abuse. That's why thousands left Him and He had only 11 disciples on whom He could depend.

Prayer

Holy Spirit, please keep me on the road of Life no matter how much it costs.

Notes: _____

_____

_____

The Heart Restoring Spirit

"Now this He said about the Spirit, which those who believed in Him were to receive; for as yet the Spirit had not been given, because Jesus was not yet glorified" (John 7:37–52).

Jesus was constantly preparing people for the Holy Spirit whom He was going to send on the Day of Pentecost. His message to people was that they (we) were suffering from a serious heart problem. While the heart was supposed to be the residence of the Holy Spirit out of which should flow *"living water,"* it was infected with sin and was developing *"all these evil things"* (Mark 7:21–23) that defile people. Every person ever born has this innate heart problem. The major symptom is a feeling of emptiness that nothing seems to satisfy. No human success in business, sports, recreation, family or religion can quench the thirst. It is a thirst for a relationship with God and a need for *"living water"* flowing through it to touch others. It takes a spiritual heart transplant to solve the problem. Jesus is the only doctor who can perform the miracle. *"If any one is thirsty, let him come to Me and drink"* (John 7:37). The restorative heart operation can be had without financial cost. There are always mixed reactions because Jesus has the monopoly on *"living water."* Regardless, it tastes wonderful.

Prayer

Holy Spirit, please fill my heart and produce rivers of living water flowing through me.

Notes: _____

_____

_____

The Paraclete Spirit

"He will give you another Counselor, to be with you forever, even the Spirit of Truth..." (John 14:12–24).

"Paraclete" is the Greek word for "defense lawyer" or "legal counselor."

Jesus knew that we could not keep His commandments, no matter how good our intentions. He knew we needed "Somebody" who could steer us through the complexities of life, whisper God's wisdom to us, strengthen our position, and essentially be on call for each one of us every moment of the day, whether awake or asleep. We needed a Heavenly legal expert who knew God's law perfectly and could safely guide us away from temptation, keeping us faithful to God's plan for our lives. Only the Holy Spirit had the capability of being able to dwell within every person at the same time and deal with each of us in a very personal, individual way. Again, the Holy Spirit was the only Person for the job. In this Scripture, Jesus calls Him the *"paraclete."* It is Jesus' intention that the Holy Spirit take up residence in our hearts to be our Guide, directing us to an increasingly loving relationship with Jesus, within the loving boundaries of His commandments.

Prayer

Holy Spirit, thank You for being my "legal Counselor." Please guide, teach, warn, and lead me at Your discretion.

Notes: _____

_____

_____

The Spirit of Remembrance

"But the Counselor, the Holy Spirit, whom the Father will send in My Name, He will teach you all things..." (John 14:25–31).

*J*esus makes it clear that the Holy Spirit is sent by the Father in Jesus' Name. The Holy Spirit has two main functions:

1) To teach us all things. This is not an excuse not to study the Scriptures in the process of showing ourselves *"approved to God, workmen who do not need to be ashamed, rightly dividing the Word of truth."* The *"all things"* that He will teach us is how to *"endure all things"* so that we can be *"vessels of honour, sanctified, useful to the Master, prepared for every good work"* (2 Timothy 2:15–21).*

2) To bring to our remembrance all that Jesus has said to us. This is not only what He has said in the Bible, but also what He has told us to do in our daily living. Whatever Jesus says to us personally will never be contrary to what is in the Bible.

The Holy Spirit is our guarantee for faithfulness.

*The Gideon Bible, The Gideons International, 501 Imperial Road, Guelph, Ont. N1H 7A2

Prayer

Holy Spirit, please teach me all things and remind me of all Jesus said – both in the Bible and to me personally – as He purposed to show me what He wants me to do in serving Him.

Notes: _____

_____

_____

The Witnessing Spirit

"But when the Counselor comes, whom I shall send to you from the Father, even the Spirit of Truth...He will bear witness to me..." (John 15:26–16:4).

*A*nother work of the Holy Spirit is to bear witness to Jesus – through us. Just as it is with the Holy Spirit, that is our major calling. Jesus sends the Holy Spirit into our lives so that we can have "power" to be His witnesses. A witness is a person who gives testimony to other people about what they have personally seen or heard. Spreading hearsay or gossip is not being a witness.

We are often unaware of the influence our words can carry when empowered by the Holy Spirit. The impact of witnessing, just sharing a personal testimony, can be enormous. The evidence of the life of another can deeply penetrate the minds and hearts of those who hear it, leading them to conclude that if Jesus can do it for another, He can and will do it for them. It plants hope for miracles of Divine intervention. According to Revelation 12:11, when the devil attempts to rob us of the assurance of our salvation, we overcome him when we witness to others.

Prayer

Holy Spirit, please help me become an effective witness for Jesus so that many other people will be able to call Him Saviour, Lord, Healer and Deliverer.

Notes: _____

_____

_____

The Working Spirit

"It is to your advantage that I go away, for if I do not go away, the Counselor will not come to you; but if I go, I will send Him to you" (John 16:4–11).

Jt must have been almost impossible for the disciples to imagine that it would be better for them if Jesus were to go back to Heaven. What counselor could be better than Him?

Jesus knew that until He returned to Heaven and sent His Holy Spirit to dwell within all who would accept Him, His ministry on Earth would be limited to those with whom He had personal contact, because when He became flesh, He took on the same physical limitations that we have. However, with His Spirit indwelling and empowering thousands and eventually millions of His followers, the fruit of His work on Earth would be enormously multiplied. Not only that, but those in whom His Spirit dwelled would deepen in their faith and grow in His wisdom and grace as He personally led and guided them, giving the completely personal attention needed. It is really quite amazing that He is "God (Jesus) in us," the assurance of our salvation.

Prayer

Holy Spirit, You are welcome in my heart and life. Please feel free to do in me the work that Jesus sent You to do.

Notes: _____

_____

_____

The Work of the Holy Spirit

"And when He has come, He will convict the world of sin, and righteousness and judgment..." (John 16:5–15).

This passage contains the Holy Spirit's job description:

1) He will convict us of our sin – showing us that we are guilty of breaking God's law and are under the penalty of death.
2) He will convict us of righteousness – revealing the understanding of righteousness, showing us that we are not in right relationship with God until we have accepted Jesus as our Saviour and Lord.
3) He will convict us about judgment – revealing the understanding of judgment and the knowledge that because the ruler of this world, the devil, has been judged, he is going to Hell along with those who (by default) follow him instead of following Jesus.

The Holy Spirit is not an independent agent who operates on His own authority. His authority comes from Jesus and the Heavenly Father who have apportioned to Him the responsibility of revealing to us the truth and such future events as we are to know. Throughout all, He glorifies Jesus.

Prayer

Holy Spirit, please speak to me about sin, righteousness and judgment so that I too can glorify Jesus.

Notes: _____

_____

_____

The Spirit of Jesus

"Father, into your hands I commit my Spirit"

(Luke 23:44–49).

*J*esus did not face death alone. The Holy Spirit, who is His Spirit (Romans 8:9), took Him through it. As I have previously mentioned, there are two words for "spirit" used in the Greek: "pneuma" which is used of the Holy Spirit and "psyche" which is used of the human spirit or soul. Here, Jesus is committing His Holy Spirit (pneuma) to the Father because the ministry that He was about to accomplish next could not be done with His human spirit (psyche). He did not go to suffer in Hell. Rather, *"being put to death in the flesh but made alive in the Spirit* (pneuma)*; in which He went and preached to the spirits in prison"* (1 Peter 3:18–20).

Jesus established His authority when He died on the Cross of Calvary and paid for our sin, arose from the dead, and ascended into Heaven. He proves His Lordship by baptizing us with the Holy Spirit. With Jesus as our Saviour and Lord, we no longer have to fear death, but can joyfully look forward to going to Heaven.

Prayer

Holy Spirit, thank You for your work of establishing the Kingdom of God in my heart so that Jesus can be my Resurrection and my Life.

Notes: _____

_____

_____

The Spirit of the Trinity

"Make disciples of all nations, baptizing them in the Name of the Father and of the Son and of the Holy Spirit..."

(Matthew 28:16–20).

*E*vident in John 3:16, *"For God so loved the world that He gave His only begotten Son that whoever believes in Him should not perish but have eternal life,"* is the humility, cooperation, love, and ambition of the God-head – Father, Son and Holy Spirit – unified as One in its focus on salvation. The saving of people is the order of every day for Christians; an imperative for every Christian.

Jesus has given us "all authority" to do one thing: to make disciples. He has also given us the secret for receiving Heavenly food. After Jesus' disciples came back with food for Him to eat, He told them that He had already eaten. *"My food is to do the will of Him who sent Me and to accomplish His work"* (John 4:34). Disciple-making is not a specialist's job; it's everyone's commission. Until we have known the fulfilling experience of leading somebody to Jesus and seeing them become disciples, we'll never know the fulfillment of the Christian life.

Prayer

Holy Spirit, please give me the boldness that I need to joyfully carry out "the Great Commission" in the Name of the Father and of the Son and of the Holy Spirit.

Notes: _____

_____

_____

The Signs-Producing Spirit

"And these signs will accompany those who believe..."
(Mark 16:15–20).

$\mathcal{H}$ere, Jesus tells us how we can identify authentic Christians. He says we are walking sign-boards after we have become born again and are baptized both in water and with the Holy Spirit. These developments result in signs (like trademarks or logos) which show the world that we are saved people who are prepared to give directions to others so that they can find Jesus.

The first sign that we are true believers is the authority to cast demons out of people who have been possessed and set them free. The second sign is the supernatural ability to speak in new tongues or new languages that we have never learned – thus demonstrating the Lordship of Jesus Christ over our lives. The third sign is the evidence of Jesus' protection demonstrated by our immunity to the effect of deadly serpents or poisoned drink. The fourth sign is the healing of sick people as a result of us laying our hands on them and praying for them, enabling God to use us as conduits for His healing touch. These exciting signs are available for all believers to experience.

Prayer

Holy Spirit, please show me how to minister to other people so that Jesus can confirm His Word with the "signs following."

Notes: _____

_____

_____

The Promised Spirit

"And behold, I send the promise of My Father upon you; but stay in the city until you are clothed with power from on high"
(Luke 24:36–49).

The disciples were on the edge of their seats with expectation as the resurrected-from-the-dead Jesus explained that everything He had done had been prophesied according to the Scriptures. They knew it was true. They were eyewitnesses. He was actually standing right there before them with the scars on his hands and sides. Some were shocked. Others were frightened at His appearance. Any who doubted, like Thomas, doubted no more. All believed.

Jesus had to prepare His disciples for *"the promise of the Father,"* who is the Holy Spirit. He told them to tarry (wait) in Jerusalem until they were clothed with power from on high. Thankfully, we do not have to wait in order to receive the baptism of the Holy Spirit today. There is no age limit to receiving the promise. Anyone, from children to senior citizens, can be baptized in the Holy Spirit. The only condition or preparation is that we must have received Jesus as our Saviour and have had our sins forgiven. To serve Jesus with full confidence we need the promised Holy Spirit.

Prayer

Holy Spirit, promise of the Father, I am looking forward with great expectation to Your fellowship with me today.

Notes: _____

_____

_____

The Limitless Spirit

"Receive the Holy Spirit" (John 20:19–23).

After rising from the dead, Jesus began to prepare the disciples for their future ministry. First, He gave them peace. Secondly, He gave them the Holy Spirit and the authority to forgive sin.

When Jesus died on the Cross, He paid the price for all sins for everybody for all time. He has done His work. *"It is finished"* (John 19:30). Without forgiveness, no one can be reconciled to God. Our job as believers is to help others to appropriate (to receive) that forgiveness. Without the power to forgive the sins of other people against God, others and ourselves, no ministry can take place. Without the power of the Holy Spirit we have neither the capacity nor the ability to forgive as Jesus wants us to do.

Forgiveness is the basis for ministry. When Peter asked Jesus how many times he would have to forgive his brother who might sin against him (Matthew 18:21–35), Jesus shocked him (along with everyone through the ages!) when He set no limits on forgiving by saying *"seventy times seven"* times each day – because that is what He has to forgive us everyday. This limitless forgiveness is what He paid for on the Cross.

Prayer

Holy Spirit, please give me the power and grace to forgive without limit so I can fulfill my ministry.

Notes: _____

_____

_____

The Baptizing Spirit

"For John baptized with water, but before many days you shall be baptized with the Holy Spirit" (Acts 1:1–5).

All of Jesus' disciples, including us, have to wait until they have been adequately prepared by Jesus to do the kind of ministry that will be relevant and effective in saving the world. After three years of the "Jesus Christ Seminary," the original twelve had to wait until Jesus said they were ready to be baptized with the Holy Spirit.

It was as difficult to share the Gospel with the generation of the early disciples as it is with ours. They offered no solutions for their own problems with ministry, but wanted to tell Jesus how to carry out His. Jesus said they were like children playing in the market, wanting people to dance to their tune and play their games. *"For John came neither eating nor drinking, and they say, 'He has a demon'; the Son of Man came eating and drinking, and they say, 'Behold, a glutton and a drunkard, a friend of tax collectors and sinners'"* (Matthew 11:18,19)! Only the Holy Spirit could figure it all out. That's why we need to be baptized in Him. He alone can show us how to share the *"foolishness of God"* (1 Corinthians 1:25) so that our generation can know Jesus Christ as its Saviour and Lord.

Prayer

Holy Spirit, thank You for coming so that I can look to you for guidance to reach my generation with the Gospel.

Notes: _____

_____

_____

The Dynamite Spirit

"But you shall receive power when the Holy Spirit has come upon you; and you shall be My witnesses..." (Acts 1:6–11).

*J*esus wants us to receive "power." This is translated from the Greek word, "dunamis," which means power, might, strength, force, and from which we derive the word "dynamite." We need this dynamite power to have the freedom to tell other people about what He has done and is doing in our lives. It takes that explosion of God's love to blow away the sin that encrusts people's lives, and to set them free to know Jesus.

With the power of the Holy Spirit, we can set aside our fears about other people's reactions when we share our testimonies about what Jesus has done in our lives. Usually we fear the worst, thinking that we might turn them off or away from Jesus, or that they might get so angry that they will never become Christians. With the power of the Holy Spirit, we can set aside our fears and trust the Holy Spirit to give us the right words to say. As this happens, people will be blown away into accepting Jesus Christ as their Saviour no matter where they are – from Jerusalem, to Judea, to every country in the world.

Prayer
 Holy Spirit, please give me this power so that I can witness for Jesus everywhere I go.

Notes: _____

_____

_____

The Choosing Spirit

"...the Scripture had to be fulfilled, which the Holy Spirit spoke beforehand by the mouth of David, concerning Judas...'His office let another take'" (Acts 1:15–26).

*W*henever one of God's chosen people in leadership, like Judas, betrays Jesus or turns away from Him, backslides, falls away into sin or causes problems in the church and has to be removed, his or her position has to be filled with somebody else. Somehow, the Holy Spirit always warns ahead of time that the person is going to fail Jesus and us. When it does happen, while very sad, we have to remember that all leadership can be replaced. No one is indispensable in the Kingdom of God.

The beautiful thing about the Gospel is that it is not always necessary to replace fallen leadership if they will repent and return to God's plan. Such was the case with King David who repented of his affair with Bathsheba and was restored. With the picture of the Good Shepherd going out from the 99 to find the one lost lamb, we must be very mindful of restoration. Unfortunately, like Judas, not all respond. When it is necessary to place or replace anybody in a church position, it is important to pray and find out who God wants and select that person. This is how Matthias was chosen.

Prayer

Holy Spirit, please show me when You want to use me to help restore fallen leadership, or to replace it with God's choice.

Notes: _____

_____

_____

The Day of Pentecost Spirit

"And they were all filled with the Holy Spirit and began to speak in other tongues..." (Acts 2:1–13).

The Holy Spirit fell upon the 120 believers. They saw fire bursting through the ceiling of the Upper Room and heard a rushing wind as the Holy Spirit filled them. With no known words to express a response to their awesome God, they all began to speak in legitimate languages that they had never learned. Then, with no thought of any inhibitions they might have once had, they went out into the streets speaking in these tongues / languages. The people on the streets heard them speaking in their own languages and dialects about *"the mighty works of God"* and were amazed.

This is the "normal" experience of Christian believers when they are baptized by the Holy Spirit. While not all hear wind or see fire, they all receive power to be witnesses and can begin to speak in tongues, which is both the initial evidence of the baptism of the Holy Spirit (Acts 11:16; 15:8) and a gift (Mark 16:17; 1 Corinthians 12:10) given to show that Jesus Christ has control of their mouths and that they are now under His Lordship. It is a sign to unbelievers of the reality of God. This baptism with the Holy Spirit empowers us to do what Jesus wants us to do.

Prayer   (For those who have not yet received the baptism.)

Holy Spirit, please baptize me so that I can have my Day of Pentecost, speak in tongues, and witness for Jesus.

Notes: _____

_____

_____

The Question-Answering Spirit

"...I will pour out My Spirit upon all flesh..." (Acts 2:14–37).

In answer to the confused crowd's question, *"What does this mean?"* Peter explained that what they were witnessing was the fulfillment of a prophecy of Joel. God was now pouring out His Holy Spirit upon both men and women, young and old. No longer would there be only a special chosen few. God wanted to give His Spirit to all who called on His Name, Jesus, and He would save them from their sin. Their sons and their daughters would prophesy. God would use both men and women. Young people would see visions from God. Elderly people would dream God's dreams. The last days had begun. It was going to be exciting.

And it has been exciting to this very day. The Holy Spirit is still being poured out whenever and wherever people ask Jesus to baptize them with the Holy Spirit. The biggest obstacle today is us. It's like one young couple I met who were afraid to ask Jesus to baptize them with the Holy Spirit; she was afraid that the Spirit wouldn't come and he was afraid that He would! He came and all their fears evaporated as He baptized them.

Prayer

Holy Spirit, please baptize me and let me speak in tongues and prophesy, or dream dreams or have visions. I want everything You have for me.

Notes: _____

_____

_____

The Truthful Spirit

"Repent and be baptized every one of you in the Name of Jesus Christ for the forgiveness of your sins; and you shall receive the Holy Spirit" (Acts 2:14–47).

*J*esus poured out the promise of the Holy Spirit from the Father that day on His people. The crowd could hear and see the results themselves. In an impassioned message, Peter, the once shy fisherman, explained the fulfillment of Joel's prophecy. He challenged the crowd with the witness of those who had obviously been baptized in the Holy Spirit. The purpose of the baptism of the Holy Spirit was – and is – to give people power to witness about Jesus Christ so that others can be saved. Salvation for the crowds was the motivation of Peter's heart that day. Without any personal study or planning, he knew what had to be said to these people as he had never known before. As promised, the Holy Spirit gave him the words to speak – as He does for us today.

Peter called the people to repent and be baptized in the Holy Spirit. Like Peter, we have to love people enough to tell them the truth and not be worried about offending them. He gave it straight from the shoulder. All 3,000 people repented and were saved and baptized in the Holy Spirit and spoke in tongues.

Prayer
Holy Spirit, please guide me so that I can minister salvation and the baptism of the Holy Spirit.

Notes: _____

_____

_____

The Defending Spirit

"Then Peter, filled with the Holy Spirit, said to them..."
(Act 3:6–8; 4:1–22).

Peter and John were arrested because they ministered healing to a 40-year-old lame man who had been begging money at the temple's "Beautiful Gate." They had had no money to give him, but recognized that his real need couldn't be satisfied with money anyway. As he pulled the man to his feet, Peter said, *"I have no silver and gold, but I give you what I have; in the Name of Jesus Christ of Nazareth, walk."* Instantly, the man was healed and ran around the temple telling everybody what had happened. Money cannot buy good health! Unfortunately the result was that Peter and John were arrested.

Today, when we use the authority and ministry gifts with which the Holy Spirit has equipped us, most people will be happy but there are those who won't like it when God uses us to heal others – or whatever He has in mind. Nevertheless, we must be willing to allow Him to use us so that others can praise God. If we are brought before any church council to explain our actions, the Holy Spirit will tell us what to say to defend ourselves.

Prayer

Holy Spirit, please tell me what to say if I need defense when I minister healing to other people.

Notes: _____

_____

_____

The Place-Shaking Spirit

"When they had prayed, the place in which they were gathered together was shaken; and they were all filled with the Holy Spirit..." (Acts 4:23–35).

It is always amazing that certain people get angry whenever God works miracles, and attribute wrong motives to His children. David certainly puzzled over this: *"Why did the Gentiles rage and the peoples imagine vain things?"* (Acts 4:25). But this is always the reaction of sin to the presence and work of God – and I guess it will always be this way. Jesus uses those of us who make ourselves available to Him. He has a plan for our lives and that often means that we will be misunderstood, hated, maligned, and accused of all sorts of evil motives that never crossed our minds.

There is a process for dealing with such accusations. First of all, we have to honestly explain what God is doing. Second, we need to forgive those who have become angry and attacked us. Third, we need to get together with some fellow Christians and *"rejoice and be glad."* Fourth, we need to pray that the Holy Spirit will fill us afresh and even shake the place where we're meeting. Then we can speak the word of God even more boldly.

Prayer

Holy Spirit, when I have been misunderstood, please help me to "rejoice and be glad" and pray, and please fill me afresh with Your Spirit.

Notes: _____

_____

_____

The Promise-Keeper's Spirit

"Why has Satan filled your heart to lie to the Holy Spirit..."
(Acts 5:1–15).

No Christian is beyond being tempted and falling. Ananias and his wife Sapphira had promised the Holy Spirit that they would give the proceeds from selling a piece of property to the church. Nobody told them they had to do it. After selling the land, they changed their minds and lied about the selling price, keeping part of it for themselves – but they forgot that the Holy Spirit saw what they were doing. He told Peter that they were lying. Like many people today, Ananias and Sapphira thought that they could cheat God and lie to the Holy Spirit without any consequences. When confronted by the truth individually, they both dropped dead. I don't think that God killed them, but I believe that every time we lie to God, Jesus, or the Holy Spirit, we kill ourselves. We remove ourselves from God's protective care. There are consequences to lying to the Holy Spirit.

If we promise the Holy Spirit anything, we have to be careful not to arbitrarily change our minds. That is lying to God. We must keep our promises.

Prayer

Holy Spirit, please strengthen me to keep my promises to You that my life may be blessed.

Notes: _____

_____

_____

The Supporting Spirit

"And we are witnesses to these things, and so is the Holy Spirit..." (Acts 5:27–42).

The apostles were arrested a second time and thrown into prison for preaching about Jesus Christ and healing those who were sick or tormented by unclean spirits. That night, an angel released them and said, *"Go and stand in the temple and speak to the people all the words of this Life."* Again they were found and arrested and brought before the ruling council of Jerusalem. Reminded that they had been told to stop teaching in the Name of Jesus, they answered, *"We must obey God rather than men."* Here is a lesson in obedience for us. Like the apostles, when criticized, attacked, and (who knows?) even arrested, we must say and do what Jesus has called us to do.

We too need to stand up for Jesus – regardless of the cost. We must afflict the comfortable and comfort the afflicted in Jesus' Name. Thus far, it has not cost many of us very much to follow Jesus. We ourselves cannot get comfortable until every person around us knows Jesus as Saviour and Lord. He has given us the Holy Spirit to help us speak *"all the words of this Life"* to all within our range.

Prayer

Holy Spirit, please renew my boldness so that I can speak words of life.

Notes: _____

_____

_____

The Spirit of New-Wine

"And no one after drinking old wine, desires new; for he says, 'The old is good'" (Luke 5:37–39; Matthew 9:17; Mark 2:22).

Before the Holy Spirit can come into our lives, we have to be transformed into *"new wineskins."* Our old wineskins, or old lives, can't handle the power of the Holy Spirit because, like old wineskins, they have lost their flexibility to cooperate with God because of sin. And so, in order to receive the Holy Spirit and handle the Holy Spiritual fermentation process called sanctification, we have to be transformed into *"new wineskins"* by being *"born again."* After that, we can be filled with the Holy Spirit and be flexible enough to be used by Jesus Christ.

Once this happens, old religion built on tradition will never satisfy us. The Holy Spirit will transform us, help us to know Jesus intimately and witness for Him. He will give us the gifts (Romans 12:6–8; 1 Corinthians 12:8–11) and the fruit (Galatians 5:22,23) of the Spirit, as well as a wonderful desire to worship. Nothing can compare to the "new wine." Unbelievably, Jesus warns us that there are people who, after receiving the Holy Spirit, will say they liked the old life better.

Prayer
Holy Spirit, thank You for being "new wine" in my life. Please keep me flexible and responsive to Your guidance.

Notes: _____

_____

_____

The Deacon-Choosing Spirit

"and they chose Stephen, a man full of faith and of the Holy Spirit, and Philip, and Prochorus, and Nicanor, and Timon, and Parmenas, and Nicolaus..." (Acts 6:1–7).

*W*henever people are needed to take positions of leadership in the church, like deacons, they must be chosen through prayer, not by popular vote. They must be God's choice and must meet the requirements laid out by the Holy Spirit.

The Greek Christians felt that their widows were being neglected in the food distribution. In response to the problem, the apostles called the church together in order to choose seven men who could take on this ministry since the apostles did not feel called to *"give up the preaching of the Word of God to serve tables."*

The seven who were considered were found to meet God's requirement of being people of *"good repute, full of the Spirit and wisdom."* Thus the apostles prayed with them and set them aside for this new ministry. It is always important that we do not try to decide ourselves where we should serve Jesus. If He wants us to give leadership in the Church, He will tell others who will recognize us if we meet the requirements.

Prayer

Holy Spirit, please equip me to be a person of good reputation and full of the Spirit and wisdom.

Notes: _____

_____

_____

The Disputing Spirit

"But they could not withstand the wisdom and the Spirit with which he spoke" (Acts 6:1–15).

Stephen started his public ministry by serving widows their meals. Like anything we do for Jesus, if we are faithful, He takes notice of it and says, *"Well done, good and faithful servant; you have been faithful over a little, I will set you over much; enter into the joy of your Master"* (Matthew 25:21,23). Soon, he was doing *"great wonders and signs."* Some Jews attempted to argue publically with him about Jesus, but the Holy Spirit gave him wisdom to answer their questions. They couldn't convince him that their religious beliefs were right and he was wrong. Finally, they made up false charges against him and had him accused and arrested for speaking blasphemy.

You can argue with a person who has a theory – but not with a person who has had a life-changing experience with Jesus Christ. Faithfulness has its own reward: eternal life. After we have said all we can say, then all we can do is to *"be aglow with the Spirit"* (Romans 12:11), and let the Holy Spirit do His work.

Prayer

Holy Spirit, please teach me how to be faithful over a little so that I can have more opportunities to serve Jesus.

Notes: _____

_____

_____

The Eloquent Spirit

"...you always resist the Holy Spirit"
(Acts 7:1–3; 42–53).

We may forget our history, but God does not. The Holy Spirit, through Stephen, eloquently reminded the ruling council of their history. He spoke of Abraham and Joseph, of Moses and the Exodus, of Israel's sin and rebellion, of Joshua, David, and of Solomon building the temple. He reminded them about the killing of the prophets, and of Jesus, who was betrayed and murdered.

Some people think Stephen shouldn't have been so forthright and direct, but a Christian has to do and say what he believes the Holy Spirit tells him. If we want to be effective for Jesus Christ, we can't always be subtle in calling people to repent.

People who disregard their past are almost certain to repeat it. The Holy Spirit is a good history teacher. God gave us the Bible so that we would not forget the sins of our forefathers and how God dealt with them. It is the Bible that points us to Jesus Christ and our New Covenant with Him. It shows us how to cooperate with the Holy Spirit and be obedient to say what He tells us.

Prayer

Holy Spirit, please use me to share the Gospel with stiff-necked people who are like I used to be, so that You can draw them to Jesus Christ as their Saviour.

Notes: _____

_____

_____

The Martyr Spirit

"But he, full of the Holy Spirit, gazed into Heaven and saw the glory of God, and Jesus..." (Acts 7:54–8:3).

Stephen was the first of us to be killed, or martyred, as a result of serving Jesus and carrying out ministry through the power of the Holy Spirit. He dealt with his murderers by asking God to forgive them and praying, *"Lord Jesus, receive my spirit."* The more powerful the presence of God, the more violently sinful people will react. In fact, as Jesus warned, *"Then they will deliver you up to tribulation, and put you to death; and you will be hated by all nations for My Name's sake"* (Matthew 24:9). Today, we have many examples of modern-day martyrs, because people still react violently when they are brought under the conviction of their sin by the Holy Spirit.

From Stephen, however, we learn that Christians die differently than other people. God allowed Stephen to see into Heaven, where He saw Jesus standing at the right hand of God. I believe Jesus does the same for each of His martyrs. We are not alone and we know we are going to Heaven. The good news is that we don't have to be afraid of dying because the transition into eternity is painless. Exciting, isn't it!

Prayer

Holy Spirit, please guide me so that I can be a faithful witness for Jesus even unto death.

Notes: _____

_____

_____

The Samaritan-Pentecost Spirit

"Then they laid their hands on them and they received the Holy Spirit" (Acts 8:4–8; 14–17).

During the persecution of the church in Jerusalem, Philip escaped to Samaria and began to preach, set people free from evil spirits, and heal people. Amazed at the miracles, and hearing his message, many became believers in Jesus Christ and were baptized with water. The apostles in Jerusalem sent Peter and John to Samaria to see if these new believers had received the Holy Spirit. They had not. *"Then they laid their hands on them and they received (*were baptized in*) the Holy Spirit."*

Not everyone receives the baptism of the Holy Spirit when they become believers. For many, salvation and the baptism in the Holy Spirit are two separate experiences. For others, the two occur at the same time. If a person is a believer and has not been baptized with the Holy Spirit, he or she should seek out someone who has a ministry of praying for Christians to receive the baptism of the Holy Spirit with the laying on of hands. One sign of the need for the baptism of the Holy Spirit is a continual sense that "something is missing" in a Christian's life.

Prayer   (For those who have not yet received the baptism.)

Holy Spirit, please guide me to somebody who can lay hands on me to be baptized in the Holy Spirit, and then use me to lay hands on others so that they can receive Your Spirit.

Notes: _____

_____

_____

The Spirit Who Won't be Bought

"...he offered them money, saying, 'Give me also this power, that any one on whom I lay my hands may receive the Holy Spirit'" (Acts 8:9–13, 18–24).

The baptism of the Holy Spirit can't be bought or sold. Simon, the former magician, discovered this the hard way. Not everyone who becomes a Christian acts and thinks like Jesus. *"Not every one who says to me, 'Lord, Lord,' shall enter the Kingdom of Heaven,"* (Matthew 7:21) warned Jesus. Simon saw the financial potential of having the power of the Holy Spirit in his life. There are people today who, like Simon, are spiritual con artists, trying to make money from Christians by pretending to do things for God. Peter confronted Simon and told him that he was *"in the gall of bitterness and in the bond of iniquity"* (Acts 8:23). Simon asked Peter to pray that nothing bad would happen to him as Peter had said.

Trying to buy the things of God has become known as "simony." We still have to minister to Christians who have fallen to the temptation of the love of money and confront them with their sin so that they can repent.

Prayer

Holy Spirit, please help me to seek You with the right intention of serving Jesus faithfully, like Peter.

Notes: _____

_____

_____

The Carrying-Away Spirit

"And the Spirit said to Philip, 'Go up and join this chariot'"
(Acts 8:26–40).

An angel told Philip to go to the Gaza road. When he got there, he saw a chariot approaching, carrying the treasury minister of the Queen of Ethiopia. The official was returning home, reading the book of Isaiah. The Holy Spirit told Philip to go and join him. It must have been a strange sight to see Philip running alongside the chariot talking to the man. But he did it. He asked him, *"Do you understand what you are reading?"* The man didn't, and invited Philip to ride with him to explain. When Philip told him that Isaiah was talking about Jesus, the Ethiopian believed. When they came to some water, he asked Philip, *"What is to prevent me from being baptized?"* So Philip baptized him.

Because of Philip's obedience to the Holy Spirit, the mission was accomplished. The official became the first person to carry the Gospel into Ethiopia. With that assignment completed, the Holy Spirit carried Philip away to Azotus so he could preach in that area. Our simple obedience to the Holy Spirit to do unusual things can mean amazing things for the Kingdom of God.

Prayer

Holy Spirit, please teach me to obey quickly when You speak so that others may be saved and baptized.

Notes: _____

_____

_____

The Enemy-Transforming Spirit

"Brother Saul, the Lord Jesus has sent me that you may regain your sight and be filled with the Holy Spirit"
(Acts 9:1–19).

*E*ven our worst enemies are not beyond the reach of Jesus Christ. Saul, who was responsible for the death of Stephen, was traveling up to Damascus to arrest any Christians he could find there. On the road, Jesus Himself confronted him, blinded him and told him to go into the city where he would be told what to do. Saul didn't have much choice but to allow himself to be led there by his men. Jesus then told Ananias to go to Saul and pray for him with the laying on of hands so that he could recover his eyesight and be filled with the Holy Spirit. Despite his fear of Saul, Ananias obeyed. The result was that Saul was baptized in the Holy Spirit and spoke in tongues (1 Corinthians 14:18).

Whenever we do what Jesus tells us to do, even the people whom we fear the most can be saved, baptized with the Holy Spirit, speak in tongues, and go on to serve Jesus Christ faithfully. Like Saul, they could become God's instruments to carry the Name of Jesus to the whole world.

Prayer

Holy Spirit, please help me to cooperate with Jesus so that I can minister Your baptism to every person for whom Jesus instructs me to pray.

Notes: _____

_____

_____

The Barnabas Spirit

"So the Church had peace and was built up; and walking in the fear of the Lord and in the comfort of the Holy Spirit it was multiplied" (Acts 9:26–31).

We must be willing to receive into the Church every person who has been saved by Jesus; welcoming them with open minds and hearts, anxious to listen to their testimonies. It is vital that we never forget what we were like before we were saved. If Jesus could save us, then He can save anybody.

When the Church heard that Saul had become a Christian, they couldn't believe it. Finally, thanks to Barnabas, he was welcomed into their fellowship and began to do ministry. When we are obedient to Jesus and are led by the Holy Spirit, He will cause the church to have peace, be built up and multiply.

New Christians don't come with pedigrees. Some may arrive at a church still reeking from the stench of offensive labels like, "God-hater" or "Christian-basher." However, after Jesus reaches them, regardless of how – whether by appearing to them personally, through a television or radio ministry, by means of a tract or a newspaper article, or through another believer – they need a modern-day Barnabas to welcome and accept them just as they are, in the Church.

Prayer

Holy Spirit, let me be a "Barnabas" who welcomes new believers into our church.

Notes: _____

_____

_____

The Preparing Spirit

"And while Peter was pondering the vision, the Spirit said to him, 'Behold, three men are looking for you, for I have sent them'" (Acts 10:9–23).

God always prepares us ahead of time for any new ministry He has for us. More than that, the Holy Spirit will bring the people to us with whom He wants us to share the Gospel. It is not by accident that we meet certain people every day, because the Holy Spirit arranges for our paths to cross. In this Scripture, God was going to teach Peter that lesson – a demonstration from which we can all learn.

God gave Peter a vision of a large sheet being let down, filled with all sorts of unclean animals, birds and reptiles. A voice told him to *"Rise, Peter; kill and eat."* He refused three times, unwilling to eat anything that was unclean. God told him, *"What God has cleansed, you must not call common."* The Holy Spirit then told him that there were three men looking for him who had been sent by Him. *"Rise and go down, and accompany them without hesitation; for I have sent them."* Peter went with them to Cornelius' house.

Prayer

Holy Spirit, please prepare me to do ministry in such a way that whenever I hear Your voice, I shall go without question to anybody, anywhere, at any time.

Notes: _____

_____

_____

The Gentile-Pentecost Spirit

"While Peter was still saying this, the Holy Spirit fell on all who heard the Word" (Acts 10:24–48).

*C*ornelius was both a Gentile and one of the Roman soldiers who had conquered and ruled Israel. But he wanted to know God. He did everything he could to find Him. He attended worship, tithed, gave offerings, and gave alms to help the poor.

Cornelius caught God's attention. God knew his heart. In a vision, an angel told him that God had heard his prayer and he was to send for Peter. Simultaneously, God prepared Peter to minister to Cornelius. Having learned through the vision of the sheet that, *"God shows no partiality,"* he went to Cornelius' house to preach about Jesus to all assembled there.

While Peter was speaking, the Holy Spirit fell upon all who heard the Word. *"Peter was amazed, because the gift of the Holy Spirit had been poured out even on the Gentiles."* He knew, because they were speaking in tongues and praising God (the evidence). We have to be careful not to put limitations on God. We need to set aside all of our prejudices and share the Gospel to anybody who will listen regardless of race, religion, age or sex.

Prayer

Holy Spirit, please remove any partiality in me so that I can minister the Gospel with love to anyone who will listen.

Notes: _____

_____

_____

The Consistent Spirit

"As I began to speak, the Holy Spirit fell on them, just as on us at the beginning" (Acts 11:1–18).

When the church leadership heard that the Gentiles (anyone who is not Jewish) had received the Word of God, a meeting was called so that Peter could explain what had happened. Some criticized him for going to uncircumcised men and eating with them. Peter explained everything, starting with the vision that God had given him and told how the Holy Spirit had directed him to go with the three men *"making no distinction."* He also told how an angel had instructed Cornelius to send for him so that Cornelius and his whole household could be saved. When he related how the Holy Spirit fell on those people just as He had come on the first Day of Pentecost, with all of them speaking in tongues and praising God, the church leadership was silenced.

As the news sunk in that the Gentiles too had been granted repentance, they glorified God. It was just as John the Baptist had said it would be: Jesus baptized them with the Holy Spirit – so how could Peter have questioned God? When we follow the Holy Spirit's leading, the very people that we don't expect to be saved and baptized with the Holy Spirit – are.

Prayer

Holy Spirit, please surprise me by the people who Jesus saves and baptizes in You, and who begin to speak in tongues.

Notes: _____

_____

_____

The Encouraging Spirit

"for he was a good man, full of the Holy Spirit and of faith."
(Acts 11:19–30).

When we take our place in the Church and serve Jesus faithfully, we do not have to recommend ourselves to do ministry. The Holy Spirit will do it when we are ready.

Barnabas was a man who had proven himself in the church. The Holy Spirit was visible in him. A Levite from Cyprus, his real name was Joseph. However, everyone called him "Barnabas," meaning "son of encouragement," because he was always there to help anyone who wanted to serve Jesus. Having sold his land and given the money to the church's ministry, he was a true believer who would do anything for his Lord. It was he who introduced Saul to the apostles when nobody wanted to believe that Saul had become a believer.

When the apostles heard that a revival had started in Antioch, they sent Barnabas to help the new believers because he was *"a good man, full of the Holy Spirit and of faith."* He had a teaching ministry in which he encouraged the believers to be faithful. It was there in Antioch, studying under Barnabas, that the disciples were, for the first time, called Christians.

Prayer

Holy Spirit, please help me to encourage believers to be faithful to Jesus so they will be called "Christians."

Notes: _____

_____

_____

The Setting-Apart Spirit

"...the Holy Spirit said, 'Set apart for me Barnabas and Saul for the work to which I have called them.'" (Acts 13:1–5).

Here is a lesson for all who are in leadership in our churches. When the leadership takes the time to pray and seek God's will for the church, the Holy Spirit will tell them what Jesus wants the church to do, where to do it, who should do it, the kind of problems they'll run into, and how to solve those problems. The result will be that many people will become Christians and the church will grow and mature. Conversely, any church that will not consult the Holy Spirit and follow His guidance will quickly get into trouble and lose their ministry. The same thing is true in our personal lives.

This Scripture tells of a group of prophets and teachers who were fasting, praying and seeking God's plan for their church. The Holy Spirit told them to set apart Paul and Barnabas for the work to which He had called them. They did it. The two men went out and preached with great success.

Prayer

Holy Spirit, please show me what You want me to do and then tell the church leadership so that I can be set apart to do that ministry.

Notes: _____

_____

_____

The Disciplining Spirit

"...Paul, filled with the Holy Spirit, looked intently at him..."
(Acts 13:4–13).

During the course of their ministry, Barnabas and Paul encountered a magician, a Jewish false prophet named Bar-Jesus. This man opposed their ministry and tried to turn the Roman proconsul against believing in Jesus Christ. Paul confronted him and disciplined him, pronouncing a judgment upon him. Under the guidance of the Holy Spirit, he exposed him as a spiritual fraud who was *"an enemy of righteousness, full of all deceit and villainy."* He also told him that, *"the hand of the Lord is upon you, and you shall be blind and unable to see the sun for a time."* Immediately, Bar-Jesus was blinded and had to be led out. The proconsul was astonished by the power of the Lord and he believed in Jesus.

Paul was not a prophet. He was a Christian who took his relationship with Jesus seriously, and developed his prayer life to the extent that he could really hear the Holy Spirit and do what He was asked to do. In this case, the Holy Spirit led him to discipline a false prophet – which He still does today.

Prayer

Holy Spirit, please help me to develop my prayer relationship with You so that when You speak to me I will recognize Your voice and will know to cooperate without question.

Notes: _____

_____

_____

The Joyful Spirit

"And the disciples were filled with joy and with the Holy Spirit"
(Acts 13:44–52).

This is an account of a very unusual reaction to persecution. Nevertheless, it is a pattern for the way Jesus wants us to handle it (Matthew 5:11–12).

Paul and Barnabas were preaching in Antioch. The Jews reacted against the Gospel and opposed them. Paul explained that *"It was necessary for the Word of God to be spoken to you first; but since you reject it, and judge yourselves unworthy of everlasting life, behold, we turn to the Gentiles."*

The Gentiles were happy to hear this and *"as many as were ordained to eternal life believed."*

With every revival, there are always two reactions. There are those who get excited and become believers; and those who get angry, and stir up persecution of those doing the ministry. When this happened to the disciples, they didn't feel like failures; they simply said, *"Even the dust of your town that clings to our feet, we wipe off against you"* (Luke 10:11), and moved on to the next town *"filled with joy and the Holy Spirit."* No matter how careful we are, Jesus said we would inevitably be persecuted (Luke 21:12), but He will be with us as we continue serving Him.

Prayer

Holy Spirit, please use me to preach the Gospel. If I am persecuted, fill me with joy and Your Spirit as you lead me to the next place.

Notes: _____

_____

_____

The Accepting Spirit

"God, who knows the heart, bore witness to them, giving them the Holy Spirit, just as He did to us" (Acts 15:1–12).

In the early Church, there was division between those who believed that people are saved by circumcision alone and those who believed that people are saved by faith alone. They argued "works-righteousness" against "faith-righteousness." The bone of contention was the claim that non-Jewish, uncircumcised Gentiles were being accepted into the Church. So, a Church council meeting was called to deal with the growing problem. Peter testified that God gave the Holy Spirit to the Gentiles, *"just as He did to us,"* in reference to the Day of Pentecost when they all were filled with the Holy Spirit and spoke in tongues (Acts 2:4). Finally, faced with the evidence, they all believed him.

However, the "works vs. faith" controversy is still heard in our churches today. The fact is that no one can earn his or her way into Heaven. Jesus told us that we had to *"be born again"* in order to enter the Kingdom of God. Today, to all who have faith in Him and ask, He still gives the Holy Spirit with the accompanying proof that He has accepted us and saved us.

Prayer

Holy Spirit, please be my constant reminder that I am saved by faith and not by works so I can boast only about Jesus and pray in the Spirit.

Notes: _____

_____

_____

The Directing Spirit

"For it has seemed good to the Holy Spirit and to us..."
(Acts 15:22–29).

*W*hen any person or group of people pray in order to seek God's guidance, He will give it. In this passage, the church leaders, the apostles and elders, had sought it and God gave it to them via the Holy Spirit. Having discussed the question of being saved by faith or circumcision, the council had come to one accord. Previously, people had acted on their own authority and had upset many new believers.

Thus, three men were sent to the troubled churches with a letter giving instructions for what I call, "The First New Believers' Course of Instruction." Many of us need to read this letter today and receive encouragement because the "works-righteousness" people are on the loose again!

"It has seemed good to the Holy Spirit and us to lay upon you no greater burden than these necessary things." They gave four instructions for Christian living: first, abstain from eating food offered to idols; second, abstain from blood; third, abstain from eating the meat of strangled animals; and fourth, abstain from sexual immorality.

Prayer

Holy Spirit, thank You for protecting me from unnecessary burdens so that I can be free to listen to you and follow Jesus.

Notes: _____

_____

_____

The Guiding Spirit

"having been forbidden by the Holy Spirit to speak the word in Asia they attempted to go into Bithynia, but the Spirit of Jesus did not allow them..." (Acts 16:6–10).

Too many Christians want to run off on their own, assuming they know what God wants them to do. We can presume wrongly that we know where Jesus wants us to go. Too often it's where we would like to go and not where the Holy Spirit is trying to send us. By not taking the time to listen, we can end up defeated and angry with God. There is nothing more frustrating than being in a place where Jesus has not called us.

Paul was careful to pray before he went anywhere. He thought at first that God wanted him to go into Asia and then into Bithynia; but each time he prayed about it, the Holy Spirit said no. The rule is: go only where the Holy Spirit sends you. There can be at least three answers to our prayers: yes, no and wait. Like Paul, we have to learn to wait. He waited and was given a vision of a man calling, *"Come over to Macedonia and help us."* He knew where he was to go. Waiting can mean the difference between success and failure.

Prayer

Holy Spirit, please guide me. Teach me to wait and listen so I will not miss Jesus' plan for me.

Notes: _____

_____

_____

Spirit-Led Days

The Unknown Spirit

"'Did you receive the Holy Spirit when you believed?'
"'No, we have never even heard that there is a Holy Spirit.'"
(Acts 19:1–10).

Paul discovered 12 disciples in Ephesus who were saved people. They sound like a lot of people in our churches today. He asked them if they had received the Holy Spirit when they believed. They didn't know anything about the Holy Spirit. They had come to believe in God through the ministry of John the Baptist. Paul told them that John was preparing people to believe in Jesus. When he laid hands on them and prayed with them, they were baptized with the Holy Spirit and all began to speak in tongues and prophesied. This was the day when they were *"sealed"* by the promised Holy Spirit (Ephesians 1:13).

The Holy Spirit is the best kept secret and a stranger in our churches today. Sadly, there are many saved people who have had a believer's water baptism but have simply assumed that they received the Holy Spirit when they believed. But they didn't. They have no power to witness and do not have the *"signs following"* (Mark 16:17,18). They need Spirit-filled believers to pray with them, as Paul did, to receive the baptism of the Holy Spirit.

Prayer

Holy Spirit, please use me to baptize others with Your Holy Spirit so they'll know You personally.

Notes: _____

_____

_____

The Compelling Spirit

"And now, behold, I am going to Jerusalem, bound in the Spirit, not knowing what shall befall me there; except that the Holy Spirit testifies to me in every city..." (Acts 20:16–27).

Paul knew what he was facing when he went into Jerusalem. The Holy Spirit had told him ahead of time that he would be arrested and imprisoned, and Jesus had told him how much he would suffer for His sake (Acts 9:15,16). Paul wanted only to *"finish the race and complete the task"* the Lord Jesus had given him of *"testifying to the Gospel of God's grace."* He knew he would not be back in Ephesus again. He believed he was *"innocent of the blood of all men"* because he never missed any opportunity to declare the whole counsel of God. Thus, he knew that no one would ever be able to point a finger at him and say, "You never told me about Jesus Christ so that I could be saved." Paul had a clear conscience.

We need to be in such a close, personal relationship with the Holy Spirit that He can compel us to go anywhere Jesus wants us to go. We need an intimate relationship with the Holy Spirit so that when given the opportunity to share the Gospel with others, we'll not miss it.

Prayer

Holy Spirit, please compel me to go only where Jesus wants me to go and give me the words to declare the whole counsel of God.

Notes: _____

_____

_____

The Giving Spirit

"Take heed to yourselves and to all the flock, in which the Holy Spirit has made you overseers" (Acts 20:28–38).

To be chosen as an elder by the Holy Spirit is not just an honour; it is a responsibility with authority which can't be given by people. This is true about all positions in the Church. Paul encouraged the believers to pay attention to what was happening in the Church because there are people who will try to take advantage of Christians, not just from outside the Church, but from the inside. Not everyone who claims to be a Christian is one. *"Beware of false prophets, who come to you in sheep's clothing but inwardly are ravenous wolves. You will know them by their fruit,"* Jesus warned (Matthew 7:15,16). Wolves distort God's truth and take advantage of others. Jesus is our example of a "Good Shepherd" (John 10:11).

Paul demonstrates that good shepherds look after the weak and the poor – they don't exploit them. Jesus sends them to us for ministry and how we treat them determines our judgment (Matthew 25:31–46). Jesus said: *"It is more blessed to give than to receive"* (Acts 20:35). All of us, as Christians, have a responsibility to look after the sheep as the Holy Spirit guides us.

Prayer

Holy Spirit, please teach me to be a giver and a good shepherd to the weak and the poor, just like Jesus, so that I can be a blessing to the sheep.

Notes: _____

_____

_____

The Prophesying Spirit

"Thus says the Holy Spirit, 'So shall the Jews at Jerusalem bind the man who owns this girdle and deliver him into the hands of the Gentiles'" (Acts 21:1–14, NIV).

While Paul was in Caesarea, Agabus, a prophet, had a prophecy for him. He took Paul's belt and tied his own feet and hands and told those assembled that Paul would be tied up, arrested and turned over to the Gentiles. Everyone in the meeting got upset and some began to cry. They begged Paul not to go up to Jerusalem. Agabus, along with everybody else, interpreted it to be a warning telling Paul not to go. Paul, however, saw it as just the opposite – as confirmation that he was to go to Jerusalem! Jesus had told Ananias that he must suffer for His sake. The Holy Spirit had told Paul the same thing. Now he was ready.

It is not the responsibility of prophets to explain or interpret their prophecies. Their responsibility is simply to give them. The Holy Spirit will explain or interpret each prophecy to the person or people for whom it is intended. The rule is: *"No prophecy of the Scripture is of private interpretation because no prophecy ever came by the impulse of man, but men moved by the Holy Spirit spoke from God"* (2 Peter 1:20).

Prayer

Holy Spirit, please give us Your prophecies and explain them Yourself so that we can receive Your direct guidance.

Notes: _____

_____

_____

The Warning Spirit

"The Holy Spirit was right in saying to your fathers through Isaiah the prophet..." (Acts 28:16–31).

After Paul arrived in Rome, under arrest, he had a meeting with the Jewish leaders who brought people to hear Paul testify about Jesus and the Kingdom of God. There was a mixed reaction. Some believed and some didn't. Paul reminded them what the Holy Spirit had spoken through the prophet Isaiah. It wasn't very complimentary. Isaiah had warned Israel that because, spiritually speaking, their hearts had grown dull, their ears deaf and their eyes blind, they could not understand and accept what God was doing. If they would understand what God was doing they would turn to Him and He would heal them. Since they wouldn't, God had sent His salvation to the Gentiles.

The Gospel is for anybody who will listen and receive Jesus. This problem that Paul ran into with the Jews is the same as we have in our churches today. Many thousands of people have been inoculated with enough religion to prevent them from accepting Jesus Christ as their Saviour. Because they have been blinded by tradition and rocked into apathy by the drone of vain ramblings, they can't see and understand what God is doing today.

Prayer

Holy Spirit, please open my understanding so that I can cooperate with Jesus and turn to Him for my total healing.

Notes: _____

_____

_____

The Wise Virgins' Spirit

"Then the Kingdom of Heaven shall be compared to ten maidens who took their lamps and went to meet the bridegroom. Five of them were foolish, and five were wise" (Matthew 25:1–13).

Here Jesus tells us how the Kingdom of Heaven works. The Church is like ten bridesmaids who are waiting for the Bridegroom, Jesus, to arrive. The Bridegroom takes longer than expected to arrive. The bridesmaids are supposed to keep their oil lamps burning. However, because the Bridegroom takes so long, some foolish bridesmaids run out of oil and ask the wise ones, who brought along extra containers of oil for their lamps, to give them some oil. But, knowing that only those who didn't run out of oil were allowed into the wedding, the wise ones wouldn't share. They had only enough for themselves.

The oil represents the Holy Spirit. The oil lamps, when burning, represent the ministry of the Church. Because Jesus is delayed, we need to keep the Holy Spirit burning brightly within us and go to Him continuously for fresh infilling to remain faithful and do the ministry that He wants done before He returns. Each person receives the Holy Spirit for himself or herself. Only those who are ministering in the Holy Spirit when Jesus returns will be allowed into the Kingdom.

Prayer

Holy Spirit, please replenish Your oil in me daily, so I can be ready when Jesus returns.

Notes: _____

_____

_____

The Circumcising Spirit

"...and real circumcision is a matter of the heart, spiritual and not literal" (Romans 2:23–29).

How can you identify a real Christian? How to recognize an authentic believer was the problem in the early Church, just as it is today.

Circumcision was always the sign of a Jew. However, physical scars don't guarantee faithfulness to God, Paul pointed out, because even those who had been physically circumcised broke God's law and sinned. The value of circumcision is seen only if a person observes the law. Otherwise, its purpose is lost.

When the Church (body of believers) first began, it was composed entirely of Jews. It wasn't until the believers were called Christians in Antioch that the name stuck. When salvation was extended to the Gentiles, both believing Jews and Gentiles were equally called Christians. We have always been a part of the true Israel. However, the New Covenant changed how we could recognize true believers. The real Jew or Christian is the person whose heart has been circumcised by the Holy Spirit and who serves Jesus Christ faithfully. Appearance does not make a person a Jew, but faithfulness does. And so, today, Christians are the spiritual Jews who inherit the promises of Israel.

Prayer

Holy Spirit, please circumcise my heart so that my faithfulness to Jesus will prove that I am a real (spiritual) Jew.

Notes: _____

_____

_____

The Pouring Spirit

"...because God's love has been poured into our hearts through the Holy Spirit..." (Romans 5:1–11).

When the Holy Spirit takes up residence in our hearts, He immediately begins pouring a continuous stream of God's love into us. One infilling is not enough. God's love is quite different from other kinds of love. His love (agape) is unconditional. It does not keep a record of wrongs, which would imply, "I'll love you and help you only if you will do exactly what I want." No. It is the kind of love that leads us to lay down our lives for our enemies. *"But God showed His love for us in that while we were yet sinners Christ died for us."* Only this kind of love can rejoice in suffering; knowing the hope we have in Jesus shall not disappoint us, but will produce endurance and depth of character. God's love within us is proof to other people of our salvation.

In turn, Jesus commands us to love (agape) others regardless of how they react (John 15:17). This supernatural love changes our attitude toward people who we once enjoyed hating. As we allow the Holy Spirit to pour His love through us to touch them, they are set free from our hatred and released to be changed by God as we minister to them in the power of the Holy Spirit.

Prayer

Holy Spirit, please pour your love continuously into my heart so I can love unlovable sinners as Jesus did for me.

Notes: _____

_____

_____

The New-Life Spirit

"...we serve not under the old written code but in the new life of the Spirit" (Romans 7:1–6).

There are still people today who think that if they keep the Ten Commandments, they will be acceptable and pleasing to God and so will go to Heaven. It doesn't work that way. God gave His commandments so that we could experience the impossibility of meeting God's standards for righteousness and recognize our need for a Saviour. No one can keep all the commandments because *"None is righteous, no, not one"* (Romans 3:10). Human efforts to live by them produce not righteousness, but guilt. Jesus said, *"The law and the prophets were until John; since then the good news of the Kingdom of God is preached, and everyone enters it violently"* (Luke 16:16). When we repent and accept Jesus as our Saviour, we die to the law so we can begin to live life directed by the Holy Spirit, according to the *"law of Christ"* (Galatians 6:2), a New Covenant. Despite the way some people keep trying to put us back under the law, disregarding the new life of the Spirit, we are free. No longer captives of the law living in guilt, we can live our new life by grace, in the power of the Holy Spirit. Jesus paid for our freedom on the Cross.

Prayer

Holy Spirit, please keep my attention on Jesus so that I will not go back to the law, but with Your help, I will live by grace.

Notes: _____

_____

_____

The Lawful Spirit

"We know that the law is spiritual; but I am carnal, sold under sin" (Romans 7:13–25).

The law comes from the Holy Spirit. It is not sinful. It was given to us in order to define sin. Paul shares with us the principles of sin. First, we can't do what we want to do but we do the very thing that we hate. *"I can will to do what is right but I can't do it."* Second, whenever we decide not to do something wrong, we end up doing it. *"For I do not the good I want, but the evil I do not want is what I do."* There is a war inside of us. It makes us wretched, miserably unhappy. Because of sin, we can't deal with it. There is only one solution.

"Thanks be to God through Jesus Christ our Lord!" Jesus Christ is the only one who can rescue us from the war that leaves us continually at the mercy of the sin working in our bodies. After accepting Jesus as our Saviour and Lord and being baptized in the Holy Spirit, we redirect control of our lives from sin to the Holy Spirit. We have real choice for the first time: to sin or not to sin – to obey the voice of the Spirit or to cave in to the demands of the flesh. Before, we could only sin; but now we can do the things that we want to do, and not the things that we don't want to do.

Prayer
Holy Spirit, please continuously remind me that through Your power, I am free to do what Jesus wants without sinning.

Notes: _____

_____

_____

The Spirit of Life

"For the law of the Spirit of life in Christ Jesus has set me free from the law of sin and death" (Romans 8:1–8).

Until we receive forgiveness for our sins, we carry guilt for breaking God's law. After confessing, repenting and receiving Jesus' forgiveness, however, the guilt is gone. The condemnation evaporates and we experience peace. Like Paul, we can say, *"There is therefore now no condemnation for those who are in Christ Jesus."*

Predictably, however, soon after feeling the wonderful freedom of life in Christ, most Christians begin to second-guess His grace and succumb to a continuous problem with guilt. Remembering their past sins, they once again dwell on their failings and experience condemnation. They mistake the memory of sin for unforgiven sin. This prevents them from going ahead and doing what Jesus wants them to do. Whenever we remember or are reminded of past sin, it is not an opportunity for Satan to condemn us. It is a reminder by the Holy Spirit to thank Jesus for forgiving us for those past sins. When we say, "Thank You, Jesus, for forgiving me," the guilt goes away; the devil is defeated and we can experience abundant new life and peace.

Prayer

Holy Spirit, when You remind me of Jesus' gift of forgiving my sin, please remind me to thank Him and keep my peace.

Notes: _____

_____

_____

The Belonging Spirit

"Anyone who does not have the Spirit of Christ does not belong to Him" (Romans 8: 9–11).

*A*fter we have been born again and baptized in the Holy Spirit, we belong to Jesus. We are no longer under the control of the flesh or the power of sin in our bodies. The sad thing for those who have come into the fullness of the Holy Spirit is seeing the sincerity, but incomplete understanding and consequential frustrations of those who haven't; they want Jesus to forgive their sin and be their Saviour, but stop short of letting Him be Lord over their lives. Because being baptized with the Holy Spirit requires the Holy Spirit to take up residence in them, they pull back.

It is possible to have one's sin forgiven and not have received the Holy Spirit. Evidence the disciples before the Day of Pentecost (Acts 2); Philip's new believers in Samaria (Acts 8:16); and the disciples to whom Paul ministered near Ephesus (Acts 19). None of them had received the Holy Spirit when they believed. The sign that a Christian needs to be baptized in the Holy Spirit is a feeling that, "something is still missing." When the Holy Spirit, who raised Jesus from the dead, dwells in us, He gives life to our dying mortal bodies, assures us of eternal life with Jesus, fills up our empty spaces and empowers us to live this life.

Prayer

Holy Spirit, please renew me every day and empower me to lead others into Your baptism so they can be complete in Jesus.

Notes: _____

_____

_____

The Spirit of Sonship

"When we cry 'Abba! Father!' it is the Spirit Himself bearing witness with our spirit that we are children of God"
(Romans 8:12–17).

*Y*ou can tell those people who have been adopted into the Family of God (Galatians 4:5). We call God *"Abba! Father."* The Holy Spirit within us is proof of our adoption.

The only person to whom we are spiritually in debt is Jesus Christ. He is the One who shed his blood as the price to purchase our redemption, and filled us with His Holy Spirit. If we follow the leading of the Holy Spirit we can escape the slavery of sin which stops us from serving God. We can put to death the sinful works of the body and live life without guilt, free to serve God.

When we are led by the Holy Spirit to live in freedom as the children of God, it shows. People can see that we're God's kids. Not only that, the Holy Spirit causes us to constantly cry *"Abba! Father!"* To call God anything else: mother, sister or whatever, proves that the Holy Spirit is not the one who is guiding our lives.

The Holy Spirit is the proof that we are God's heirs whose inheritance we'll receive if we are willing to suffer with Jesus so that we can also be glorified with Him.

Prayer

Holy Spirit, cause me to cry "Abba! Father!" so the world will know I am a child of God and I can serve Jesus in freedom.

Notes: _____

_____

_____

The First-Fruits Spirit

"...but we ourselves, who have the first fruits of the Spirit, groan inwardly as we wait for adoption as sons, the redemption of our bodies" (Romans 8:18–25).

Only the Spirit-filled Christian who is cooperating with the Holy Spirit understands what Paul is saying here. No matter what our circumstances are as we serve Jesus Christ, good or bad, the Holy Spirit is constantly working inside us, giving us an overwhelming sense of expectation for Jesus' return. That "eager longing" will not let us settle peacefully on Earth, but gnaws away at us. It is the longing to go to our new home in New Jerusalem. The old hymn says, "This world is not my home; I'm just a passin' through."

While the whole of Creation experiences this yearning, Christians experience it most, because the Holy Spirit lives within us and will not let us get fully comfortable here on Earth. The best way to describe this restlessness (it is a physical experience) is to compare it with the relentless labor pains a woman experiences in childbirth. No Christian will have total physical peace until the first fruits arrive, the redemption of our bodies on the Day of Resurrection. Every pang of restlessness reminds us of the promise of that day.

Prayer

Holy Spirit, as You groan within me in the birth pains of redemption, remind me that my hope is firmly established daily.

Notes: _____

_____

_____

The Interceding Spirit

"Likewise the Spirit helps us in our weakness but the Spirit Himself intercedes for us..." (Romans 8:26–30).

*I*magine that! The Holy Spirit prays for us, according to God's will, interceding for us continuously – 24 hours a day. He even prays in words that can't be spoken, expressing His prayer in groans or sighs. It's encouraging to know there's never a time when we don't have Somebody very special interceding on our behalf and praying that we would know God's will for our lives. Because the Holy Spirit is praying, we know that everything cooperates for good for those who love God and who are called according to His purpose (Romans 8:28).

Since we know that the Holy Spirit helps us in our weakness, we can have confidence that we can overcome through His power. Paul's encouragement to remember that nothing can separate us from the love of Christ, rings true. As long as the Holy Spirit is in our hearts, there is nothing in all of Creation – neither tribulation, distress, persecution, famine, nakedness, peril nor sword – that *"is able to separate us from the love of God in Christ Jesus our Lord."*

Prayer

Holy Spirit, thank You for interceding for me so that all things can work together for me to be more than a conqueror through Jesus Christ our Lord.

Notes: _____

_____

_____

The Conscience-Cleansing Spirit

"...my conscience bears me witness in the Holy Spirit..."
(Romans 9:1,2; 19–32).

Our consciences are shaped by the people who try to teach us the difference between what they think is right and wrong. Before we become Christians, our consciences conflict with God's law because every conscience is infected with sin, and everyone has different structures shaping his or her conscience. Every unredeemed conscience flows out of a different value system and is in constant disagreement with God's law and plan. There are as many conscience structures as there are people. After we accept Jesus as our Saviour and Lord, our consciences are cleansed through forgiveness and reprogrammed by the Holy Spirit. Then, when we speak God's Word to other Christians, our consciences cooperate and agree with the Holy Spirit.

For this reason, Paul pointed out that God, as our potter, has a right to shape the clay (us) into vessels of mercy or of wrath. Because of Israel's rebellion in refusing to accept a righteousness based on faith, God said He would save only a small remnant of Israel; those who would allow Him to reprogram their consciences.

Prayer

Holy Spirit, please cleanse and reprogram my conscience, so that I can speak with conviction the truth about God's plan to other people.

Notes:

_____

_____

_____

The Irrevocable Spirit

"For the gifts and calling of God are without repentance"
(Romans 11:16–36, KJV).

Paul tells us that Israel is God's olive tree. Because of unbelief, the natural branches (the Jews) were broken off and replaced by wild olive branches (the Gentiles) which were grafted onto the tree because of faith. This is no basis for Gentile pride, however, because we too can be broken off and replaced if we should fall into unbelief. God has allowed this *"hardening"* on the part of Israel *"until the full number of Gentiles come in,"* and then *"all* (spiritual) *Israel will be saved"* (Romans 11:26) according to God's everlasting mercy.

God's plan is accomplished through the power of the Holy Spirit who equips us with the charismatic gifts of the Holy Spirit which we are to use for ministry both in the Church and outside to draw people to Jesus. Both His gifts and His call on us to do ministry are irrevocable. They are proof of God's faithfulness throughout eternity. Our response determines our faithfulness. The gifts and calling of God on us are the means by which the olive tree can produce fruit of saved people.

Prayer

Holy Spirit, please guide me to fulfill God's call by using Your gifts in ministry.

Notes: _____

_____

The Gifting Spirit

"Having gifts that differ according to the grace given us, let us use them..." (Romans 12:1-8).

These are the "other" charismatic spiritual gifts of the Holy Spirit that have been overshadowed by the more spectacular ministry gifts described in 1 Corinthians 12. Like the others, these gifts are distributed by the Holy Spirit and, when used skillfully, draw people to Jesus Christ as their Saviour, Lord, Healer and Deliverer. Every gift of the Holy Spirit has an evangelistic purpose. Paul says all are *"inspired by one and the same Spirit, who apportions to each one individually as He wills"* (1 Corinthians 12:11). In other words, the Holy Spirit decides which gifts we should receive. He directs their use both inside and outside the Church. They are given for our encouragement and edification. All have their place in the body of Christ and are important for the growth and maturity of the Church and individual Christians. None are more important than the others. The only condition for receiving gifts of the Holy Spirit is that we must be saved and baptized with the Holy Spirit.

Through the gifts of the Holy Spirit, Jesus exercises His Lordship and enables us to do ministry.

Prayer

Holy Spirit, please equip me with Your gifts so that I can serve You in the Church.

Notes: _____

_____

_____

The Spirit in Prophecy

"...if prophecy, in proportion to our faith..." (Romans 12:1–8).

The "gift of prophecy" is the means by which Jesus can tell us what He is going to do before He does it. The person with this gift is God's *"watchman"* for *"the house of Israel* (the Church)*"* (Ezekiel 3:17). It is the responsibility of the prophet to tell us what God has said. The gift of prophecy requires faith for its use and is given for our protection. Prophecy is used by God to call His people to repent so that He can use them in ministry. By means of this gift, the Lord can reveal His plans for both the local and the universal Church; the kind of problems that we'll run into, and how to solve them so that it can grow and complete its ministry. It is important to keep a record of every prophecy, check it out according to the Bible, and, when it is fulfilled, give thanks to Jesus for giving it.

The Holy Spirit will never tell us to do anything that is contrary to the Bible. The purpose of the gift of prophecy is to prepare us to cooperate with God's plan for the Church.

Prayer

Holy Spirit, please give me the gift You want me to have. If it is prophecy, teach me how to use it.

Notes: _____

_____

_____

The Spirit of Service

"...if service in our serving..." (Romans 12:1–8).

The "gift of service" is the gift of practical help. This is a supernatural gift given to help people with everyday problems such as business decisions, repairing vehicles, household repairs, cooking, preparing meals, serving food or cleaning houses; looking after the physical needs of the sick, handicapped or shut-ins; providing transportation for people so that they can go to worship, Bible studies or prayer meetings; or making it possible for others to do their ministry. Those who have this gift never complain about looking after other people's needs because they are doing it under the direction and power of the Holy Spirit. They always see the possibilities of serving Jesus and do it with praise and thanksgiving. The first deacons who were chosen to wait on the tables appear to have had this gift.

The joyful use of the gift of serving opens the door of opportunity to introduce many people to Jesus as their Saviour and Lord.

Prayer

Holy Spirit, if You give me the "gift of service," please teach me how to use it skillfully under Your guidance, that I may give honour to Jesus.

Notes: _____

_____

_____

The Spirit of Teaching

"...he who teaches in his teaching..." (Romans 12:1–8).

The "gift of teaching" can't be learned. It is a supernatural ability to explain the Gospel of Jesus Christ, as well as the rest of the Bible and its promises. Just because some people earn their living teaching school or instructing other people to learn business and job skills, does not mean that they have the "gift of teaching." Those who have the "gift of teaching" are given special insight by the Holy Spirit that they can not learn by studying on their own. However, this does not mean that people with the "gift of teaching" do not have to study and prepare before they teach the truths that the Holy Spirit shows them. In fact, they may have to study even more so that they can *"rightly handling the word of truth"* (2 Timothy 2:15). Since the natural mind cannot understand the Gospel, which requires spiritual discernment, the Holy Spirit is needed to explain spiritual truth.

People with this gift can answer the questions of both believers and unbelievers, who can then go on to serve Jesus with the confidence they need.

Prayer

Holy Spirit, if You decide to give me the "gift of teaching," please show me how to use it so I can encourage others to live by faith according to Your Word.

Notes: _____

_____

_____

Spirit-Led Days

The Spirit of Exhortation

"...he who exhorts, in his exhortation" (Romans 12:1–8).

The "gift of exhortation" is a supernatural ability to encourage people to do what God wants them to do, both individually and in the Church. People so gifted can see the potential in others. When Christians become discouraged through trying times, or because of difficult people, or through struggling with their own apparent weaknesses and inconsistencies, people with the gift of exhortation encourage them to keep going. They confirm the call of Jesus Christ on the lives of people who can't see their own potential and gifting, encouraging them to go ahead into whatever ministry God has for them. Those with this wonderful gift can give the needed encouragement for individuals, groups, and whole churches to continue their ministries. They are usually found quietly, confidently encouraging believers of all ages to get on with their Heavenly Father's business. Not only that, they will often help those who need encouragement by assisting them with their ministries. They provide the "Yes and Amen" that Christians need to hear to spur them onward.

Those with this gift draw out our spiritual potential and always encourage excellence in the work of ministry.

Prayer

Holy Spirit, if You want to give me the "gift of exhortation," please show me how to use it with sensitivity.

Notes: _____

_____

_____

The Spirit of Giving

"...he who contributes, in liberality..."   (Romans 12:1–8).

The "gift of giving" (sharing or contributing) is the gift of supplying fellow Christians or non-Christians with what they need to live and meet their requirements. Those in ministry often reap the outworking of this gift through those made sensitive to their needs in order to serve Jesus Christ.

This is a very special gift. It often involves money, but is not necessarily financial. No matter what form it takes, however, it must be ministered with kindness, sensitivity, obedience and generosity. There are few people who can be trusted to give money to other people without question, even under the direction of the Holy Spirit. Such people will be good stewards of their finances, tithing and giving offerings and alms joyfully. They are cheerful givers who know that whatever they have is not theirs, but belongs to the Lord and is to be used at His discretion. This is a supernatural gift exercised in the assurance that those so gifted will receive joy as they supply the needs of the saints.

Prayer

Holy Spirit, if You give me "the gift of giving," please teach me to give with unquestioning obedience so I can know the joy that comes from helping the saints.

Notes: _____

_____

_____

The Spirit of Administration

"...he who gives aid, with zeal..." (Romans 12:1–8).

The "gift of administration" (leadership or aid) is of vital importance in our churches and fellowships. It comes from a Greek word that means to stand in front, to give leadership, or to rule. This gift is not based on natural ability. Those who have it do not draw attention to themselves, having learned from the Holy Spirit, who makes Himself completely transparent, enabling people to see Jesus but never see Him. These people organize ministries, church programs and itineraries, and help other Christians achieve their goals without taking or expecting praise. Their praise comes from Jesus and the satisfaction of seeing that they were able to help equip the saints to do the ministry that Jesus called them to do. The "gift of administration" brings God's order into the church and its ministries. Those with this gift are shown by the Holy Spirit how to deal with problems. This gift is vitally needed so that our churches can be organized to provide worship, teaching and fellowship, and make disciples of all nations.

Prayer

Holy Spirit, if You give me the "gift of administration," please show me how to be invisible like You.

Notes: _____

_____

_____

The Spirit of Mercy

"...he who does acts of mercy, with cheerfulness..."
(Romans 12:1–8).

*T*he "gift of mercy" is the ability to give and show mercy and forgiveness to people with gracious kindness. The motto of people with this gift is "seventy times seven, every day for every person" (Matthew 18:22). It is a supernatural gift of compassion and understanding. In our world with all of its sin, selfishness, misery and every-man-for-himself attitude, mercy is desperately needed. Jesus shows mercy to all those who call on Him and ask Him to forgive their sins. He expects no compensation. Jesus' attitude towards the woman caught in adultery was full of mercy. Standing naked before Jesus, after her judges had dropped their "stones of judgment and death," Jesus asked with gentle mercy, *"Has no one condemned you?"*

She replied, *"No one, Lord."*

And Jesus said, *"Neither do I condemn you: go, and do not sin again"* (John 8:10,11). Oh, the compassionate mercy of Jesus! It's this gift of mercy that extends God's generosity to look after other people's needs. As Christians, we all have a measure of mercy to extend to others: *"Truly I say to you, as you did it to one of the least of these my brethren , you did it to Me"* (Matthew 25:40).

Prayer

Holy Spirit, whether You have given me the "gift of mercy" or not, please give me a heart that is merciful to all.

Notes: _____

_____

_____

The Kingdom Spirit

"...for the Kingdom of God is not food and drink, but righteousness and peace and joy in the Holy Spirit"
(Romans 14:4–23).

*W*e live in a time when many are diet-conscious; either because of being overweight, or worse, because they think God will condemn them for what they eat. The Old Testament food laws no longer apply (Luke 16:16). There are only two food restrictions for us today: do not eat food offered to idols, or animals that have been strangled (Acts 15:29). God doesn't really care what we eat. Jesus may call us to fast occasionally, but generally, He just wants us to be healthy. Jesus said it's *"not what goes into the mouth that defiles a man, but what comes out of the mouth* (what we say)*...this defiles a man"* (Matthew 15:10–20).

So, let's not get bent out of shape over eating habits and diets which have nothing to do with serving Jesus but which can drive people away from Jesus. The Kingdom of Heaven isn't about diets: it's about righteousness (a right relationship with God), peace (from forgiven sin), and joy (happiness serving Jesus) which comes from the Holy Spirit living inside of us and being our Counselor.

Prayer

Holy Spirit, please help me to be healthy and to concentrate more on righteousness, peace and joy, than on what I eat and drink.

Notes: _____

_____

_____

The Spirit of Hope

"...so that by the power of the Holy Spirit you may abound in hope" (Romans 15:1–13).

Hope is a desire resting on future situations, with its foundation anchored in the promises of God as they are written in Scripture. As we read the Bible, we discover that God always did what He promised – for the patriarchs, for the Jews, and for the Gentiles. Jesus came to give us hope. He came not to please Himself, but to save us. When we receive Jesus as our Saviour, He gives us the hope of eternal life!

Hope is God's "I.O.U." like a postdated cheque. Because of hope, we can envision Heaven as reality and keep our eyes fixed on the New Jerusalem (Revelation 21:2). Because of hope, we look forward to being amongst the great crowd that no man can number, standing before God's throne (Revelation 7:9). Because of hope, we see the possibility of saving the unsaved as we witness to them.

It is the Holy Spirit who gives us strength through joy, the serenity of peace, and the certainty of hope that assures us of our place in Heaven as we help others.

Prayer

Holy Spirit, please give me not only abounding hope for Heaven, but also hope for those who need to be saved as You empower me to be Your witness.

Notes: _____

_____

_____

The Priestly Spirit

"...so that the offering of the Gentiles may be acceptable, sanctified by the Holy Spirit" (Romans 15:14–17).

When we become Spirit-filled Christians, we discover that part of the purpose for which we have been saved is for doing ministry. We belong to what Peter describes as *"a chosen race, a royal priesthood, a holy nation, God's own people, that* (we) *may declare the wonderful deeds of Him who called* (us) *out of darkness into His marvelous light"* (1 Peter 2:9).

Paul tells us that we are more than ministers of Jesus Christ who witness and preach. We are *"a royal priesthood."* We have a responsibility to do priestly things. A priest represents God to His people and represents God's people to their God so that they can be "sanctified," which means "to be fit for holy use." Jesus is our High Priest (Hebrews 5:5) who has made the only and final sacrifice for our sin (Hebrews 10:12).

Since Jesus has saved us, we have a priestly responsibility, not only to bring people to know Jesus as Saviour, but also to lead them into sanctification through the Holy Spirit. Thus, our priestly service is to make believers acceptable to God by ministering the baptism in the Holy Spirit to them.

Prayer

Holy Spirit, please teach and empower me to be a sanctifying priest for Jesus.

Notes: _____

_____

_____

The Spirit of Wonders

"...to win obedience from the Gentiles, by word and deed, by the power of signs and wonders, by the power of the Holy Spirit..." (Romans 15:17–21).

*L*ike Paul, we should all be proud of our work for God – proud in the sense of the God-given satisfaction that comes from work that's well done when people are saved, baptized in the Holy Spirit, healed and delivered. It's pride in the Holy Spirit we feel from the work He has done through us when we hear those sweet words from Jesus: *"Well done, good and faithful servant; you have been faithful over a little, I will set you over much; enter into the joy of your Master"* (Matthew 25:21,23).

We need to learn ever more how to cooperate with the Holy Spirit to effectively reach those who are not saved. It takes a combination of God's Word, deeds, and a *"demonstration of the Holy Spirit and power"* (1 Corinthians 2:4,5) with signs (Mark 16:17,18) and wonders. That is how Jesus ministered and continues to do so today, through His Holy Spirit. Signs and wonders convince unbelievers to believe in Jesus as their Saviour, Lord, Healer and Deliverer. They happen through the power of the Holy Spirit who convicts, converts, and convinces them to believe in Jesus. How proud we can be of our awesome God!

Prayer

Holy Spirit, please show me how to minister with You so that signs and wonders will follow.

Notes: _____

_____

_____

The Spiritual-Blessings Spirit

"...for if the Gentiles have come to share in their spiritual blessings, they ought also to be of service to them in material blessings" (Romans 15:22–29).

Whenever we receive "spiritual blessings" which means blessings from the Holy Spirit (pneumatikos), we have a responsibility not only to encourage those who introduced us to Jesus Christ and the Holy Spirit, but also to help them materially or financially. It was in giving alms to God's people that Cornelius caught God's attention and was saved and baptized in the Holy Spirit (Acts 10). Paul received an alms offering from the churches in Macedonia and Achaia for the poor Christians in Jerusalem. What a privilege Jesus gives us, to be able to help meet each other's needs!

Making us aware of any Christian in need is the Holy Spirit's way of telling us that we are to do something to help, even if it means giving our last dollar, like the widow who gave out of her poverty (Mark 12:44). In the Kingdom of God, we do not look for excuses – we look for opportunities to help each other so that we can experience *"the fullness of the blessing of Christ."*

Prayer

Holy Spirit, please show me both the spiritual and material needs of people and enable me to help them.

Notes: _____

_____

_____

The Spirit of Love

"...by the Lord Jesus Christ and by the love of the Spirit, to strive together with me in your prayers to God on my behalf..."
(Romans 15:30–32).

Here is a lesson that we all need to learn: we need other people to pray with love and in cooperation with us so that we can accomplish whatever ministry Jesus has called us to do. "Lone Ranger" Christians who think they can serve God alone, without being a part of the Church and having support from fellow Christians, end up frustrated, lonely and disappointed. Paul not only recognized the importance of prayer as our lifeline to God, but he understood the critical nature of being strengthened through praying for and with other Christians.

If Paul were living today, he would probably have telephoned, faxed or e-mailed the church in Rome to ask the believers to pray with him that his ministry would be accepted by those in Jerusalem. As it was, he wrote, asking them to strive, to struggle, and to agonize with him in prayer that any opposition to Jesus Christ and the love of the Holy Spirit would be broken down. It is the prayer prayed in love that makes miracles happen. Paul's ministry was accepted.

Prayer

Holy Spirit, please teach me to strive together in prayer with other believers that any barriers to ministry will be torn down through Your love.

Notes: _____

_____

_____

The Demonstrating Spirit

"...but in demonstration of the Spirit and of power..."
(1 Corinthians 2:1–5).

How do we know who to believe when we hear somebody give a message – supposedly, from God? Paul tells us that plausible words are not enough. He says it is necessary for us to receive *"a demonstration of the Spirit and of power"* to prove the preached Gospel. We must see people respond to the message and experience its power – through people receiving salvation, receiving the baptism of the Holy Spirit, exercising gifts of the Holy Spirit in ministry, people receiving healing or demons being cast out. We need to see signs, wonders and miracles, or else what we are hearing are empty words. Jesus said, *"he who believes in Me will also do the works that I do; and greater works than these will he do"* (John 14:12). The *"signs following"* (Mark 16:17,18) which are for all believers, are signs of authenticity and demonstrations of the Spirit and power.

The "spirit of the world" (Satan) tells us that God stopped doing miracles and using the ministry gifts. What a lie!

Prayer

Holy Spirit, please teach me to share the Gospel simply, but with a demonstration of Your wonder-working power.

Notes: _____

_____

_____

The Revealing Spirit

"Now we have received not the spirit of the world, but the Spirit which is from God..." (1 Corinthians 2:6–12).

God's wisdom can't be learned, discovered or accepted by people who do not have either the capacity or the spiritual ability to understand it. God's wisdom is a secret and hidden wisdom which He established and decreed from the beginning. No ruler, politician or religious person can understand God's wisdom apart from the Holy Spirit. Natural people can't see, hear, or conceive what God has prepared for us. The only way to understand God's wisdom is by means of a revelation through the Holy Spirit. His job is to reveal things that we could not ordinarily understand.

It is only by means of the Spirit of God *that we might understand the* (charismatic) *gifts bestowed on us by God."* The Holy Spirit must interpret "spiritual truths" or else we could never understand them. For instance, unless the Holy Spirit explains salvation to us, it makes no sense according to worldly wisdom. Unless explanations of what God has done, is doing, and will do, are communicated through the power of the Holy Spirit, we can't effectively share the Gospel with others.

Prayer

Holy Spirit, please reveal to me what I need to understand so that I can draw others to Jesus.

Notes: _____

_____

_____

The Discerning Spirit

"The spiritual man judges all things, but is himself to be judged by no one" (1 Corinthians 2:14–16).

The spiritual man is any person who has been baptized with the Holy Spirit. Spirit-filled Christians are not smarter than other people. They just have the advantage of having the Holy Spirit living in them. Spiritual people have the Heavenly lawyer, the Counselor, at their disposal 24 hours a day. The "unspiritual" people do not have the Holy Spirit living in them and so do not receive or understand the gifts of the Holy Spirit which are "spiritually discerned." This means that they can only be recognized, understood, and used by people who have been saved and baptized with the Holy Spirit.

The gifts (1 Corinthians 12:4–11) are powerful ministry tools which are to be used to minister to the needs of people so that they can receive salvation, the baptism of the Holy Spirit, direction and guidance, healing and health, and develop an intimate relationship with God. The advantage that the Holy Spirit gives us is that in Him "we have the mind of Christ" because He is the Spirit of Jesus.

Prayer

Holy Spirit, help me to recognize and receive Your gifts so I can use them to bring other people to Jesus.

Notes: _____

_____

_____

The Spirit of Spiritual People

"But I, brethren, could not address you as spiritual men..." (1 Corinthians 3:1–15).

*L*isten to this! Paul was talking to Christians, saying that they were not spiritual men. That means they had not yet received the Holy Spirit into their lives. They were babies in Christ. Jesus had forgiven their sins but they had not yet allowed the Holy Spirit to be in control. In calling them unspiritual, Paul was drawing a conclusion based on all the divisions and problems they were having. Whenever the Holy Spirit is in control of people's lives, there is unity and cooperation. Anyone who has the Holy Spirit can see clearly what is going on.

The people being addressed in this passage would not listen to the Holy Spirit. They were too busy following preachers the way people chase after television stars today. Some liked Paul, while others liked Apollos. These men weren't in competition with each other – they were fellow workers in God's field.

Only one Person should be followed, one foundation recognized, and that is Jesus Christ. We all need to learn from the church at Corinth that if we do not live and worship according to the Holy Spirit, we are just immature babies.

Prayer

Holy Spirit, teach me to be a spiritually mature person, following only Jesus in the Church.

Notes: _____

_____

_____

The Temple Spirit

"Do you not know that you are God's temple and that God's Spirit dwells in you" (1 Corinthians 3:16–23).

Paul is reminding us here that God's real temple is not the building in which Christians meet and worship. In the same way, the Church is not a building – it is the people who join together as God's family. When Paul says, *"you are God's temple,"* he is using the plural form of *"you"* or *"all of you believers together are God's temple."* Thus, because the Holy Spirit lives in God's temple, which consists of all believers, no one person has a monopoly on the Holy Spirit. However, the Holy Spirit wants to have a monopoly on every person, so that He can get us to cooperate in worship and in ministry. He has only one mind. When different people want to do different things out of rivalry, jealousy and strife, it means that they are not listening to the Holy Spirit.

When we come together as the Church or temple of the Holy Spirit and set aside our own personal wishes in deference to the Holy Spirit, all things are ours. If anyone destroys God's temple, however, God will destroy him. How much better to take Paul's advice and become mature spiritual people who serve Jesus together in unity and in the power of the Holy Spirit.

Prayer

Holy Spirit, please help me to be a mature member of the temple in which You dwell so I can honour Jesus.

Notes:

_____

_____

_____

The Body-Temple Spirit

"Do you not know that your body is a temple of the Holy Spirit within you, which you have from God"

(1 Corinthians 6:9–20).

Yesterday, we talked about the corporate nature of the temple of the Holy Spirit. In this passage, Paul addresses the individual aspect. When we receive the Holy Spirit, our bodies become the dwelling place of the Holy Spirit – His temple.

There are still people who think that after they have become Christians, they can do anything they please. But that is not true. Jesus saves us from evil so that by living life according to His plan, we can be free from all kinds of immorality which Paul lists in this passage. God does not approve of any kind of sexual activity outside of marriage between a man and a woman. Paul tells us that anyone, including church members, who indulges in immorality, will not inherit the Kingdom of God. We are forgiven, sanctified, and empowered by the Holy Spirit to live lives that honour God. Freed from the law which stirs us to rebellion, we can choose to disregard the demands of the flesh and live in the peace of the Holy Spirit. Misusing our bodies sexually, or in any other way, dishonours Jesus who came to set us free. Our bodies are not our own. He bought us with a price.

Prayer

Holy Spirit, please teach me how to glorify God in my body; and with Your help, to live a moral and righteous life.

Notes: _____

_____

The Spirit in Marriage

"And I think that I have the Spirit of God"

(1 Corinthians 7:1–40).

Paul's concern is that, whether married or single, all people must: *"lead the life which the Lord has assigned to him, and in which God has called him."* As a married man himself (1 Corinthians 9:5), Paul knew that the advice he was giving could only be followed if both marriage partners were saved and baptized with the Holy Spirit (Acts 9:17) as he was. Otherwise, his advice was worthless and impossible. Only the power of the Holy Spirit can give *"self-control"* (Galatians 5:23) over our powerful sexual desires. Only the Holy Spirit could give husbands and wives the sensitivity *"to rule"* over each other's bodies. Only the Holy Spirit could help us to follow Paul's directive that *"everyone should remain in the state in which he was called,"* either as a single (I Corinthians 7:24-26) or a married person. Only the Holy Spirit is able to renew marital love so adultery (Matthew 5:27) will not be committed and result in a painful divorce (Matthew 19:8,9). We are to change our "marital state" only when the Holy Spirit prepares us and Jesus changes it. This way, we can give our "full attention" to the Lord's work.

Prayer

Holy Spirit, please teach me to be content in the "marital state" to which Jesus has called me, and to serve Him faithfully, whether He changes it or not.

Notes: _____

_____

_____

The Spirit of the Talents

"For it will be as when a man called his servants and entrusted to them his property..." (Matthew 25:14–30).

The *parable of the talents* tells us how the Kingdom of Heaven operates. The man called in his three servants and gave them his property in talents to look after and invest. Now, a talent is a measurement of gold weighing 158 pounds – worth about $961,514.40 in US dollars. To the first servant, he gave five talents ($4,807,572.00). To the second, he gave two talents ($1,923,028.80). To the third, he gave one talent ($961,514.40). Each man invested the money entrusted to him. The first doubled his gold and returned ten talents ($ 9,615,144.00), as did the second who returned with four talents ($3,846,057.60). The master was very impressed with these two: *"Well done, good and faithful servant; you have been faithful over a little, I will set you over much; enter into the joy of your master."* The third servant hid his talent in the ground because he said, *"I knew you to be a hard man, reaping where you did not sow."* His reward was to be *"cast into the outer darkness."* The Holy Spirit shows us that the *"Master"* is not a hard man but one who loves us and died for us and who gives us responsibility to operate His Kingdom.

Prayer

Holy Spirit, please help me to know the Master more deeply, so I can appreciate Him more fully.

Notes: _____

_____

_____

The Talent-Equipping Spirit

"For to every one who has will more be given, and he will have abundance..." (Matthew 25:14–30).

This Scripture contains a parable. Its purpose is to tell us how the Kingdom of Heaven operates here on Earth. Jesus is the *"Master"* and we are the *"servants."* However, He does not literally give each of us 158 pounds of gold to invest. Obviously, we must discover what He is telling *us* here.

- The talents are spiritual abilities for servants of the household (the Church).
- The talents are extremely valuable.
- The talents are for temporary use until the Master returns.
- They are to be invested so they can increase the Kingdom.
- They have to be returned to the Master.
- How we use them will result in promotion or demotion.
- The key to their use is obedience.

"Talents" are not *natural* talents and abilities. The only things in the Bible that fit these seven conditions are "the gifts of the Holy Spirit" (Romans 12:6–8; 1 Corinthians 12:4–10). These are distributed for use until Jesus returns (1 Corinthians 13:10). Using them faithfully will result in us being given more gifts and seeing more people being saved and receiving ministry.

Prayer

Holy Spirit, please equip me with Your gifts or "talents of gold" so I can serve the Master faithfully and fruitfully.

Notes: _____

_____

_____

The Lord's Spirit

"...and no one can say "Jesus is Lord" except by the Holy Spirit" (1 Corinthians 12:1–4).

Paul wants us to understand that the source of the spiritual gifts is the Holy Spirit. There was controversy in the Corinthian Church. Some said the gifts were from the devil and others said they were from God.

Prior to conversion, most Christians were led astray by dumb idols which, of course, meant that evil spirits deceived people into worshiping them by elevating them to the status of the things most important in life. These idols could take many forms – movie stars, houses, personal appearance, intellect, career, power – or whatever one esteems above God. Satan and all evil spirits (demons) hate God, Jesus and the Holy Spirit, and do not give Christians anything that will help them to serve God.

As the Holy Spirit would never prompt anyone to say, "Jesus be cursed!" and Satan would never nudge anyone to say "Jesus is Lord," the only way that anybody can say, "Jesus is Lord!" is by the power of the Holy Spirit. When people are born again, they say, "Jesus is my Saviour!" When they are baptized with the Holy Spirit, they say, "Jesus is my Lord!" *"For out of the abundance of the heart the mouth speaks"* (Matthew 12:34).

Prayer

Holy Spirit, please encourage me daily to freely proclaim "Jesus is my Saviour and Lord."

Notes: _____

_____

_____

The Spirit of Variety

"Now there are varieties of gifts but the same Spirit..."
(1 Corinthians 12:4–7).

Paul wants us to know that all of the charismatic gifts have the same source – the Holy Spirit – the Lord Jesus – God. Each gift has a different ministry or service and its own method of working or functioning. God inspires them individually in each person. Every born-again, Spirit-filled person will receive at least one gift or manifestation of the Holy Spirit for the common good of those in the church. When believers see God meeting their needs through fellow believers who dare to step out and exercise the gifts God has given them, their faith skyrockets. The evangelistic effect of the gifts can also be very dramatic, because they demonstrate to unbelievers that the Gospel, with its signs and wonders, is unarguably for us today.

Since each Spirit-filled believer receives at least one gift, each person discovers that he or she has a unique ministry. When these gifts of the Holy Spirit are used in the church, fellowship deepens because the aspects of giving and receiving strengthens bonds between individuals, thereby contributing to the common good of all of the believers.

Prayer

Holy Spirit, please equip me with Your charismatic gifts so I can minister to those inside and outside the church.

Notes: _____

_____

_____

The Spirit of the Word of Wisdom

"To one is given through the Spirit the utterance of wisdom..." (1 Corinthians 12:7,8).

The "word of wisdom" is a problem-solving gift with very practical applications. Through it, the Holy Spirit will impress a person who has this gift with the knowledge that there is someone in the Church body who has a problem. It can be any kind of a problem that might cause distress – financial, spiritual, family or any personal concern. The Holy Spirit will tell the person with the gift what the problem is *and the solution to it*. For instance, a Christian might be having a problem with his car and doesn't know what to do. Through the word of wisdom, the Holy Spirit might tell what is wrong or how to repair it. He will rarely give the name of the person for whom it is directed. It is the responsibility of the person receiving the word of wisdom from the Holy Spirit to simply speak it out so that the person with the problem can receive it.

The word of wisdom was not what James described in James 1:5: *"If any one of you lacks wisdom, let him ask God and it will be given him."* That wisdom is received as an answer to prayer. This is a supernatural gifting given to us by the Holy Spirit.

Prayer

Holy Spirit, if You give me "the word of wisdom," please teach me to listen to You so I can use it skillfully.

Notes: _____

_____

_____

The Spirit of the Word of Knowledge

"...and to another the utterance of knowledge..."
(1 Corinthians 12:8).

The "word of knowledge" is a supernatural knowing what Jesus wants to do in the midst of a meeting or worship service. It most often has to do with healing. The Holy Spirit will tell the person who has this gift that Jesus wants to heal certain people of physical diseases, psychological problems or emotional disorders. As an example, He might say that Jesus wants to heal people who who have arthritis, or a tumour located in a specific place in the body, or an infected prostate gland, or a skin rash, or cancer or whatever. The people for whom the word of knowledge is given are generally required to go to the front of the church (or the altar) for prayer to receive healing for their various conditions. As with any of the gifts of the Holy Spirit, the person with the gift has a responsibility to step out and tell the people at the meeting what Jesus wants to do for them so that they can receive from Him.

The word of knowledge is a supernatural gift that can't be learned by studying.

Prayer

Holy Spirit, if You give me this gift, please teach me to minister it with sensitivity.

Notes: _____

_____

_____

The Spirit of the Gift of Faith

"...to another faith by the same Spirit..."

(1 Corinthians 12:9).

The "gift of faith" manifests as a complete trust in Jesus Christ and the promises of the Bible. The "faith people" never have any doubts about what God can or can't do. Every person has a measure of faith, but the person with the "gift of faith" has it in full measure. This is not the *"mustard seed faith"* that Jesus described (Matthew 17:20) which grows depending upon the spiritual climate. The people with the gift of faith are the ones who stir the faith of the rest of the people in the church. They constantly remind us that God can and will do what He has said in His Word. They have access to all of the promises of the Bible and continuously reaffirm them. Most of all, their faith is built upon a daily personal relationship with Jesus Christ through the power of the Holy Spirit.

If you do not have the gift of faith, then use your "mustard seed" faith, which is enough to tell Jesus what you need and to respond to His love and direction. This may come either from the Bible or from discerning His personal word to you – if the latter, however, it must line up with Scripture. The result will be a mustard tree faith that grows large enough for the birds to nest!

Prayer

Holy Spirit, if You give me the gift of faith, please give me opportunities to encourage others to trust in Jesus and His Word.

Notes:

_____

_____

_____

The Spirit of Gifts of Healing

"...to another gifts of healing by the one Spirit..."
(1 Corinthians 12:9).

The "gifts of healing" are given as a supernatural ability to heal people of their sicknesses or diseases – physically, mentally or emotionally. The Greek word is "gifts" in the plural which can mean that there are different giftings for healing different illnesses, like a specialist. Or it can mean that a person has the gift of healing many or all sickness like a general practitioner. The important thing to understand is that if the gifts of healing are used, people will be healed – but if they are not used, people will remain sick and could die.

In our healing ministry, I have observed that when we pray for healing, either with the gift of healing or with the laying on of hands, Jesus heals in two different ways. He heals a person completely the first time – or He heals them a little each time we pray, over a period of time, until the person is completely healed. If you have the gift – use it. If not, pray for healing with the laying on of hands. Regardless, people will be healed.

Prayer

Holy Spirit, if You give me the gifts of healing, please give me the boldness to use them so others can be healed and serve Jesus.

Notes:

_____

_____

_____

The Spirit of the Gift of Miracles

"...to another the working of miracles..."

(1 Corinthians 12:10).

The "gift of miracles" gives a person the ability to apply the supernatural power of God to a natural situation and change it. The Greek does not use the word "miracles" but it says that it is the gift of "energizing power" which, when applied to people's lives and situations, creates a miracle which is ordinarily defined as "an event or action that apparently contradicts known scientific laws...due to...an act of God." We hear most frequently about "healing miracles," which are different from gifts of healing, in that a miracle results in actual re-creation of organs, bones, or parts of the body which have been completely destroyed by disease or some related factor.

Water being turned into wine, or the multiplication of food, are examples of this gift being used today. Walking on water is another miracle that has been recently reported. Whenever a person falls down under the power of the Holy Spirit, or is "slain in the Spirit" (Isaiah 28:13), the gift of miracles is in operation. When this occurs, a person can experience any number of miracles – salvation (the greatest miracle!), the baptism of the Holy Spirit, healing or other ministry.

Prayer

Holy Spirit, if You give me this powerful gift, please show me how to exercise it wisely.

Notes: _____

_____

_____

The Spirit of the Gift of Prophecy

"...to another prophecy..." (1 Corinthians 12:10).

The "gift of prophecy" is the only charismatic gift that is mentioned in both Romans 12 and 1 Corinthians 12. This is a gift through which the Holy Spirit will give the gifted person a message from Jesus about some future happening. Paul tells us that prophecy is for our "edification, exhortation, and comfort" (1 Corinthians 14:3). A person with this gift does not go into an ecstatic state, but is self-controlled and alert to hear clearly what the Holy Spirit is saying. All prophecy should be written down, just as God instructed Jeremiah to do, and checked out according to Scripture (1 Corinthians 4:6). If the message runs contrary to anything in the Bible, it is clearly not from God.

There are three sources of prophecy: God, the devil and self. It goes without saying that the first is the only valid source: the second and third being not only unreliable, but possibly destructive. Prophecy is necessary because, *"Where there is no prophecy the people cast off restraint, but blessed is he who keeps the law"* (Proverbs 29:18). Although God does give personal prophecy, it is usually only to confirm what He has already told a person to do, and so it can be dangerous to seek after personal prophecies. It is a confirmation, never a substitute for prayer.

Prayer

Holy Spirit, if You give me this gift, please teach me to listen carefully before I tell the people what Jesus wants them to hear.

Notes: _____

_____

_____

The Spirit of the Gift of Discernment

"...to another the ability to distinguish between spirits..."
(1 Corinthians 12:10).

The "gift of discerning of spirits" or distinguishing or differentiating between spirits is to be used in the Church and is given for the protection of individual Christians and the Church. We are engaged in spiritual warfare and the enemy often comes disguised as *"false prophets," "wolves in sheep's clothing," "angels of light," "who show signs and wonders, to lead astray, if possible, even the elect"* (Matthew 24:24).

Those with this gift are "spiritual policemen" equipped with a "spiritual x-ray vision" by which they can identify the enemy (the devil or evil spirits) who try to attack us and disrupt our worship. Some with this gift have visual discernment, some audio discernment, and others have Scriptural discernment.

Whenever the enemy gets involved in a church, there will be Christians who fall for the deception, which often appears as a "good, but non-Biblical spiritual experience" that will stealthily draw them away from Jesus. Those with this gift have a responsibility to inform the church's pastor or leadership about what they discern so they can deal with it.

Prayer

Holy Spirit, if You give me this gift, please give me the courage to use it.

Notes: _____

_____

_____

The Spirit of the Gift of Tongues

"...to another various kinds of tongues..."

(1 Corinthians 12:10).

The "gift of tongues" should be properly translated as "the gift of other national languages," according to the original Greek. When a person receives tongues, he or she receives a legitimate language that is spoken either somewhere in the world today, or has been spoken in the past. This gift is the supernatural ability to talk in a language that the speaker has not learned. It is the only gift that is given to everybody (Mark 16:17) who receives the baptism of the Holy Spirit. The evidence of tongues proves that Jesus is Lord because it demonstrates that He has taken control of the most uncontrollable organ in the body – the tongue (James 3:6–10). Contrary to critics, tongues is not an ecstatic experience, but completely under the control of the speaker. The gift of tongues has two purposes:

1) Privately, it is to be used in prayer so that we can pray in cooperation with the Holy Spirit.

2) Publically, it is to be used when the Holy Spirit wants to deliver a message to a meeting.

When used properly, tongues serve to assist in the development of an intimate relationship with the Holy Spirit.

Prayer

Holy Spirit, please make me sensitive to Your direction as You guide me to use my tongues language.

Notes: _____

_____

_____

The Spirit of the Gift of Interpretation

"...to another the interpretation of tongues."
(1 Corinthians 12:10).

The "gift of interpretation of tongues" is a supernatural gift of interpreting, translating, or explaining a message that has been given in tongues from Jesus to a church or meeting through someone with the gift of tongues. The person who gives the message in tongues must have been inspired or directed by the Holy Spirit to give the message. Following the tongues, the Holy Spirit will give the interpretation to someone in the gathering. It is the responsibility of that person to tell the others in the service or meeting what the message means. If there is more than one person with the gift of interpretation, the others can confirm what has been said. In some meetings, more than one person may share in giving the interpretation of tongues.

It is important keep a written record of all messages received from Jesus through tongues and interpretation. Through this unique communications system Jesus can guide us both as a Church and individually. However, He will never give a message, or any kind of direction, that does not line up with Scripture.

Prayer

Holy Spirit, if You give me this gift, help me to listen so that I can accurately interpret what Jesus wants to communicate.

Notes: _____

_____

The Distributing Spirit

"All these are inspired by one and the same Spirit, who apportions to each one individually as He wills"
(I Corinthians 12:4–11).

The Holy Spirit decides who should receive which of the charismatic gifts. He is the Person who distributes them and makes them work according to His will. He gives them to us according to our ability, and the needs of the Church as He sees them. No one receives all of the gifts of the Holy Spirit. Otherwise, that person would be a little one-person church who didn't need fellowship. Only Jesus has all of the gifts. When we learn to faithfully and skillfully use whatever gift He gives us, He will add more.

When gifts are given, they are not taken back until Jesus returns. They operate continuously as we are guided by the Holy Spirit. *"The gifts and the call of God are irrevocable"* (Romans 11:29). All of the gifts are supposed to be used every time Christians get together for fellowship and worship. Prayer and the gifts of the Holy Spirit are to be used together for effective ministry. They complement each other.

Prayer

Holy Spirit, please teach me how to be faithful every day in using the the gifts that You have given me.

Notes: _____

_____

_____

The One Spirit

"For by one Spirit we were all baptized into one Body...and all were made to drink of one Spirit" (1 Corinthians 12:12–26).

Paul gives us an interesting picture of the Church. Referring to it as the "Body of Christ," he compares it to a human body with all of its organs such as eyes, hands and ears. Each person with his or her gift of the Holy Spirit is an organ of the body. For instance, one person who has the gift of discerning of spirits might be considered an eye. Or another, with the gift of tongues, might be considered a mouth. Someone with gifts of healing might be considered a hand. Every born-again, Spirit-filled Christian is a vital organ in the Body of Christ, His Church. Every person with his or her spiritual gift is essential to the healthy functioning of the Church. It is not for anyone to say that another Spirit-gifted person is not needed.

God has made the Body so that certain parts or people should be treated with modesty while other parts or people should be shown greater honour. If any part or person of the body suffers, everyone suffers, and if any part or person of the body is honoured, everyone should rejoice.

Prayer

Holy Spirit, thank You for placing me in the Body of Christ. Please show me how to function to give Jesus the highest honour.

Notes: _____

_____

_____

The Spirit of the Body of Christ

"Now you are the Body of Christ and individually members of it" (1 Corinthians 12:27–31).

Paul was faced with an interesting problem – one we often run into in our churches today. There were individuals in the church at Corinth who wanted to do everything themselves. They wanted to be the apostles, the prophets, the teachers, the workers of miracles, ministers of healing, ministers of helping people, administrators, the ones who give messages in tongues and interpreters of tongues. They didn't want to share ministry with other people. They were "super-spiritual Christians." According to them, nobody else could do any ministry correctly. They knew it all and they did it all, leaving no opportunities for anyone else. They were "one man shows." This is a prevalent problem in many churches today.

Paul had to deal with the problem of whether every believer had all of the gifts of the Spirit and could do all of the ministry. Seven times He said, *"No! No! No! No! No! No! No!"* because *"Now you* (plural) *are the Body of Christ,"* and everyone is supposed to use their ministry gifts in the Church, like interdependent parts of a body.

Prayer

Holy Spirit, teach me how to encourage people to use Your gifts so that each member can minister.

Notes: _____

_____

_____

The Spirit Who Gives Love

"But earnestly desire the higher gifts. And I will show you a still more excellent way" (1 Corinthians 12:31–13:13).

The church in Corinth was in deep trouble, and the believers couldn't see it. They wanted to serve God and childishly attempted to prove who was the best Christian by trying to out-perform each other in ministry and worship. They were in a "spiritual gift competition." They saw themselves as super-apostles (2 Corinthians 11:5), even more spiritual than Paul. They boasted about *"their"* gifts and wouldn't give each other the opportunity to exercise the gifts of the other. In the process of clarification and bringing balance into the picture, Paul encouraged them (us) to earnestly desire the higher (charismatic) gifts (1 Corinthians 14:1-5).

He went on to show them *"a more excellent way"* that was missing in their ministry: agape love. Love is the oil that makes the charismatic gifts function as they should. It makes room for others in the Church to use their gifts and serve God. It is patient, kind, not arrogant or rude, doesn't keep a record of wrongs, rejoices in right and never ends. When the perfect end of history comes, all the gifts will cease but love will remain.

Prayer

Holy Spirit, please show me how to use Your gifts with love and to encourage others to use their gifts.

Notes: _____

_____

_____

The Spirit Who Acts

"Make love your aim, and earnestly desire the spiritual gifts..." (1 Corinthians 14:1–25).

Paul tells us how to use the charismatic gifts of the Holy Spirit properly. We should pray in tongues daily in our private prayer time: first in our own language and then, thinking with our minds about the situations that need prayer, pray in tongues until we receive the Holy Spirit's peace, which indicates that He is acting on our requests. When we pray in tongues, we are (without interpretation) speaking *"mysteries in the Spirit"* to God who alone can understand us. Praying in the Spirit (tongues) aids in the development of an exciting prayer life. The believer is at once being edified and developing an intimate relationship with the Holy Spirit.

Speaking in tongues publicly must be accompanied with interpretation if unbelievers are present, or they won't understand what is said. *"Tongues is not a sign for believers but for unbelievers."* Tongues with interpretation draws people supernaturally to believe in Jesus. Its proper use results in a harvest of believers, as on the Day of Pentecost when 3,000 people were saved.

Prayer

Holy Spirit, show me how to use my gift of tongues correctly so I can be an instrument for You to draw people to Jesus.

Notes: _____

_____

_____

The Spirit Who Leads Correctly

"...earnestly desire the spiritual gifts, especially that you may prophesy" (1 Corinthians 14:1–25).

Prophecy is an important gift when used properly. The prophet speaks to people in the language they normally speak. It is given for our *"upbuilding, encouragement and consolation"* – for our strength, help, encouragement and comfort. A prophecy can call us to repentance when we have sinned, give direction for our church, and comfort us through tragedy or grief. By means of prophecy, the Holy Spirit can tell us what God wants us to do so that we can get equipped for that particular ministry – or warn us of impending danger so that we can avoid it.

All prophecy should be written down and its accuracy checked according to the Scriptures (1 Corinthians 4:6). If it conflicts with the Bible, it isn't from Jesus Christ. We do not have to explain a particular prophecy (2 Peter 1:20). It speaks for itself and will be fulfilled in God's time. We don't have to run around to make sure it happens. Our response to prophecy should be to simply prepare ourselves and the Church for its fulfillment by faithfully serving Jesus. Unbelievers are drawn to God by seeing prophecy fulfilled.

Prayer

Holy Spirit, please speak through prophecy so that I can look forward with anticipation to that which Jesus is going to do.

Notes: _____

_____

_____

Praying in the Spirit

"I will pray with the Spirit and I will pray with the mind also" (1 Corinthians 14:13–19).

When Paul commanded us to, *"Pray constantly"* (1 Thessalonians 5:17), it sounded like an impossibility. In the natural realm, it is impossible – but not in the realm of the supernatural – the realm of the Holy Spirit. The person who has been baptized in the Holy Spirit and speaks in tongues can be in a constant state of prayer – not necessarily constantly speaking to God, but sometimes simply in enjoying God's presence. We can pray in tongues when we run out of words during our prayer time or when we know that we should pray for others, but don't know exactly what their needs are. As well as praying in the Spirit (in tongues), we can sing in the Spirit (in tongues) as we develop an intimate relationship with the Holy Spirit. Praying in tongues allows Him to shape and change us more into the character of Jesus, reflecting Him in our lives and responding with sensitivity as the Holy Spirit guides us to do ministry.

Paul learned the key to using tongues. *"I thank God that I speak in tongues more than all of you."* He was sensitive to the right time to pray in the Spirit, whether in private or in public.

Prayer

Holy Spirit, please teach me to pray and sing in the Spirit.

Notes: _____

_____

_____

The Spirit of Worship

"When you come together..." (1 Corinthians 14:26–40).

This is the only "order of worship" in the New Testament. Sadly, very few churches follow these instructions from Paul. Instead of aligning ourselves with God's meaning of *"all things should be done decently and in order,"* we have developed our own boring concept of orderly worship. God is never boring.

Rather than simply attending meetings as spectators, when everyone gathers together to worship God, each person is supposed to arrive prepared to share something from the Holy Spirit: a hymn, a lesson, a revelation, a message in tongues or an interpretation of tongues. The service should be open so that everyone has an opportunity to be obedient to the leading of the Holy Spirit to share something. There should be no more than two or three messages in tongues with interpretation. If there is no one there with the gift of interpretation, there should be no tongues. Only two or three prophets should give their prophecies and they should be checked according to the Bible. Any revelation from God should be shared. Prophecy should be encouraged, and tongues should not be forbidden. The key-note is *"self-control."* There should be no confusion because *"God is a God of peace,"* and of exciting order.

Prayer

Holy Spirit, teach me how to worship under Your guidance so God can be glorified and I can be edified.

Notes: _____

_____

_____

The Spirit of Recognition

"If any one thinks that he is a prophet, or spiritual, he should acknowledge that what I am writing to you is a command of the Lord" (1 Corinthians 14:37–40).

People who are "spiritual" will agree with everything that Paul teaches. Those who don't are not led by the Holy Spirit. We still have people who try to impress us with their spiritual credentials; whose ministries are devoid of Biblical prophecies, signs, wonders and spiritual gifts. Recently, I visited a group that has been getting a lot of attention because of their manifestations – but these manifestations do not follow the Biblical pattern.

"Why can't God do something that isn't in the Bible?" I was asked.

"Because God tells us that He will not do anything that is not in the Bible," I answered. Paul taught *"not to go beyond what is written, that none of you may be puffed up in favour of one against the other"* (1 Corinthians 4:6). The Bible is a blueprint for the workings of God, a plumb line for recognition of authenticity. People who tout signs, wonders and prophecies that are not in the Bible are offside. Anyone who forbids speaking in tongues or prophecy is not being led by the Holy Spirit. Run for the exit!

Prayer

Holy Spirit, please guard me to participate only in the ministries of those who operate according to the Bible.

Notes: _____

_____

_____

The Life-Giving Spirit

"The first Adam became a living being; the last Adam became a life-giving Spirit" (1 Corinthians 15:35–49).

Paul is sharing with us, in this passage, about the resurrection of the dead. It seems impossible that a dead body can go into the grave and a new living body can be raised to eternal life. He tells us that *"it is sown a physical* (natural) *body."* The word that is translated "physical" is the word from which we get "psyche" or "psychology" which refers to the human soul or spirit, which is infected with sin. *"It is raised a spiritual body."* The word that is translated "spiritual" is from the word that refers to the Holy Spirit (pneuma) which is not infected with sin. Thus, Paul is telling us that the core and power of our dying bodies is a human spirit or soul (psyche). The core and power of our resurrected bodies will be the Holy Spirit (pneuma) so we shall never die. What an amazing transformation!

The first Adam was a living, sin-infected (psyche) being; but the last Adam, Jesus Christ, is a life-giving (pneuma) Spirit. When we are saved and baptized with the Holy Spirit, we are given the assurance that when *"the trumpet will sound, the dead will be raised imperishable, and we shall be changed."*

Prayer   (For those who have received the baptism in the Holy Spirit.)

Holy Spirit, I am so grateful that Jesus baptized me in You, the life-giving Spirit, and that I will rise imperishable to be with Him at the sound of the trumpet.

Notes: _____

_____

_____

The Guarantee Spirit

"He has put His seal upon us and given us His Spirit in our hearts as a guarantee" (2 Corinthians 1:15–24).

Paul wanted the Corinthians to know that he was not trying to insult them by not accepting their hospitality in not staying with them. He was sorry for having to disappoint them, but had planned to visit them so they could help him financially with his ministry. It is a rare occasion today for a church to be disappointed because an evangelist couldn't come around to pick up their offering and spend time with them!

Like God, Paul wanted people to know they could count on whatever he said to be trustworthy. He didn't want them to think his "Yes" could mean "Maybe" or "No." When Jesus says He will baptize us with the Holy Spirit, He does. His "Yes" means "Yes."

The proof of God's "Yes" is that He establishes all of us believers in Christ by anointing us with the Holy Spirit, and placing His seal (mark of ownership) on us so that the angels, the devil, and the demons can see it. He deposits the Holy Spirit in our hearts as a guarantee or down payment of eternal life. The down payment yields interest through the gifts of the Holy Spirit as a witness to other people.

Prayer

Holy Spirit, please shine through me and show others that Your anointing, God's seal, proves God's "Yes" in my life.

Notes: _____

_____

_____

The Epistle-Writing Spirit

"You are a letter from Christ...written not with ink but with the Spirit of the living God..." (2 Corinthians 3:1–6).

What a wonderful way to look upon people who have been saved through our ministry! Sometimes people forget who it was who introduced them to Jesus and the Holy Spirit. They start getting sophisticated and want letters of recommendation. Paul points out that each person who has been saved through his ministry *is* a letter of recommendation or reference.

Christians, whether they realize it or not, are open books to people who look at them. Their stories and ours are written not with ink on stone tablets like the commandments God gave to Moses; but by the Holy Spirit on tablets of flesh, which are their hearts. We are living letters or *"demonstration(s) of the Spirit and power"* (1 Corinthians 2:4,5). The point is that every one of us Christians who has been saved and baptized with the Holy Spirit is an epistle or a letter mailed directly to every person that we meet. We can't hide the story. They see the changed life. They hear the changed language. They hear our testimonies. They experience the new love that is flowing out of our hearts.

Prayer

Holy Spirit, please let me be an epistle that will show others how wonderful Jesus is.

Notes: _____

_____

_____

The Spirit Who Gives Life

"...for the written code kills, but the Spirit gives life"
(2 Corinthians 3:4–6).

*M*ost people who want to know God think that they can please Him by living their lives according to the Bible. Keep the rules and you can go to Heaven. Break them and you go to Hell. Most still think that if they keep God's laws they can earn eternal life. They think that they are sufficient by themselves – but they quickly discover that living by the letter of the law doesn't work. The Old Covenant didn't generate righteousness (Hebrews 8:7,13).

Fortunately, God gave us a New Covenant by which we can be made right with God. Jesus paid for our sin. Now we can receive forgiveness and receive the Holy Spirit into our hearts so that we can have a personal relationship with God and enjoy living by the *Spirit* of the law. Jesus explained the purpose of the Bible: *"You search the Scriptures, because you think that in them you have eternal life; and it is they that bear witness to Me; yet you refuse to come to Me that you may have life"* (John 5:39). The Scriptures are given to point us to Jesus so we can have eternal life starting now.

Prayer

Holy Spirit, please teach me how to enjoy living by the Spirit of the law today.

Notes: _____

_____

_____

Spirit-Led Days

The Spirit of Liberty

"...where the Spirit of the Lord is, there is freedom"
(2 Corinthians 3:7–18).

*W*hen the glory of the Lord, the Holy Spirit, comes into our hearts, we can't hide it! When Moses received the stone tablets with the Ten Commandments, he couldn't hide the fact that he had spent time with God, even though he covered his face with a veil. It shone with God's glory and people could not look at him because it was so bright. Sinful people can't look at God's glory for their minds are blinded. They have a veil over their minds and hearts.

In Jesus Christ we have something greater than the ministry of condemnation. We have the ministry of righteousness. When we receive the baptism of the Holy Spirit, an even greater glory shines through us because the veil over our minds is taken away. We can look at the Lord! *"Now the Lord is the Spirit; and where the Spirit of the Lord is, there is freedom."* That freedom allows us to see ourselves being transformed by the Holy Spirit, step by step, glory to glory, into the image of Christ.

Prayer

Holy Spirit, please transform me into the image of Jesus and give me the freedom to carry out God's will for my life.

Notes: _____

_____

_____

The Same Spirit of Faith

"Since we have the same spirit of faith..."

(2 Corinthians 4:13–18).

Paul reminds us in this passage that we have the same Spirit of faith that David had when he said, *"I believed, and so I spoke."* We believe, which means *"I know whom I have believed, and am persuaded that He is able to keep that which I have committed unto Him against that day"* (2 Timothy 1:12, KJV). The Holy Spirit gives us a once-and-for-all-time assurance that we shall be raised from the dead with Jesus. But, even so, we must maintain our daily relationship with God through the Holy Spirit so our hope will be maintained.

Every time we feel alone, we need to use our gifts of the Holy Spirit. They confirm, over and over again, that our hope is real. When we pray with our minds, we are encouraged. But, when we pray in the Spirit, we *"look at things that are not seen"* and *"eternal"* and understand that God is *"preparing for us an eternal weight of glory beyond comparison."* We can then speak about what we believe and extend grace to more people. We *"lift up the cup of salvation and call on the Name of the Lord"* (Psalm 116:13), offering *"the sacrifice of thanksgiving"* (Psalm116:17).

Prayer

Holy Spirit, thank You for being there so I can see what is not seen.

Notes: _____

_____

_____

The Spirit as our Guarantee

"...has given us the Spirit as a guarantee"

(2 Corinthians 5:1–20)

Paul compares our aging bodies, which are like temporary, deteriorating tents – with our resurrected bodies, which will be like houses that will not wear out. As long as we live on Earth, we shall always have a groaning desire to put on our "spiritual bodies." This deep yearning comes from the Holy Spirit within us who is longing to go Home. The Holy Spirit is like a deposit, pledge or first installment – a Heavenly guarantee that we are going to be raised from the dead.

Those of us who have given ourselves to Him are controlled by Christ's love and so we live for Him. This is the reason why we no longer look at people from a human point of view. Each of us is *"a new creation."* We have become reconciled to God through Christ who has given us *"the ministry of reconciliation,"* so we can be the mediators who help others become reconciled to God. We are ambassadors for Christ, with full power and authority to represent God today. We do not have to wait until Jesus comes back because *"now is the day of salvation"* (2 Corinthians 6:2). Isn't this exciting! We prove our hope over and over again by using the gifts of the Holy Spirit daily.

Prayer

Holy Spirit, thank You for being my indwelling guarantee that I have a place in Heaven.

Notes: _____

_____

_____

The Commending Spirit

"...but as servants of God we commend ourselves in every way: ...by the Holy Spirit" (2 Corinthians 6:3–10).

Paul's résumé does not summarize what most of us consider "abundant life." Few Christian celebrities today would give a testimony like Paul's. We have the mistaken idea that after we become Christians, only good things will happen to us. If a candidate for pastor were to submit a résumé like Paul's to a pulpit committee, the group would quickly conclude that there was something seriously wrong with this man's ministry. Look at Paul's references: troubles, hardships, distress, beatings, imprisonments, riots, hard work, sleepless nights, hunger, bad reports, regarded as an imposter, dying, beaten, sorrowful, poor, having nothing.

Most churches today are looking for social acceptability, numerical and financial success, respectability, polished speaking skills and good appearance. But Jesus has not changed. He wants hearts so filled with the fire of the Holy Spirit that our world will be turned upside down (Acts 17:6); workers so impassioned with the message of the Gospel that any benefits the world has to offer are meaningless. If there is no cross (Matthew 16:24), there is no crown (Revelation 2:10). No controversy means poor ministry.

Prayer

Holy Spirit, please commend me when my life reflects Your power and the Cross.

Notes: _____

_____

_____

The Spirit of Jesus

"...if you receive a different spirit from the one you received..." (2 Corinthians 11:1–15).

Not everyone who comes in the Name of Jesus serves Jesus. And not everyone who comes with "a spirit" brings the Holy Spirit. The Jesus whom we preach is exactly as He is described in the Bible. Likewise, the Holy Spirit we preach is exactly as He is described in the Bible. His gifts, fruit, and signs have not changed. He does nothing that is not patterned for us in the Scriptures. This is our protection for staying on track.

Paul had to deal with the same problem we have today. False apostles abounded – preachers who were saying that Paul was wrong, the Jesus they accepted was wrong, and the Holy Spirit was not the real one. Like dumb sheep, many in the church accepted these false apostles' teaching. The same "serpent" who deceived Eve is still at work today, disguised as an angel of light. His false apostles portray themselves as servants of righteousness. There are even those who falsely claim there will be a "third covenant."

Our protection from being deceived by false teachers is to know Jesus personally, the Holy Spirit intimately, and the Scriptures so well that we can recognize the deception at a glance.

Prayer

Holy Spirit, please teach me how to discern the real servants of Jesus Christ by their fruit, gifts and "signs following."

Notes: _____

_____

The Spirit of Fellowship

"The grace of the Lord Jesus Christ and the love of God and the fellowship of the Holy Spirit be with you all"

(2 Corinthians 13:5–14).

The Holy Spirit is the One who brings us together in unity. Christian fellowship is a special family relationship of those who joyfully look forward to spending eternity together. There is no relationship like it on Earth. The bond of unity created by oneness in the Spirit is uniquely trusting and peaceful. Whenever there is quarrelling, jealousy, anger, selfishness, slander, gossip, conceit or disorder, the Holy Spirit is being ignored. When included, He will convict any Spirit-filled Christian of sin and wrongdoing. That is why Paul commanded the Corinthians: *"Examine yourselves to see whether you are holding to your faith."* And again, *"Test yourselves. Do you not realize that Jesus Christ is in you? – unless indeed you fail to meet the test!"*

We all need to examine ourselves by reading the Bible, and test ourselves by talking to Jesus through the Holy Spirit who lives inside us. He will speak if we listen. If we have gotten out of line, we can ask for forgiveness, and get back into comfortable relationship with both Jesus and our fellow Christians. Everyone will be blessed in the process.

Prayer

Holy Spirit help me to examine and test myself so I can stay faithful to Jesus and stay in fellowship with other Christians.

Notes: _____

_____

_____

The Spirit We Hear with Faith

"Let me ask you only this: did you receive the Spirit by works of the law, or by hearing with faith?"

(Galatians 3:1,2).

"*O foolish Galatians!*" might be better addressed to all of us as "O foolish Christians!" Like the Galatians, many believers don't know what to do after they have been baptized with the Holy Spirit. They are so accustomed to having to earn their way and justify their existence, that they return to a life of *"works."* Although they know Jesus forgave them for their sin, they forget about the keeping power of the Holy Spirit. They're not sure how far they can trust Him to do the job. They don't understand that He is a real Person. He is our Counselor. He's not just an impersonal power that sort of helps us earn our way to Heaven with our well-intentioned efforts to live by the law.

When new Christians leave the Holy Spirit back at the starting gate, the result is discouragement, feelings of failure and fear of loss of salvation. Eternal life is given to us as a free gift. The Holy Spirit is "God-in-us," to speak with us and guide our lives so that we can live out God's wonderful plan. *"Faith cometh by hearing and hearing by the Word of God"* (Romans 10:17, KJV).

Prayer

Holy Spirit, remind me often that You came into my life by faith, and not by works of the law, as proof of my salvation.

Notes: _____

_____

_____

The Beginning Spirit

"Having begun with the Spirit, are you now ending with the flesh?" (Galatians 3:3,4).

How foolish can we be? How short are our memories! We can't begin to walk with God apart from His Holy Spirit – so why do we fall back on our own resources? The real problem is that we live most of our lives as "religious" people who think we have to earn our way to Heaven by keeping laws that will make us acceptable to God. Many still view Him as a white-haired ogre sitting in the clouds waiting for us to sin so He can punish us.

I remember a church music director who tried to live her life by the "Sermon on the Mount." Not having been baptized in the Holy Spirit, she had a total nervous breakdown. She made the mistake, like a lot of people do, of trying to use the New Testament as a law book. We can't live the "Sermon on the Mount" until we have become born-again, Spirit-filled Christians. Then, in a love relationship with Jesus, we can walk in His ways almost automatically with the power of the Holy Spirit – not so we can earn our way to Heaven, but because Jesus has already given it to us as a gift. Oh, by the way, the music director became a born-again, Spirit-filled Christian who lives "the Sermon" in good health.

Prayer

Holy Spirit, teach me how to continue in the Spirit and enjoy serving Jesus.

Notes: _____

_____

_____

The Spirit of Faith

"Does He who supplies the Spirit to you and works miracles among you do so by works of the law, or by hearing with faith?"
(Galatians 3: 5–9).

God sent the Holy Spirit to us because we heard by faith and believed in Jesus as our Saviour. Pleasing God was never just simply a matter of not sinning – it has always been about relationship – faith in Him. The Holy Spirit was poured out on the Day of Pentecost upon 120 believers, not because they had kept the law, but because Jesus had paid for their sin by dying on the Cross of Calvary. At the point at which Jesus forgave those who believed in Him, they were total "religious" failures. When Jesus shouted, *"It is finished!"* that meant " paid in full" for all of our sin. He knew that the believers needed the power of the Holy Spirit to keep them faithful and to guide them wherever He sent them. They all received the Holy Spirit on that first Day of Pentecost and spoke in tongues (initial evidence) (Acts 2:4; 1 Corinthians 14:21). Because of their faith in Jesus Christ, God worked miracles through them.

We all need to have our own "Day of Pentecost" when we are baptized in the Holy Spirit, so we can live by faith and God can work miracles amongst and through us.

Prayer

Holy Spirit, baptize me with Your Spirit and teach me to live by faith and enjoy God's miracles.

Notes: _____

_____

_____

The Spirit of Adoption

"And because you are sons, God has sent the Spirit of His Son into our hearts, crying, 'Abba! Father!'" (Galatians 4:1–11).

*B*efore we accepted Jesus as Saviour and Lord, we were slaves to the "elemental spirits" or evil spirits whom (by default) we mistakenly worshipped as gods. But we have been redeemed through Jesus and adopted into God's family. As such, we are no longer slaves but sons and daughters, heirs of our Father's estate. Proof of our adoption is God's deposit of the Holy Spirit in our hearts. The Holy Spirit gives us an overwhelming desire to be with our Father. He cries out, yes even screams and shouts continuously, day and night, *"Abba! Father!"* ("Abba" being the intimate form of the Greek word for "father," similar to "dad.") The cry of the Holy Spirit within us to be with our "Heavenly Dad" is like a continuously ringing telephone which is temporarily answered when we pray and talk to our Father in Heaven or our Saviour Jesus Christ. As we pray in the Spirit, we spend intimate time with Abba Father. The desire, or longing of our hearts, will never be completely satisfied until we receive our inheritance of Heaven.

Prayer
    Holy Spirit, thank You for continuously reminding me that I can spend time with my Heavenly Father who is only a prayer away.

Notes: _____

_____

_____

The Spirit of the Free Children

"But as at that time he who was born according to the flesh persecuted him who was born according to the Spirit, so it is now" (Galatians 4:21–31).

*S*piritually, we have two family trees, both going back to the two wives of Abraham: Sarah and Hagar. Sarah was a free woman whose son, Isaac, was born through a promise of God. Hagar was Sarah's slave. Hagar's son, Ishmael, was born according to the flesh. Hagar represents Mount Sinai, the Old Testament, and the present-day city of Jerusalem because she was in slavery to sin along with her children. Sarah, on the other hand, represents the New Jerusalem, because she was free, along with her children who are saved by faith through Jesus Christ. Just as those who were in spiritual slavery persecuted the spiritually free (born of the Holy Spirit) then, the same thing happens today.

We experience the residual spiritual conflict in our churches. Those who have not been born again and baptized with the Holy Spirit (religious people) persecute those who have been. When it happens, we need to do what Jesus said: *"Rejoice and be glad"* (Matthew 5:12). Those living in the freedom of the Spirit, under the New Covenant, shall not be turned away from their mother – New Jerusalem. The Holy Spirit within us is proof.

Prayer

Holy Spirit, please teach me how to live as a wholeheartedly free person in Jesus Christ, regardless of the way I am treated.

Notes: _____

_____

_____

The Spirit of Freedom

"For through the Spirit, by faith, we wait for the hope of righteousness" (Galatians 5:1–12).

"**Y**ou can't have it both ways," Paul says in this passage. It's salvation through Jesus – or the law. The law failed to save us, and circumcision is a sign of that failure. Anyone who depends on circumcision for their justification, sets aside the great salvation available to them, ignores the love of Christ, and does not partake in His grace. Nobody receives the baptism of the Holy Spirit by keeping the law.

There were people in the Galatian church who tried to make Christians go back and live under the Old Testament law which called for circumcision. To do that meant to go back into the slavery of sin, and to lose their freedom in Christ. There are people like that today who would rob us of our freedom. It didn't work then, and it doesn't work today. These people are like "sinful leaven" who can infect the whole church. Paul suggests that if they want to go back under the law, let them go ahead and mutilate themselves. But, let us stay on track and follow the Holy Spirit so we won't lose our hope of Heaven.

Prayer

Holy Spirit, please help me to stand fast in my freedom and thank You for being inside of me as a reminder to live by faith.

Notes: _____

_____

_____

The Spirit Who Opposes the Flesh

"But I say, walk by the Spirit and do not gratify the desires of the flesh" (Galatians 5:13–21).

The desires of human nature, when out of line with the laws of God, are at odds with the workings of the Holy Spirit. For instance, sexual desire within the context of marriage is a beautiful, God-given pleasure. Outside of marriage, however, it falls into the realm of a lustful work of the flesh. It is sin in us, fighting the Holy Spirit. We know what sin is because God's Word clearly names the things that separate us from Him. These sinful desires constantly try to prevent us from doing what God wants. There is a principle that says: the more you try not to do something the more you'll want to do it. What's the solution? The Holy Spirit sets us free from the desires of the flesh. By the power of the Holy Spirit, we can say, "No! No! No!" to the sinful lusts of the flesh. The Holy Spirit gives us the freedom to say, "Yes! Yes! Yes!" to Jesus and to love (agape) our neighbours as ourselves (Luke 10:27).

The works of the flesh destroy us as individuals and can destroy our churches as well. Paul warns that those who continuously keep doing the works of the flesh without seeking forgiveness and changing their ways with the help and power of the Holy Spirit will not inherit the Kingdom of God.

Prayer

Holy Spirit, thank you for giving me the power to say "No" to sin and "Yes" to Jesus.

Notes: _____

_____

_____

The Fruit of the Holy Spirit

"If we live by the Spirit, let us also walk by the Spirit"
(Galatians 5:22–26).

It is very interesting to notice that the Greek word for *"fruit"* is singular. The fruit of the Spirit is like an orange that is made up of sections or segments. This fruit has nine segments *"love, joy, peace, patience, kindness, goodness, faithfulness, gentleness (meekness) and self-control."* We do not have the option of picking and choosing amongst these. The fruit must grow as one, so that we can grow to maturity in a balanced way. The Holy Spirit makes the changes that are needed. He works like a microwave oven, ripening us from the inside out, starting with our hearts. He usually does it so discretely that we don't notice the changes ourselves. I believe that is why we can't say that we ourselves have the fruit of the Spirit. We have to hear from other people that the Holy Spirit has ripened the fruit within us as they taste of it.

The fruit of the Holy Spirit describes the character of Jesus. Thus, the Holy Spirit develops the character of Jesus in us, so that we can be more like Him, and live and walk in His Holy Spirit.

Prayer

Holy Spirit, please grow and ripen the fruit of the Spirit in me, and make me more like Jesus.

Notes: _____

_____

_____

The Spirit of the Fruit of Love

" *The fruit of the Spirit is love...*" (Galatians 5:22–23).

In the Greek language, there are four different words for "love": friendship, sexual love, family love and Christian love (agape). Christian love is the only kind that is not a conditional love. All other kinds of love are extended arbitrarily to people as long as they are returned – but if the conditions are broken, the love disappears. Agape love is the only kind of love that can be commanded (John 15:7) and includes the unloveable. Unlike the other kinds of love which are based on emotions, Christian love flows from a redeemed, Spirit-empowered will that encompasses all of a person's heart, soul, strength and mind.

Paul gives us the best description: *"Love is patient and kind...not jealous or boastful...not arrogant or rude...does not insist on its own way...not irritable or resentful...doesn't rejoice in wrong, but rejoices in right...bears...believes...hopes...endures all things. Love never ends"* (1 Corinthians 13:4-8). Love does not keep a record of wrongs, is long-suffering and lays down its life for its enemies. This love can be given to others only after we have received it from Jesus through the Holy Spirit (Romans 5:5).

Prayer

Holy Spirit, please grow agape love in me so that I can love others the way Jesus loves me.

Notes: _____

_____

_____

The Spirit of the Fruit of Joy

"But the fruit of the Spirit is...joy" (Galatians 5:22,23).

Joy is the wellspring of real faith and meaningful religion. It's a fountain of inner happiness, totally independent of circumstances. Its source is found in God's river of life and flows from a personal relationship with Jesus Christ. The first thing we discover after being saved and baptized in the Holy Spirit is that it is fun to be with Jesus! Our joy increases as we serve Him. That is what two of the three men in the parable of the talents discovered when their master rewarded them: *"enter into the joy of your master"* (Matthew 25:21). Joy comes from doing what Jesus commands. We quickly discover increased strength flowing from the joy of knowing Him: *"the joy of the Lord is your strength"* (Nehemiah 8:10). *"For the Kingdom of God is not food and drink but righteousness and peace and joy in the Holy Spirit"* (Romans 14:17).

In worship, our joy is renewed. In prayer, our joy is increased and multiplied. When we witness to others, our joy abounds. When we study the Scriptures, our joy expands. In Jesus, we *"rejoice with unutterable and exalted joy"* when we go through *"various trials"* (1 Peter 1:6–8). We must beware of "sour puss" Christians who try to rob us of our joy.

Prayer
Holy Spirit, please fill me with the joy that no one can steal from me.

Notes: _____

_____

_____

The Spirit of the Fruit of Peace

"But the fruit of the Spirit is...peace" (Galatians 5:22,23).

"*Peace*" is the tranquility, the serenity of heart which is enjoyed under our benevolent and just King, Lord, Saviour, God. Peace brings order into our lives. It is not just freedom from trouble, but it is peace in the *middle* of troubles or storms. Jesus had this peace when He fell asleep in the boat and a storm threatened to sink it. He said, *"Peace, be still"* (Mark 4:39). It is His peace that stills the storms in our lives and gives us a calmness in our hearts that comes from the all-pervading consciousness that we are safely in the hands of God. Paul tells us to *"let the peace of Christ rule in your hearts"* (Colossians 3:15). Absence of peace is the Holy Spirit's warning light, signalling that something is wrong, flashing, "Stop! Do not proceed."

Peace is not always a *welcomed* emotional experience. I remember one woman, a very hyperactive person living a high energy life, who was disappointed when she was baptized in the Holy Spirit. She spoke in tongues but felt empty. Her so-called emptiness was "peace" that she had never before experienced! I couldn't help but be amused when her children became Christians – because of the change Jesus made in their mother!

Prayer

Holy Spirit, please give me the peace of God that passes understanding.

Notes: _____

_____

_____

The Spirit of the Fruit of Patience

"But the fruit of the Spirit is...patience" (Galatians 5:22,23).

*T*oo many people mistakenly think that *"patience"* means "unflappability." Others think that it means immunity to emotional pain or sorrow. Nothing is further from the truth! Patience is the ability to endure a bad situation without complaining. It implies the bearing of suffering or provocation with calmness and self-control. I like the King James version which translates it as *"long suffering."* Patience is most often used to describe God's attitude towards us as sinners.

People often mistake God's patience for permission to sin. We can't get away with it. *"Or do you presume upon the riches of His kindness and forbearance and patience? Do you not know that God's goodness is meant to lead you to repentance?"* (Romans 2:4). We need to have the same patience with other people that God has with us. No wonder Peter was shocked when Jesus instructed him to forgive his brother 490 times every day (Matthew 18:22)! The patience that we show to other people convinces them that Jesus loves them, too.

Prayer

Holy Spirit, please develop patience in me so that I can lead others into salvation, the baptism of the Holy Spirit and healing.

Notes: _____

_____

_____

The Spirit of the Fruit of Kindness

"But the fruit of the Spirit is...kindness" (Galatians 5:22,23).

*"K*indness*"* is also translated "gentleness" and "sweetness." God treats us with kindness *before* we turn to Him as well as after. When confronted with the woman caught in adultery who was dragged naked before Him, He gently asked, *"Has no one condemned you?"*

"No one, Lord," she replied.

"Neither do I condemn you; go and do not sin again" (John 8:2–11). With the same kindness He extended to the distraught woman, Jesus bestows His kindness upon us when we are caught in sin. The Holy Spirit is described as the *new wine* or good wine which means mellow and sweet. We sing, "There's a sweet, sweet Spirit in this place, and I know that it's the Spirit of my Lord."

Jesus said, *"Come to Me all you who labor and are heavy laden, and I will give you rest. Take My yoke upon you, and learn from Me, for I am gentle and lowly in heart, and you will find rest for your soul. For My yoke is easy and My burden is light"* (Matthew 11:28,29). As He kindly takes our burdens, being yoked with Jesus is sweet.

*P*rayer

Holy Spirit, please develop kindness (sweetness) in me so that I can be sympathetic and generous, just like Jesus is.

*N*otes: _____

_____

_____

The Spirit of the Fruit of Goodness

"But the fruit of the Spirit is...goodness" (Galatians 5:22,23).

"Goodness" means to be virtue-equipped at every point. Goodness encourages people to accept Jesus as their Saviour and Lord. Goodness prays for people's needs. Goodness rebukes people when they sin arrogantly. Goodness corrects and disciplines. *"For the Lord disciplines him whom He loves, and chastises every son whom He receives"* (Hebrews 12:6). Jesus showed goodness when He drove the money changers out of the temple (Matthew 21:13) because He wanted to turn it back into a House of prayer.

As a young pastor, I had a man who was an English teacher offer to correct the grammatical errors that I made during my Sunday sermons. I accepted his offer and his goodness improved my ministry. Goodness can only help. It offers only constructive criticism.

As Christians, we need a goodness that will help people without destroying them. Paul confidently tells Roman believers, *"I am satisfied about you...that you yourselves are full of goodness...and able to instruct one another"* (Romans 15:14). Goodness is both kind and gentle.

Prayer

Holy Spirit, please help me to show goodness that helps others.

Notes: _____

_____

_____

The Spirit of the Fruit of Faithfulness

"But the fruit of the Spirit is...faithfulness"

(Galatians 5:22,23).

"Faithfulness" refers to the characteristics of trust-worthiness and reliability developed in us by the Holy Spirit. From time to time we are tempted by the devil to test whether or not we are faithful and can be trusted to do whatever Jesus tells us to do (John 2:5), and counted on to be wherever He wants us to be. Through the power of the Holy Spirit, we need to consistently demonstrate that whatever Jesus tells us to do, we'll follow through and complete it (Luke 17:10). Faithfulness comes from knowing *"whom I have believed and I am sure that He is able to guard until that Day what has been entrusted to me"* (2 Timothy 1:12).

Faithfulness guarantees that we shall be wherever Jesus wants us to be, even if we are the only ones who are there – at worship, Bible study, prayer meeting, or any other place Jesus calls us to be. We'll be there without complaining, because Jesus will be there in His Holy Spirit. Together we'll have a wonderful time of fellowship – during which we'll pray for those who didn't come! Faithfulness is the fruit of knowing Jesus as our Saviour and being baptized in the Holy Spirit.

Prayer

Holy Spirit, please teach me to be faithful, like You are, so that others can see Jesus in me.

Notes: _____

_____

The Spirit of the Fruit of Meekness

"But the fruit of the Spirit is...meekness (gentleness)"
(Galatians 5:22,23).

"*Meekness*" or "*gentleness*" is the most misunderstood of the fruit of the Spirit. One generally thinks of a meek person as a spineless, submissive, fearful individual who is afraid to assert himself. The Greek word means something quite different. It refers to a person who is submissive to the will of God in all things; someone who is perfectly under the control of the Holy Spirit, who is teachable in all things, who is considerate of the needs of other people, and who acts on the command of Jesus and the Holy Spirit to meet the needs of others.

Meekness disregards natural, human feelings of inadequacy when confronted with the need of another. Often we pray with people who, in the natural, are beyond any hope of healing. But putting our natural feelings aside, we pray for them out of obedience, according to the promises of the Bible – with the result that Jesus heals them. Meekness means to be so firmly under God's control that we act on command, no matter how things may appear

Prayer

Holy Spirit, please make me a meek person, submissive to Jesus, always teachable and considerate.

Notes: _____

_____

_____

The Spirit of the Fruit of Self-Control

"But the fruit of the Spirit is...self-control"
(Galatians 5:22,23).

"*Self-control*" is sometimes translated as "temperance." It is the characteristic responsible for controlling or mastering human desires, emotions and love of pleasure. Paul refers to it to describe an athlete's discipline of his body (1 Corinthians 9:25). Like the athlete, a Christian must exercise self-control over his or her body to prevent disqualification after preaching the Gospel. Self-control is particularly important for a Christian's mastery over extramarital sex (1 Corinthians 7:9). The Holy Spirit strengthens us.

Self-control is foundational for the Christian who masters his own desires to the extent that he can be a servant of all. Jesus said, "*If anyone would be first, he must be last of all and servant of all*" (Mark 9:35). Actually, the translation should read, "*slave of all*." Slaves have no rights, but servants do. We have been bought with a price. We do not belong to ourselves, but to Jesus. When Jesus washed his disciples' feet (John 13:5), He was demonstrating self-control. He expects us to exercise our Spirit-ripened self-control by looking after the hungry, the thirsty, the stranger, the naked, the sick and those in prison (Matthew 25:40,45).

Prayer

Holy Spirit, please teach me self-control so that I can minister to Jesus and everyone to whom He leads me.

Notes: _____

_____

_____

The Spirit of Gentleness

"If we live by the Spirit, let us also walk by the Spirit"
(Galatians 5:25–6:6).

If we are going to "talk the talk" then we must "walk the walk." It means nothing to say, "I am a Spirit-filled Christian with the gifts and fruit of the Spirit evident in my personal life," without gently fulfilling our duty to look after each other's spiritual and physical needs. On the first Day of Pentecost, the Spirit-filled believers didn't just walk by the Spirit – they *ran* by the Spirit out into the streets speaking in tongues. It's no wonder their little church grew to 5,000 within a week. Despite their fervent enthusiasm, however, the Spirit of gentleness in them was so compelling that it drew people to Jesus. It wasn't a fellowship of selfishness: they gently shared everything in common. *"Great grace was upon them all"* (Acts 4:33).

Paul tells those of us "who are spiritual," or who have received the Holy Spirit, to exude a ministry of gentle restoration, not condemnation. *"Bear one another's burdens"* (Galatians 6:2). We must regularly test our own walk in the Spirit, gently sharing the good things of God.

Prayer

Holy Spirit, please teach me how to walk in a Spirit of gentleness, and so fulfill the law of Christ.

Notes:

_____

_____

_____

The Spirit of Sowing and Reaping

"...but he who sows to the Spirit will from the Spirit reap eternal life" (Galatians 6:7–18).

There is a law of sowing and reaping. We need to sow the seed of the Word of God so that people can be saved (Matthew13:1–9; 18–23). Contrary to the teachings of the prosperity preachers, this law is not about expecting God to reward us financially for giving Him money. We sow the fruit of the Holy Spirit into the lives of other people, both believers and unbelievers. When we cooperate with the Holy Spirit, He develops the character of Jesus in us. We have a choice. We can sow "the works of the flesh" that will harvest people to Hell *or* we can sow "the fruit of the Spirit" which harvests people to eternal life.

Many people would like to make a choice between having "the fruit of the Spirit" or "the gifts of the Spirit." It is not a matter of either / or but of both / and. We need the fruit of the Spirit, the character of Jesus, in order to the preach the Word and do ministry with the gifts of the Holy Spirit. The fruit of the Spirit makes the ministry of the gifts acceptable, and the gifts of the Holy Spirit give credibility to the fruit of the Spirit. Without having both, we grow weary in well-doing. Using both, we sow and reap people into salvation and can do good to all people.

Prayer

Holy Spirit, please teach me how to sow and reap a harvest of souls for Jesus.

Notes: _____

_____

_____

The Spirit Who Speaks to Us

"How did the Spirit of the Lord go from me to speak to you?" (1 Kings 22:5–28,37).

*M*any Christians run from meeting to meeting, looking for someone to give them "a word from the Lord," just like the kings who chased after prophets like fortune tellers. They want to know what their futures hold. Refusing to follow God's word, the King of Israel called together 400 prophets who told him what he wanted to hear. The mistake the king made was to consult Micaiah who told him what he didn't want to hear, which was that God had put a lying spirit in the mouth of those prophets and if he went to war, he would be killed.

The lesson for people who will not listen to the Word of God and follow it, is that God will send a lying spirit to them in order to expose them, remove them, and lead them to their destruction. Real prophets, like Micaiah, usually make us angry because they tell us what God says whether we like it or not. People need to be quiet and consult Jesus Himself in prayer. We need to listen to the Holy Spirit and take our places in the Church to serve Jesus. Today, Jesus wants us all to receive the baptism of the Holy Spirit so He can speak directly to us (John 16:13–15).

Prayer

Holy Spirit, help me to listen to You and Your prophets and accept what You say.

Notes: _____

_____

_____

The Spirit of the Good Samaritan

"But a Samaritan...went to him and bound up his wounds, pouring on oil and wine..." (Luke 10:25–37).

The point of the parable of the good Samaritan is to *"Go and do likewise."* But before we can follow Jesus' command, something has to happen to us to enable us. We ourselves need ministry. In this parable, we have to recognize the parallels between us and the victim, the man left at the side of the road. Whether as the result of our own sin and foolishness or somebody else's, we once fell, bleeding on the road of life, until the Good Samaritan, Jesus, stopped at the side of life's dangerous road to help us. Many, like the priest and the Levite, passed us by *"on the other side of the road."* But Jesus stopped, ministered to us, poured on the oil and the wine and saved us. The oil was for healing. The wine was the Holy Spirit.

For us to become "good Samaritans," we have to be saved (given new life), healed (oil poured on) and baptized with the Holy Spirit (wine poured on). Then, like Jesus, we can run the risk of stopping to save other victims of sin and the devil at the side of life's road. Then we can *"Go and do likewise."*

Prayer

Holy Spirit, please give me the boldness to stop at the side of life's road and be a good Samaritan to other people, as Jesus was to me.

Notes: _____

_____

_____

The Spirit of the Lamp

"No one, after lighting a lamp, puts it in a cellar, or under a bushel, but on a stand, that those who enter may see the light" (Luke 11:33–36).

The key to understanding this "parable of the lamp" is to remember that Jesus said earlier in this sermon, *"How much more will your Heavenly Father give the Holy Spirit to those who ask Him"* (Luke 11:13). Before we can become lamps that radiate the light of Jesus, we not only have to be born-again Christians: we have to be baptized with the Holy Spirit. Jesus fills the lamp with Holy Spirit oil and lights it up. The light is a reflection of the way in which we live our lives. As we walk, talk, work, and get involved in a church, our talk and our walk changes. Often, we are the last ones to notice the metamorphosis. It has been suggested that people who have recently been "lit up" or baptized in the Holy Spirit should be locked up for six months until they calm down. No! No! No! Most "lit up" Christians do more in their first six months than they will do for the rest of their lives, because their lamps get covered by baskets. We don't have to calm down. If we do, we become "basket cases" and lose our *"first love"* (Revelation 2:4,5). Anyone complaining of the lights being too bright needs to put on his or her "Son glasses!"

Prayer

Holy Spirit, light me with Your fire so I can be aglow and shine for Jesus.

Notes: _____

_____

_____

The Spirit of Good Leaven

"The Kingdom of Heaven is like leaven..." (Matthew 13:33).

When mixed in a recipe for making bread, leaven or yeast causes the dough to expand and increase in size. There is good leaven and bad leaven. Jesus warns us to *"Beware of the leaven of the Pharisees and the Sadducees"* (Matthew16:6,11). Paul talks about the *"old leaven...of malice and wickedness."* Like a lot of things in life, leaven can be used for good or for evil purposes.

Jesus compared the way the Kingdom of Heaven spreads throughout the world to the way that leaven spreads throughout three measures of meal. It moves unnoticed, until suddenly the loaf has risen and overflows out of the pan that was holding it.

Jesus said, *"For indeed, the Kingdom of God is within you"* (Luke 17:21). It is through His Kingdom that God rules our lives. When we are baptized with the Holy Spirit, He establishes Jesus as Lord over our lives. You cannot see the Holy Spirit; but He goes to work, like leaven, changing us from the inside to the outside.

At first, His effect is not very noticeable, until suddenly, we overflow with the fruit and gifts of the Holy Spirit, visible to all.

Prayer

Holy Spirit, please work like leaven in me, making me a visible part of the Kingdom of God.

Notes: _____

_____

_____

The Shrewd Spirit

"Therefore if you have not been faithful in the unrighteous mammon, who will entrust to you the true riches?"

(Luke 16:1–13).

Jesus is not commending dishonesty in this parable. What He is pointing out is that Christians can act awfully stupid, both in material and spiritual things. The dishonest steward, a shrewd man, quickly started to make business deals that would give him a good reputation and insure himself a future in his business.

The steward was selling oil and wheat. He made one deal after another with his employer's customers by discounting their bills. His employer was impressed.

Our employer (Jesus) expects no less from us. We too are in the oil and wheat business. We need to learn to cut deals quickly with people so they can have our oil (the Holy Spirit) and our wheat (the Bread of Life). Like this steward, we have been dishonest in the way we have run God's business. Let's look at the books: how many salvations, baptisms of the Holy Spirit, and healings have we facilitated? Where is the profit (harvest)? We've been losing money (souls). The time has come to ensure our future by being faithful in keeping Jesus on the throne of our lives and being diligent in completing the work God has given us, thereby laying up treasures in Heaven.

Prayer

Holy Spirit, show me how to be a shrewd steward for God.

Notes: _____

_____

_____

The Spirit of the Kingdom Within

"For indeed, the Kingdom of God is within you"
(Luke 17:20–21).

When Jesus said *"the Kingdom of God is within you,"* He was not saying that the Kingdom of God was naturally inside everybody. His answer was in reply to a question asked by some Pharisees who wanted to know when the Kingdom would come. The word "kingdom" in Greek does not refer to a place, but rather the exercising of authority or ruling over people, or the governing of people.

The Kingdom of God can't be seen coming, because it comes by means of the Holy Spirit who can't be seen. The Holy Spirit comes to put the Kingdom of God into place and into operation in people's hearts. He is like the wind. You can't see Him coming, but you can see the results after He has come (John 3:7,8). When people are born again and filled with the power of the Holy Spirit, great changes are visible through their attitudes, values, speech, demeanour, goals and even appearance. So, on the one hand, you cannot say, "Here it is," or "There it is," but if you have the eyes to see and the ears to hear, you can identify the Kingdom of God in people's lives by both their *"witness"* (Acts 1:8) and the *"signs following"* them (Mark 16:17,18).

Prayer

Holy Spirit, thank You for bringing the Kingdom of God into my life and giving me direction.

Notes: _____

_____

_____

The Spirit Jesus Gave Up

"And Jesus cried again with a loud voice and yielded up His Spirit" (Matthew 27:45–54).

*W*hen Jesus died on the Cross of Calvary and His Holy Spirit left His body, the Spirit moved away from that hill to complete some important work. First of all, the curtain of the Temple, which was 6 inches thick, 15 feet high and 60 feet long, was torn apart from top to bottom (not from bottom to top, as man would have done). This was God's way of tearing up the Old Covenant and establishing the New Covenant (Hebrews 9:15). No longer was the high priest the only one who could talk to God. That day, God became accessible to all of His people. Jesus made it possible for each of us to deal directly with God by simply calling on His Name, Jesus, so we could be saved and baptized with the Holy Spirit. Our hearts would become His "Holy of Holies"

That day, the Holy Spirit raised some of the saints from the dead to show that He has power over death, having promised that on the last day He would raise the dead to eternal life. *"If the Spirit of Him who raised Jesus from the dead dwells in you, He...will give life to your mortal bodies also through His Spirit which dwells in you"* (Romans 8:11).

Prayer

Holy Spirit, thank You for establishing Jesus' Holy of Holies in my heart so I can speak to God in His Name.

Notes: _____

_____

_____

The Spirit of Blood and Water

"But one of the soldiers pierced his side with a spear, and at once there came out blood and water" (John 19:31–37).

This was the fulfillment of the prophecy, *"Not a bone of Him shall be broken"* (John 19:36). Some have interpreted the mixture of blood and water as proof that Jesus was really dead. However, we need to look at this a little closer. Since Jesus was not a sinner, He was not an ordinary man. Thus, the blood and water that poured out of his pierced side were extraordinary. When His sinless blood poured out, it was to give new life to everybody who would believe in Him, because with it, He paid for the sin of the world. *"...it is the blood that makes atonement"* (Leviticus 17:11).

When the water poured out, it was the "living water" that Jesus said He would give to us. *"If any one thirst, let him come to Me and drink. He who believes in Me, as the Scripture has said, 'Out of his heart shall flow rivers of living water.' Now this He said about the Spirit, which those who believed in Him were to receive; for as yet the Spirit had not been given, because Jesus was not yet glorified"* (John 7:38,39). The water was a release of the Holy Spirit. Blood and water – the elements for new birth.

Prayer

Holy Spirit, thank You for applying the blood and water to me so that I could be born again.

Notes: _____

_____

The Strong Spirit

"Now he was casting out a demon that was dumb; when the demon had gone out, the dumb man spoke and the people marvelled" (Luke 11:14–28).

Casting out demons or evil spirits is part of our ministry. Jesus empowered us to do it after giving us salvation and the baptism with the Holy Spirit (Mark 16:17). Today, this is often called "deliverance ministry" or "exorcism." Jesus showed us that we can cast out demons very easily using our authority as believers.

But, He warned that when an unclean spirit has been cast out of a person, it wanders around looking for a new person in which to live. If it finds none, it will return to its former house and, finding it clean and empty, will go and get seven other spirits and repossess the person, who will be eight times worse off than before. Before a demon is cast out, the person has to be willing to let Jesus be his Saviour and fill the empty place with a new occupant, the Holy Spirit, so that the unclean spirit will not find the space empty when it tries to return. Jesus said the Heavenly Father will *"give the Holy Spirit to those who ask Him"* (Luke 11:13).

Prayer

Holy Spirit, please give me boldness to cast out demons, setting people free to receive Jesus as their Saviour and Lord and You as their Protector.

Notes: _____

_____

_____

The Spirit Who Washes

"Then He poured water into a basin and began to wash the disciples' feet, and to wipe them with the towel with which He was girded" (John 13:1–17).

What a seemingly degrading thing for Jesus to do! He stripped off his clothes, wrapped Himself in a towel like a common slave, and began to wash the disciples' dirty feet.

Peter reacted, *"You shall never wash my feet."*

Jesus responded, *"If I do not wash your feet, you have no part in me."* At that, Peter wanted a bath!

Jesus was demonstrating a three-point message. First of all, once we receive the living waters of the Holy Spirit, it's like having a bath that cleans up our whole lives from sin. Each day, the cleansing process of sanctification is needed in order to keep us in relationship with Him. Second, Jesus was teaching His followers *"to wash one another's feet"* or, in other words, to *"minister to each other like slaves."* This can be done consistently only by the power of the Holy Spirit. *"But he who is greatest among you shall be your servant"* (Matthew 23:11). Third, Jesus washed the feet of Judas who betrayed Him, knowing what he was going to do. Only by the power of the Holy Spirit can we genuinely *"love (our) enemies"* (Matthew 5:44).

Prayer

Holy Spirit, please continue to wash me and stir me to minister to others as Jesus did.

Notes: _____

_____

_____

The Spirit of the Good Wine

"...but you have kept the good wine until now"
(John 2:1–11).

To many, it is surprising that the first "sign" of Jesus' ministry was the turning of water into wine. The setting was a wedding reception Jesus attended with His mother and His disciples. Much to the chagrin of the hosts, they ran out of wine and didn't know where they could get any. Jesus' mother asked Him to do something about it. The result was that He turned about 180 gallons of water into exceptionally good wine, and *"His disciples believed in Him."*

John the Baptist said of Jesus, *"He will baptize you with the Holy Spirit and with fire"* (Matthew 3:11). Wine is a symbol of the Holy Spirit. In our natural lives, we run out of wine (or power) because of sin, and are disgraced before God. In the spiritual realm, when Jesus gives us new wine (the Holy Spirit) we never run out. With Him, there is more than enough of the Holy Spirit to quench our *"thirst for righteousness"* (Matthew 5:6). The lesson of the first miracle was that until we receive the "new" or "good" wine, we can't enter the Kingdom of God and take our place at the marriage supper of the Lamb (Revelation 19:9), a compelling message for the beginning of the ministry of Jesus.

Prayer

Holy Spirit, please keep me supplied with Your Good Wine so that I can take my place at the marriage supper of the Lamb.

Notes: _____

_____

_____

The Spirit of the Seal

"In Him you also...were sealed with the promised Holy Spirit..." (Ephesians 1:1–14).

In Paul's day, a seal was a design, a mark, an initial or some other device, placed on a letter or document as a signature or proof of authenticity. Letters were formally closed with a wafer of molten wax, into which was pressed the distinctive seal of the sender. This process closed or fastened the letter to prove that it had not been opened before the person to whom it was sent received it.

At the moment of salvation, we Christians have a seal placed on us as proof that we have received Jesus as our Saviour and Lord, and we belong to Him. The Holy Spirit is God's seal. He is the guarantee of our inheritance until we receive it, and remains with us as our Counselor and Guide until we go on to Heaven. Evidence of the Holy Spirit's seal can be seen in our changed lives, as He ripens the fruit of the Holy Spirit in us and we exercise the gifts He bestows upon us, thereby taking our place in the Church. Other people recognize the seal of authenticity by the way we worship and serve Jesus Christ.

Prayer

Holy Spirit, thank You for being my guarantee of Heaven. I want other people to be able to see that I belong to Jesus through the evidence of His seal on my life.

Notes: _____

_____

The Spirit of Wisdom and Revelation

"...the Father of glory, may give you a Spirit of wisdom and revelation of Him" (Ephesians 1:15–23).

Paul is not praying in this passage for the Spirit of wisdom and revelation to reveal the future or anything to do with ministry. He is praying that we will be given a Spirit of wisdom and revelation about Jesus Christ. We need to know Him personally and intimately. Only the Holy Spirit can help us to understand and accept "the hope" that Jesus gives us for the future; our "inheritance" and the New Jerusalem; and His "power," which is working in us to do mighty works of ministry. Only the Holy Spirit can help us to understand Jesus' ministry, His resurrection from the dead, and that He is sitting at God's right hand. Only the Holy Spirit can help us to understand that Jesus is above all earthly authority and has all authority over everything on Earth.

It is only the Holy Spirit who can convince us that Jesus rules the Church – to the extent that we will go directly to Him if we have complaints about a particular church. It is the Holy Spirit's role to help us understand and relate our concerns to Jesus.

Prayer

Holy Spirit, please be my "Spirit of wisdom and revelation," so I can know Jesus better as my Lord.

Notes: _____

_____

_____

The Spirit Who Gives Access

"...for through Him we both have access in one Spirit to the Father" (Ephesians 2:11–22).

Paul reminds us that before we came to know Jesus as our Saviour and Lord, we followed the *"prince of the power of the air,"* which is a spirit of disobedience. Having reconciled Jews and Gentiles to each other and made one people, Jesus has made salvation through faith available to both. As proof of this reconciliation, He has given us both the same "one Spirit," who gives us equal access to God our Father.

The Holy Spirit has taken us, who were strangers, foreigners and aliens, and has transformed us into citizens of Heaven and members of God's household along with all the saints (the great people of faith who we read about in the Bible). Isn't it wonderful that He can take a bunch of nobodies and make us into God's somebodies! Like building stones, He places us according to His perfect design in the building of His Temple. Jesus is the Cornerstone. The apostles and prophets are the foundation stones. We are the walls, pillars, and courts of the Temple. Individually and corporately, we are the dwelling place of the Holy Spirit.

Prayer

Holy Spirit, thank You for giving me access to God, my Father, and cementing me into His Temple, the place of Your dwelling.

Notes: _____

_____

_____

The Spirit of the Mystery

"...as it has now been revealed to His holy apostles and prophets by the Spirit..." (Ephesians 3:1–13).

Paul shocks everyone with this "mystery story" of God. It is a thriller, with all the intrigue, twists of plot, and fascinating characters a person could want. There is God. There are other gods. There is sin. There are murders. There are rebellions. There is war. The enemies of God's people battle against God's people. There is worship. There are victories. There are prophecies. God becomes a man. Jesus ministers. There are miracles. Jesus is betrayed and killed. Jesus won't stay dead. Jesus is raised to life again. Jesus ascends into Heaven. Jesus sends the Holy Spirit, not only to Jews, but to Gentiles. God's people are promised eternal life. They go into the whole world spreading the news. What drama! It would make a great movie! It's a "whodunnit."

Amid all the mystery, we know that Jesus "did it." When we receive Him as our Saviour and Lord, the mystery is solved. The Holy Spirit begins to unravel *"the unsearchable riches of Christ"* for us, amongst which is the revelation that we, as the Church, are to share in God's eternal purpose and plan as fulfilled through Jesus.

Prayer

Thank You, Holy Spirit, for solving God's mystery for me through Jesus. Help me to share the right clues with others that will lead them to find the answers that lead to You.

Notes: _____

_____

_____

The Spirit of Might

"...He may grant you to be strengthened with might through His Spirit in the inner man" (Ephesians 3:14–21).

Paul, in this passage, is praying that we don't lose heart because of his suffering. One of the well-worn excuses for not believing in God is, "I can't believe in a God who allows people to suffer or go through so many problems."

As onlookers, we have to be very careful not to draw the wrong conclusions. Suffering is not always entirely a bad thing. Paul's sufferings resulted in a richness of relationship with Jesus that doesn't happen with a life of ease. He was honoured to know Christ in *"the power of His resurrection, and the fellowship of His suffering, being made conformable unto His death..."* (Philippians 3:10, KJV). His terrible prison conditions brought him very close to Jesus. Rather than losing faith, like some in the church in Ephesus (Revelation 2:4), he became more Christ-like.

It was because of this lack of understanding that he prayed for us *"to be strengthened with might through His Spirit in the inner man."* The word *"might"* is the "power" of the Holy Spirit. With the Holy Spirit, who is "Christ dwelling in our hearts," there are no limits to what we can do and withstand.

Prayer

Holy Spirit, please unfold Your limitless power within me, that I can know the fellowship of His suffering and be made more like Jesus.

Notes: _____

_____

_____

The Spirit of Unity

"maintain the unity of the Spirit in the bond of peace"
(Ephesians 4:1–7).

Paul encourages us to start getting along with each other in the Church. Jesus has called each of us to a certain ministry as Christians. Whether we accomplish God's plan for us, however, depends on whether or not we choose to cooperate with Jesus. Cooperating with Him means absorbing and radiating His character; being completely humble, gentle (meek, or only acting on Jesus' command), patient (long on temper or suffering) bearing (putting up with) each other with love (agape). We must make every effort to keep the unity (oneness) of the Holy Spirit. This can be done if we are willing to bind ourselves to Jesus in the same way prisoners were chained together in jail to force them to walk together in perfect cooperation or oneness.

The Lord knew that we weren't very smart when it came to spiritual things, just as we aren't in natural things. Keeping things as uncomplicated as possible, He gave us just one of everything: body, Spirit, hope, Lord, faith, baptism, God and Heavenly Father. When we finally agree to agree with the "one of everything policy," we surprisingly find that we can do all things through one source – that being Christ!

Prayer

Holy Spirit, help me to live through You, that my relationships will be peaceful, and I will fulfill God's plan for my life.

Notes: _____

_____

_____

The Spirit of the Five-fold Ministry

"And His gifts were that some should be apostles, some prophets, some evangelists, some pastors and teachers, to equip the saints for the work of ministry" (Ephesians 4:8–16).

*T*his is what is called "The Five-fold Ministry." These special offices are *"domata gifts"* of the Holy Spirit, given by Jesus Christ to build up our churches so that we can learn to work together. Most churches cannot afford to hire five full-time people working together to give this kind of leadership. However, with the exception of the pastor, the others can generally travel from church to church to encourage the believers. A wise pastor will ensure that they are brought in from time to time to build up his church. Each of these should be co-workers or fellow labourers, building on the pastors' work and helping each of the members to receive, and learn how to use, their spiritual gifts (charismata) (Romans 12:6–8; 1 Corinthians 12:4–11).

Those operating in the "Five-fold Ministry" have the responsibility of working together with the saints to equip them for the work of ministry, and to develop unity, maturity, and stability so that the whole church can grow and be built up.

Prayer

Holy Spirit, please teach me and equip me for your work through the "Five-fold Ministry."

Notes: _____

_____

_____

The Spirit Who Gives Apostles

"And His gifts were that some should be apostles..."
(Ephesians 4:11–16).

The office or ministry of an apostle is a "domata gift" of the Holy Spirit to the Church. "Apostles" are people who have proven God's call on their lives in their local churches, and have been recognized by the leadership. They are sent out from their churches under the direction of the Holy Spirit to preach the Gospel in other places, and to establish new churches and ministries all over the world. Today, they are usually called missionaries or church planters. After starting new churches, apostles normally do not stay to be the pastors. They turn the new congregations over to people who have been called to minister there. Apostles will leave a trail of new churches behind them as they travel from place to place under the guidance of the Holy Spirit. They should be supported and encouraged by those who have sent them, as well as by the churches they have established, or by existing churches they have helped.

Apostles are gifts to our churches to show us how to minister the gospel to foreign cultures, other religions and unchurched groups; and to prepare new apostles for their ministries.

Prayer

Holy Spirit, if You want me to be an apostle, please prepare me to plant new churches wherever I am sent.

Notes: _____

_____

_____

The Spirit Who Gives Prophets

"And His gifts were that some should be...prophets..."
(Ephesians 4:11–16).

The office or ministry of a prophet is a "domata gift" of the Holy Spirit to the Church. A "prophet" is someone who has "the (charismatic) gift of prophecy" and has proven the gift through using it faithfully in the local church. Gradually, the Holy Spirit may use that person to prophesy in other churches. He prophesies through the Holy Spirit for the *"upbuilding and encouragement and consolation"* of churches and occasionally to individuals. Through prophecy, God tells us what He is going to do before He does it. All prophecies should be written down and checked for Scriptural accuracy. Peter tells us *"that no prophecy of Scripture is of one's own interpretation"* (2 Peter 1:20,21). Prophets must not explain their prophecies, but must leave it to the Holy Spirit to explain them to whomever they are directed – otherwise, like Agabus (Acts 21:11–14), they will be wrong. A prophet's main responsibility is to call people to repentance. Prophets are not "fortune tellers" who tell people what they should be seeking in prayer. Personal prophecies are generally given to confirm what God has already spoken.

Prayer

Holy Spirit, if You want me to be a prophet, please teach me to use my gift faithfully in my local church.

Notes: _____

_____

_____

The Spirit Who Gives Evangelists

"And His gifts were that some should be...evangelists..."
(Ephesians 4:11–16).

The office or ministry of an evangelist is a "domata gift" of the Holy Spirit. "Evangelists" are people who are called by Jesus Christ to preach the Gospel and lead people to accept Him as their Saviour and Lord. Evangelists demonstrate their gifting in their local churches and then are sent out to help in other churches. An evangelist is like a "custom combiner," who goes from farm to farm to harvest the farmers' crops and put the crops in the barns for the farmers. An evangelist is prepared by the Holy Spirit to go into churches and lead those in whom the local church has planted seeds, to Christ.

Evangelists give credibility to local pastors in that they will confirm the pastors' teaching and ministry. They do more than simply give an invitation, however. They use their special gifting to equip the local Christians to grow and mature so that they too can become effective witnesses for Jesus Christ. Evangelists operate under a special anointing of the Holy Spirit that draws people to say "Yes" to Jesus Christ.

Prayer

Holy Spirit, if You want me to be an evangelist, please show me how to bring people to Jesus and build up the Church.

Notes: _____

_____

_____

The Spirit Who Gives Pastors

"And His gifts were that some should be...pastors..."
(Ephesians 4:11–16).

The office or ministry of pastor is a "domata gift" of the Holy Spirit to the Church. "Pastors" are people who have been called by Jesus Christ and equipped by the Holy Spirit and the Church to be responsible for a *local* church. A "pastor" is a "shepherd," whose sheep are those people who comprise a local congregation. It is a pastor's responsibility to look after his people's needs from birth to death. He or she is to lead local churches in worship, preach and teach the Word of God, baptize believers, counsel those with problems, conduct weddings, give leadership to the elders (and anyone who is in leadership in the church), visit the believers in their homes, pray for the sick, see that the hungry are fed, visit those in prison, look after the poor, bury the dead, comfort the bereaved, teach believers how to pray, and fully equip the saints for ministry by involving others who are gifted in the other aspects of the "Five-fold Ministry."

It is important for pastors to be very wise in their relationships – particularly not to be part of cliques which make outsiders feel rejected, and not to be alone with members of the opposite sex who can mistake pastoral compassion for romantic interest.

Prayer

Holy Spirit, if You want me to be a pastor, please equip me as part of "The Five-fold Ministry" to build Jesus' Church.

Notes: _____

_____

_____

The Spirit Who Gives Teachers

"And His gifts were that some be...teachers..."
(Ephesians 4:11–16).

The office or ministry of teacher is a "domata gift" of the Holy Spirit to the Church. A "teacher" is a person who has *"the gift of teaching,"* or explaining the Gospel according to Scripture – to people both inside and outside the Church. Under the anointing of the Holy Spirit, teachers are given special insight into God's Word, and can explain it clearly. They have an unusual hunger to study the Bible, taking heed to Paul's instruction to *"do your best to present yourself to God as one approved, a workman who has no need to be ashamed, rightly handling the Word of Truth"* (2 Timothy 2:15). Teachers inspire other believers to get excited about God's promises and teach us how we can appropriate them for ourselves. They are responsible to teach *"all the words of this life,"* just as a pastor is encouraged to preach *"all the words of this life"* (Acts 5:20). A teacher must not teach anything that is contrary to the Bible. After they have proven themselves in local churches and their (charismata) gifting has been tested and recognized, they can be recommended to other churches as a "domata gift" to equip the saints there.

Prayer

Holy Spirit, if You want me to be a teacher, please show me how to rightly divide the Word of Truth to encourage others.

Notes: _____

_____

_____

The Spirit Who Renews Minds

"...and be renewed in the spirit of your minds..."
(Ephesians 4:17–24).

When we receive Jesus as our Saviour and receive the baptism of the Holy Spirit, we are in for some radical changes – but they are never forced upon us. We're given a choice. Paul suggests that the transformation is like changing our clothes. Before Christ, we lived in rags that consisted of futile minds, darkened understanding, alienation from God, ignorance, hardened hearts, callous attitudes, licentiousness, and greed to practice every kind of uncleanness. They were good only to be thrown into a fire and be burned up. As our old, sinful natures, our wardrobes were embarrassing. Paul suggests that we throw away, once and for all time, the old clothes of our old natures and put on our new clothes. We can do this by letting the Holy Spirit take control of our minds. *"Do not be conformed to this world but be transformed by the renewal of your mind, that you may prove what is the will of God, what is good and acceptable and perfect"* (Romans 12:2). Our new wardrobes – our new natures – are created in the likeness of God in true righteousness and holiness. By the way, our new wardrobes are heavenly white (Revelation 7:14)!

Prayer

Holy Spirit, please renew my mind to reflect the likeness of God.

Notes: _____

_____

_____

The Spirit Who Grieves

"And do not grieve the Holy Spirit of God, in whom you were sealed..." (Ephesians 4:25–5:1).

*B*elieve it or not, the Holy Spirit has feelings. He can be hurt, feeling deep pain and sorrow. For instance when, as our divinely appointed Counselor, He counsels us to channel our anger into constructive action – but we simply flail about, slaves to our emotions, – He is grieved. It is alright to get angry, but our anger should drive us to correct wrong situations, as Jesus did when He drove the money changers out of the Temple so it could again be *"a house of prayer"* (Mark 11:17). We grieve the Holy Spirit when we will not do an honest day's work; when evil talk comes out of our mouths; when bitterness, wrath, anger, clamour, slander and malice run our lives instead of Jesus.

The Holy Spirit wants us to be imitators of God. It is His ministry to teach us to walk in love, as Christ did. He wants each of us to be a fragrant offering to God; to sacrifice our own desires, like Jesus. That is why, when people do things that cause us to get angry and we are tempted to do and say sinful things, He is there to give us power to act like Jesus. We are supposed to be so much like Jesus that other people can't help but see His reflection in us.

Prayer

Holy Spirit, please correct me to the point that other people see Jesus in me immediately.

Notes: _____

_____

_____

The Spirit Who Sings

"...but be filled with the Spirit..." (Ephesians 5:3–20).

Paul shows us two different worlds in this passage. One is the new life, lived in the light among the saints; characterized by clean living, sexual purity, responsible living, clean thoughts, clean language, a good sense of humour, thanksgiving, an inheritance in the Kingdom of Christ – a life blessed and pleasing to God. The other is the old life, lived in darkness – characterized by sexual immorality, impurity, covetousness, unclean thoughts, a filthy mouth, deception, hopelessness and despair, with the inheritance of Hell – a life lived under God's wrath.

Christians get themselves into a terrible dilemma when they try to live with one foot in each world. It is so depressing that it can drive a person to get into all kinds of sin. The solution is to keep being filled daily, continuously, with the Holy Spirit, singing psalms, hymns and spiritual songs with one's heart – then to look back over life and thank God for everything Jesus has done. The result will be nothing but distaste for the old life, and a wonderful quenching of the thirst for reality.

Prayer
Holy Spirit, fill me afresh each day so I can sing and always give thanks in Jesus' Name, to our Father God.

Notes: _____

_____

_____

The Spirit's Word

"...and the sword of the Spirit, which is the Word of God"
(Ephesians 6:10–17).

We are at war. Paul wants us, first of all, to recognize who the enemy is; and second, to learn how to use our armour to defeat him. Our enemy is not made of flesh and blood. Our enemy is the devil and different kinds of evil spirits called *"principalities, powers, and world rulers."* They sound very powerful; but our weapons are even more powerful because they are *"not worldly, but have divine power to destroy strongholds"* (2 Corinthians 10:3,4). We must learn what these weapons are and how to use them so that we shall never be defeated.

To win, we must put on *"the whole armor of God."* It includes the *"belt of truth"* (John:14:6), the *"breastplate of righteousness"* (1 Corinthians 1:30), *"shoes of the Gospel of peace"* (John 14:27), the *"shield of faith"* (Galatians 2:16), the *"helmet of salvation"* (1 Thessalonians 5:8), and the *"sword of the Spirit"* (Hebrews 4:12,13). Actually, *"the whole armor of God,"* all six pieces, is one person – Jesus Christ. When we "put on" Jesus, we defeat the enemy, because we *"can do all things in Him who strengthens* (us)*"* (Philippians 4:13).

Prayer

Holy Spirit, please show me how to put on my "Jesus-armour" daily and enable me to defeat the enemy.

Notes: _____

_____

_____

The Spirit of Prayer and Supplication

"Pray at all times in the Spirit, with all prayer and supplication" (Ephesians 6:18–24).

The key to winning our warfare is to put on our "Jesus-armour" and then to stay in daily, constant, continuous communication with our Commander. Our communications system, our lifeline, is called "prayer." Without it, we can neither talk to God nor hear Him. Rather than receiving a clear set of marching orders, we risk running around in circles, if not smack into enemy lines. We become isolated and in danger of falling victim to the foe, with the result that we can be defeated. Jesus said, *"The thief comes only to steal and kill and destroy; I came that they may have life, and have it abundantly"* (John 10:10).

Our orders are to pray continuously in the Spirit. This means we are to pray, guided by the Holy Spirit, in whatever language we normally speak, but also to pray with our spiritual language. God calls us to supplication; praying humbly and earnestly on behalf of fellow Christians, that they can overcome their circumstances and boldly proclaim the Gospel – especially for those who, like Paul, are in prison because they follow Jesus. Perseverance in prayer results in peace and victory.

Prayer

Holy Spirit, teach me to pray continuously in the Spirit.

Notes: _____

_____

_____

The Spirit Who Helps

"...through your prayers and the help of the Spirit of Jesus Christ this will turn out for my deliverance..."

(Philippians 1:12–21).

Here we have a "Thanksgiving Report" for answered prayer. Paul shows how everything has *"worked together for good"* (Romans 8:28) through his arrest and imprisonment. There were times when he was not sure whether he would live or die, but he was a winner either way. *"For me to live is Christ, and to die is gain."* God used Paul's imprisonment to get him inside the emperor's household with the Gospel. Paul saw himself as an advance guard, or an army scout, who went ahead of the main army column to make sure that it was safe for the troops to proceed that way. Paul reports that he even shared the Gospel with the praetorian guard, the most feared army legion in the world – and they received it! He encourages us with the solid message, born of experience, that if he can do it, so can we!

When we pray for each other with the help of the Holy Spirit, God can use the worst circumstances to reach the most difficult people. When we pray in cooperation with the Holy Spirit, no one is beyond the reach of the Gospel – if we are willing to pay the price.

Prayer

Holy Spirit, please help me to go wherever Jesus sends me to share the Gospel with everybody who needs to hear it.

Notes: _____

_____

_____

The Standing-Firm Spirit

"...I may hear of you that you stand firm in one Spirit..."
(Philippians 1:27–30).

*W*hen we serve Jesus Christ, the Holy Spirit never encourages us to run away from our responsibilities, no matter how difficult they may be. He wants us to stay completely focused on the Gospel, just as He is. Paul encourages us to be in unity with other believers by having "one Spirit" (the Holy Spirit), with "one mind" (Jesus Christ), fighting and struggling together for the Gospel. It is never a one-person show. We are all equipped by the Holy Spirit so that we can cooperate and complement each other, to the extent that even our worst enemies can be transformed into fellow Christians. We don't have to be afraid of our opponents. They are headed for destruction. As we stand firm in the unity of our faith, allowing the Holy Spirit to ripen our fruit and exercise the gifts He has given us, it will be obvious to all, by the way we live, that God has given us salvation.

When we really believe in Jesus Christ, the Holy Spirit enables us to stand firm, even to the point of suffering; taking up our cross for His sake! Paul is not talking about simple rejection and hurt feelings, but about even a threat to our lives (Matthew 16:24).

Prayer
Holy Spirit, give me the courage to suffer for Jesus when my time comes, so that I can share the Gospel in my circumstances.

Notes: _____

_____

_____

The Fellowship Spirit

"...if any participation in the Spirit..."
(Philippians 2:1–11).

There are wonderful benefits from following Jesus Christ that one never considers at the point of making that life-changing commitment. It is only as we grow and deepen in the Holy Spirit that we begin to appreciate the big picture. Having experienced the love of Jesus, we actually get pleasure from being servants to each other, just as Jesus was to us. Through the unity and fellowship of the Holy Spirit, we are free to look after each other's interests and not just our own. This reversal of natural motivations comes through the knowledge of our consolation in Christ and the fellowship of the Holy Spirit, renewing our minds.

The Holy Spirit not only reveals His thoughts to us, but actually reprograms us to start *thinking like Jesus* as He renews our minds (Romans 12:2). Thinking the thoughts of Jesus is radically different than thinking natural human thoughts. He set aside the form of God to minister to us, made Himself of no reputation, took the form of a slave, humbled Himself and died on the Cross. In resurrection, however, He was exalted above all, that *"every knee should bow"* and *"every tongue confess that Jesus Christ is Lord."* What a privilege to fellowship with Him!

Prayer

Holy Spirit, please transform me to think and act like Jesus in the fellowship of my church so others will see our unity.

Notes: _____

_____

_____

The Spirit of True Circumcision

"For we are the true circumcision, who worship God in Spirit..."   (Philippians 3:1–16).

There have always been, and always will be, those people who want to take us backwards because they do not understand the Gospel. These are people who revert to the Old Testament, thinking that by keeping its laws, they can earn their way to Heaven.

Paul dealt with a group who believed that before we could become Christians, we had to first become circumcised Jews. They couldn't understand the Christian life of faith because they had never been "born again" and "baptized with the Holy Spirit." That's why Paul shared his testimony. He had been a superior Jew, but was unsaved until he met Jesus and the Holy Spirit.

Paul was like many of us who were raised in churches and became members, but who were not saved. It wasn't until later, when we received Jesus as our Saviour and Lord and were baptized with the Holy Spirit, that we realized what we had been missing. Our circumcision is of the heart (Romans 2:29) according to the New Covenant, and we worship God *"in Spirit."* Like Paul, we can say that the past is behind us and we *"press on toward the goal for the prize of the upward call of God in Christ Jesus."*

Prayer

Holy Spirit, please teach me to worship God and serve Jesus as I press forward for the prize.

Notes: _____

_____

_____

The Spirit Who Gives us Love

"He...has made known to us your love in the Spirit"
(Colossians 1:3–13).

There is nothing like a good reference to build a reputation. Paul had heard from Epaphras, the founding minister, about the church in Colossae. Epaphras boasted about their love (agape) in the Spirit for all believers because of their hope of Heaven. They had a church where the Gospel was preached, people were being saved, they were bearing fruit and the church was growing. It was an exciting church. They did not compromise the Gospel, nor did they apologize for it – with the result that people were transferring out of the kingdom of darkness and into the Kingdom of God's beloved Son. They allowed themselves to be led by the Holy Spirit.

Paul's concern in this letter stemmed from his understanding of the tremendous need we all have to support each other in prayer. As we pray that our fellow believers receive spiritual wisdom and understanding in order to lead a life worthy of Jesus, the love for one another deepens and grace abounds. The pressures of the world to compromise are enormous, but when we pray for each other in agreement, God ministers strength and endurance to us individually and to our churches.

Prayer

Holy Spirit, please let my reputation be of one who prays for individuals and churches with love in the Spirit .

Notes: _____

_____

_____

The Spirit Who Keeps us in Touch

"...yet am I with you in Spirit..." (Colossians 2:1–19).

As our Counselor, the Holy Spirit can keep us in touch with other Christians more effectively than e-mail. He tells us when they are doing well, when they are sick, warns us of impending danger, or tells us of any problem so that we can pray for each other – with no apparatus beyond a listening, submitted heart. This is not any occult or mediumistic consulting of the spirit world. This is communication via the Holy Spirit who calls us to pray for each other. It is the Holy Spirit who lovingly calls us to enter the prayer closet or call together other Christians to pray for another person or another church.

Even though Paul could not be with the church in Colossae in person, he was with them via the Holy Spirit who knits Christians together in love, because we have the same Saviour Jesus Christ. Even when we have no verbal communication, we can rejoice in the Holy Spirit for others and pray for their protection from vain philosophies, deceitful teachings, and the elemental spirits of the universe. We can pray that they will not be taken back into fruitless laws, worship of angels, visions that aren't from God and fleshly living.

Prayer

Father, please call me to pray for others in Your Spirit and strengthen me to be faithful to Your call.

Notes: _____

_____

_____

The Spirit of the Gospel

"...for our Gospel came to you not only in Word, but also in power and in the Holy Spirit and with full conviction"

(1 Thessalonians 1:1–5).

The Gospel of Jesus Christ is more than words, philosophy, religion, theology and doing good things. There is a dynamic power that confirms the words. There is a living person, Jesus Christ behind it, with whom we can have a relationship. He is a Person who lived, died, rose from the dead, and continues to live by His Holy Spirit. When we do what He tells us to do, the results prove His faithfulness to His Word. He proves Himself by sending the Holy Spirit to demonstrate and do in our lives what He says He will do as a result of our belief in Him. Consequently, we are led to full conviction and total belief in Jesus as Saviour and Lord.

For instance, Jesus said that whoever believes in Him and is baptized will be saved. He also said that certain signs would follow believers to prove they belonged to Him (Mark 16:17,18). They would cast out demons, speak in new tongues (languages), be protected from serpents and deadly drinks, and pray for sick people with the laying on of hands and they would be healed. We see it all happening, just as He said! There's power in the Gospel!

Prayer

Holy Spirit, please give me full conviction so that I can confidently witness with both words and Your power.

Notes: _____

_____

_____

The Spirit Who Gives Joy

"...for you received the Word in much affliction, with joy inspired by the Holy Spirit..." (1 Thessalonians 1:6–10).

There are no uniquely "perfect" conditions in which to receive Jesus Christ as Saviour and Lord. All conditions and situations are perfect, no matter how happy or how trying. As Paul told Timothy, *"preach the Word, be urgent in season and out of season, convince, rebuke, exhort, be unfailing in patience and in teaching."* In other words, we are to share the Gospel at both the right time and the wrong time. It was not brought to us by Jesus at a time the world would have described as "perfect" for its acceptance, but rather at a time when the world did not want to accept Him. He introduced it when the Roman army ruled Israel, a period of great crisis. The good news is that the Gospel is for all situations – for peace and war, for the healthy and the sick, for the newborn and the dying, for the successful people and the failures. It was designed for all people in all circumstances.

The Thessalonians imitated Paul and those who shared the Gospel with them – even at at time of great affliction. Consequently, they received continuous *"joy inspired by the Holy Spirit."*

Prayer

Holy Spirit, please give me the continuous joy which is my strength, despite afflictions.

Notes: _____

_____

_____

The Spirit Who Gives a New Walk

"Therefore whoever disregards this, disregards not man but God, who gives His Holy Spirit to you" (1 Thessalonians 4:1–12).

The new life in Jesus Christ is quite different from all other lifestyles. The commandments, when lived in the freedom of the Holy Spirit, protect us and help us to maintain a healthy relationship with both God and people. These commandments do not call us to a "holier-than-thou life" but to a "holy life" so we can serve God in peace. For example, we are to abstain from sexual immorality as defined by God. That means that each married person should have sexual relations only with their own spouse. Marriage is to be carried on in *"holiness and honour"* which means that God must be the centre of our families. Husbands and wives must honour both God and each other, as led by the Holy Spirit. God is a jealous God and will tolerate no rival gods in our relationship with Him. In the same way, husbands and wives are to tolerate no human rivals in their marriages. When they become mutually submissive to Jesus and each other, their love will grow and last forever. The result, both in the Church and outside, is that we lack nothing of true value.

Prayer

Holy Spirit, please teach me how to properly love fellow believers, both inside and outside of marriage, through You.

Notes: _____

_____

_____

The Spirit Who Can be Quenched

"Do not quench the Spirit..." (1 Thessalonians 5:12–28).

Paul gives us some very practical advice about how to prepare for the day of the Lord and Heavenly living. In summary, he says, *"Do not quench the Spirit";* advice which, if followed, would assure believers of exciting, powerful Christian lives, lived in the unity of the Spirit, with awesome signs and wonders following!

"Do not quench the Spirit," means do not extinguish or cause the fire of Holy Spirit to be put out, by dousing Him with the water of disobedience and lack of faith. If we ignore His guidance, we can't live by faith. The Christian life becomes impossible for us and we turn the Gospel into an oppressive life of laws. We quench the Holy Spirit when we despise, or don't like what He does. Here, Paul warns specifically against rejecting His "gift of prophecy." The warning really applies to all of the charismatic gifts of the Holy Spirit. All are for us to use today, despite the fact that many turn up their noses at His gifts and try to prevent their use by saying either that they aren't for today or they are from the devil. They are quenching the Holy Spirit and so see little evidence of Him in their lives. It is in cooperating with the Holy Spirit that we are sanctified through God's peace.

Prayer

Holy Spirit, please show me how to cooperate with You so I can have Your peace.

Notes: _____

_____

_____

The Spirit Who Does Not Mislead Us

"...we beg you,...not to be quickly shaken in mind or excited, either by spirit or word...to the effect that the day of the Lord has come" (2 Thessalonians 2:1–13).

*E*very generation has people who try to prophesy when Jesus will return. They get pretty embarrassed when their dates come and go! It happened in the church at Thessalonica and it's still happening today. Paul tells us that Jesus will not return until the *"man of lawlessness"* (the man of sin) leads a rebellion and proclaims himself god. The lawless one will work by the power of Satan and will show us counterfeit signs and lying wonders. Anyone who does not receive the love of the truth will not be saved. To those who will not receive the Gospel, God will send a *"strong delusion"* to make them believe what is false. To protect ourselves from this false ministry we have to watch for the true Biblical signs, examining everything in light of the Bible – using it as a plumb line. Jesus tells us, *"But of that day and hour no one knows, not even the angels of Heaven, nor the Son, but the Father only"* (Matthew 24:36). Anybody who tries to tell us they know exactly when He is coming is wrong, and doesn't listen to the Holy Spirit.

Prayer

Holy Spirit, keep my eyes on the Bible and my ears open to Your voice so that I shall be prepared when Jesus comes to get us.

Notes:

_____

_____

_____

The Spirit of Sanctification

"...God chose you from the beginning to be saved through sanctification by the Spirit and belief in truth"

(2 Thessalonians 2:13–17).

It is important to understand that we are Christians because God chose us from the beginning of time. We are not accidents of religion. We were created to have fellowship with God. Unfortunately, Adam and Eve sinned and lost the wonderful, intimate relationship with Him. However, through our belief in Jesus Christ, it can now be restored. We are sanctified (made holy and acceptable) by the indwelling of the Holy Spirit; not by our own ability to follow a set of laws. It's a matter of "Who we know," not "what we do" that ensures us a place in Heaven.

"Sanctification" is a process that begins to take effect as soon as we receive Jesus as Saviour and have been baptized with the Holy Spirit. The word means to be made "holy" or "to be set aside for holy purposes," which means to be made ready to serve God. We are free to choose whether to cooperate or not. Cooperation means letting the Holy Spirit develop the character of Jesus in us through planting and ripening the fruit of the Spirit in our lives and giving us His gifts to equip us for the ministry Jesus planned for us.

Prayer

Holy Spirit, please sanctify me, that I may have eternal comfort as I cooperate with You.

Notes: _____

_____

_____

The Spirit Who Justifies

"He was manifested in the flesh, vindicated in the Spirit..."
(1 Timothy 3:1–16).

Paul is very specific concerning the qualifications for leadership in the church. Many people find it hard to understand why the circumstances of our lives determine our qualifications for taking positions in the church. Because we don't understand the "sinfulness of sin," we can't see how it affects our ability to serve God. In the same way, many people can't see what the condition of our physical bodies has to do with serving God. They do not understand that our physical bodies are designed for worship, and what we do physically has spiritual implications.

This lack of understanding underscores "the mystery of godliness" or "the mystery of our religion." There is no greater mystery than how God can become a flesh-and-blood person, be justified in the Spirit, and go back to Heaven. It is puzzling that God would and could do this. And yet, He did. That is why He is called "Emmanuel" which means "God with us." He proved that when our sinful bodies had been cleaned up through repentance and forgiveness, and filled with the Holy Spirit, we could be justified before Him, living a Godly life, free to worship and praise Him. He wants people in leadership who can faithfully prove, through the way they live, that they have been justified.

Prayer
Holy Spirit, please use me in leadership when I am ready.

Notes: _____

_____

_____

The Spirit Who Warns Us

"Now the Spirit expressly says that in latter times some will depart from the faith..." (1 Timothy 4:1–10).

Here is a warning that we all need to take seriously. There are always people looking for a religious *experience*, rather than an authentic relationship with God through Jesus Christ. They consider themselves super-spiritual, based on experiences rather than on Biblical doctrine. These people can be easy victims of *"deceiving spirits"* as they are preoccupied with *"doctrines of demons"* rather than learning the solid doctrines of the Gospel as revealed by Jesus through His Spirit.

Such people never settle down and faithfully take their place in a church. Manifestations are more important to them than a solid relationship with Jesus. This leaves them vulnerable to being led astray by the "angel of light" (2 Corinthians 11:14) and the "roaring lion" (1 Peter 5:8) who comes to deceive and devour them. To avoid having to be warned about getting off track, we must get grounded in solid Biblical doctrine, reject non-Biblical myths, and develop authentic godliness. It's wonderful to experience the power of God in our lives – in fact we *need* it – as long as it is truly the power of God and not a counterfeit. We must listen carefully for any warning signs from the Holy Spirit, who we can trust.

Prayer

Holy Spirit, please keep my focus on Jesus, that I shall not be deceived.

Notes: _____

_____

_____

The Gift-Giver Spirit

"Do not neglect the gift you have..." (1 Timothy 4:11–13).

*W*hen Timothy received the baptism of the Holy Spirit, like Paul, he may have received the charismatic gift of speaking in tongues (languages) which would have been the normal initial evidence (Acts 2:4; Acts 15:8;1 Corinthians 14:18). Like many of us, he did not use his gift. Problems arose which, Paul correctly concluded, were a result of Timothy neglecting to use, every day, *"the gift which he received by prophetic utterance."*

To neglect to use the spiritual gifts (Romans 12:6–8; 1 Corinthians 12:8–10) is to neglect the Holy Spirit. Physical and emotional disturbances occur when we don't use His gifts daily: fear, crying for no apparent reason, heart palpitations and a burning mouth. For any Christian, especially a pastor, the results can be devastating. When we stop using the gifts, we miss out on doing the ministry for which the gifts are given. It's true that the other aspects of the Christian walk (like being an example to others), are very important; the public reading of Scripture is important, as are preaching and teaching – but it's critical to use the gifts in order to meet other people's needs. We must use them every day. Those who have not yet received spiritual gifts will, as they receive the baptism of the Holy Spirit.

Prayer

Holy Spirit, please remind me to use the spiritual gifts you have given me every day.

Notes: _____

_____

_____

The Spirit of Laying on of Hands

"Hence I remind you to rekindle the gift of God that is within you through the laying on of my hands" (2 Timothy 1:1–6).

$\mathcal{W}$e all need to be reminded to rekindle our gifts of the Holy Spirit, especially tongues. When we don't use our gifts, anxiety shows up. Because the Holy Spirit is not an aggressive intruder who attempts to dominate and control our lives, He is easily ignored. His respectful gentlemanliness makes it easy for insensitive Christians to forget that He is there, quietly waiting to be our Counselor. Because He is purposefully transparent, wanting people to see Jesus, we often forget, in the midst of our hectic lives, that He is just a whisper away.

We stir up the gift of God through the laying on of hands, and develop a relationship with the Holy Spirit by talking with Him, consulting Him, and generally seeking His direction about the will of Jesus or the Father for us. Being in tune with the Holy Spirit requires seeking solutions through prayer for problems both personally and in our churches. He has the answers to our questions. He will never tell us anything that is not Scriptural. We develop a deeper relationship with Him through using the gifts of the Holy Spirit in obedience and according to His timing.

Prayer

Holy Spirit, please refresh my friendship with You, so that as I use my spiritual gifts, I can serve Jesus more fully.

Notes: _____

_____

_____

The Spirit of Power

"For God did not give us a spirit of timidity but a Spirit of power and love and self-control" (2 Timothy 1:7–10).

The Holy Spirit is not a coward – nor does He cause people to act like cowards. He develops strength in us. We need to have the same strength that enabled Jesus to die on the Cross, walk through death and come back into life again. The Holy Spirit gives us the same courage that Paul exhibited throughout his prison term. He takes away fear and replaces it with His power. This is the power Jesus said the Holy Spirit would give us so that we could be witnesses (Acts 1:8) – the dynamite power that would allow us to talk about Jesus to anybody, anywhere, under any circumstances. In no sense an abusive, self-seeking power, it is evidenced within the context of (agape) love, invariably for the spiritual benefit of all.

When the Holy Spirit comes into our lives, He does not make us sick, physically, mentally or emotionally. He gives us *"self-control."* As one pastor said, "I thought that when the Holy Spirit came into our lives He made us more normal." That is true. Weirdness, sickness, and emotional instability are not from the Holy Spirit. He makes us normal.

Prayer

Holy Spirit, thank You for taking away my fear and replacing it with power, love and self-control.

Notes: _____

_____

_____

The Spirit Who Gives a Pattern

"Guard the truth that has been entrusted to you by the Holy Spirit who dwells within us" (2 Timothy 1:12–18).

The key to serving Jesus Christ, regardless of our circumstances, is knowing Him and recognizing the pattern He established for us through His life, death and resurrection – and through His Word. The Holy Spirit holds that key. *"Anyone who does not have the Spirit of Christ does not belong to Him"* (Romans 8:9). As we spend time with the Holy Spirit, our confidence in Jesus Christ and the hope of eternal life grows. He not only convicts us of our sin but also convinces us of our eternal life. As we follow the pattern of Paul's sound teaching, we can guard the truth that has been entrusted to us by the Holy Spirit. Paul reminds us that the Holy Spirit dwells within us, so therefore, He is always close at hand; always there to reinforce the pattern or model of the new life we have in Jesus Christ.

The pattern demonstrates that we don't have to be ashamed of the Gospel; on the contrary, knowing what Jesus accomplished fills us with overflowing gratitude and esteem for it. Knowing Jesus in His death and resurrection makes us, like Paul, unashamed to suffer for Him. The pattern is clear: that which Satan means for evil, God will turn around and use for good.

Prayer

Holy Spirit, thank you for showing me the pattern of the new life in Jesus Christ, and helping me to live it.

Notes: _____

_____

_____

The Spirit of Godliness

"...holding the form of religion but denying the power of it. Avoid such people" (2 Timothy 3:1–13).

Paul warns that these last days are perilous times in which to serve Jesus Christ. Counterfeits abound. Any true Christian can spot counterfeit Christians. They might look just like normal, religious people, but that's the problem – they are normal religious (but not Christian) people. Outwardly, they look like Christians: they attend church services and go through all the motions, but are simply self-centered manipulators who take advantage of other people in the Name of God. They deny the power of God, particularly with regard to miracles and signs and wonders. They have no desire to be "born again" Christians for fear that they will lose their freedom and look like fanatics. They deny the need to be baptized with the Holy Spirit for fear that they will lose control of their lives. They fight the gifts of the Holy Spirit because they don't want to be embarrassed. They know that unless they submit to the Lordship of Jesus, they won't receive anything beyond themselves, but they don't want Jesus to have control over their lives. Like Jannes and Jambres, they try to control their churches with their corrupt minds. We are warned to turn away from people who deny the power of the Gospel.

Prayer

Holy Spirit, please develop true godliness in me so that I can serve Jesus faithfully whether I am persecuted or not.

Notes: _____

_____

_____

The Spirit Who Gives Scriptures

"All Scripture is inspired by God and is profitable..." (2 Timothy 3:14–4:5).

The Scriptures are technically the Word of the Spirit of God (Acts 1:16). They are "God-breathed" or "theopneuso." The Holy Spirit directed the authors in writing them. They are given so that we will have correct doctrine about God and not fall prey to a false religion. The Bible is the only acceptable Spiritual covenant because it was given to us through Jesus Christ. The Scriptures are necessary for *"reproof"* or showing where people are wrong or sinful. They are given for *"correction"* in order to show us when people are off track in their teaching so they can get back to the truth. They are also given for *"instruction in righteousness,"* as a guide for developing a right relationship with God through Jesus. The Scriptures are given to us so that we can become mature believers, complete in our understanding of God and His plan for individuals, churches and the world. They prepare us to be thoroughly equipped for every good work that Jesus wants us to do. The Scriptures (the Bible) are given for our protection because God won't do anything that is not in them; just as we are not to act outside the pattern He established in His Word, so we can stay faithful.

Prayer

Holy Spirit, teach me from the Scriptures so I can be completely equipped to fulfill the ministry You have given me.

Notes: _____

_____

_____

The Spirit Who Renews

"...He saved us,...by the washing of regeneration and renewal in the Holy Spirit, which He poured out upon us richly through Jesus Christ our Saviour..." (Titus 3:1–11).

God's mercy, not our own efforts, saved us. It was *"not by works of righteousness we have done."* But, simply saving us was not enough; God needed to be able to guarantee that, despite our humanity, we could walk with Him and live according to His plan. The "guarantee," both for God and for ourselves, is the Holy Spirit. We experience *"the washing of regeneration"* when He forgives us our sins; then the *"renewing of the Holy Spirit"* as we seek Him, submit to Him, and heed His direction every day. This enables us to live out God's plan for our lives. We are not saved by works but we are saved to *do* good works.

There is no shortage of the Holy Spirit. He has been poured out on us abundantly so that when sin abounds, grace can abound even more. The Holy Spirit is inexhaustible. It is only through Him that we can do the things that Paul suggests with regard to submitting to government authorities, exercising self-control and relating to other people in the Church. Living the Christian life is impossible without the power of the Holy Spirit.

Prayer

Holy Spirit, please renew me each day so I can live daily as an heir of eternal life.

Notes: _____

_____

_____

The Spirit of Gifts

"...God also bore witness by signs and wonders and various miracles and by gifts of the Holy Spirit..." (Hebrews 2:1–9).

This passage contains a strong reminder about the bottom line of our ministry: it is all about salvation. It is important to focus on the essence of life so we don't drift away from God. He gave us His own witness regarding the message of salvation; with signs and wonders, various miracles, and gifts of the Holy Spirit which are distributed according to His will. These are the elements through which God proves to us, over and over again, that He wants us to live out our salvation. He confirmed the critical importance of salvation through these three unarguable facts: 1) it was spoken by the Lord; 2) the apostles heard it; 3) the witness of the Holy Spirit's ministry through miracles, signs (Mark 16:17,18) and gifts (1 Corinthians 12:8–11) confirms how vital it is.

All of these elements are necessary for the Church today. They prove that Jesus is Lord and that all things have been placed in subjection to Him. They help us to see Jesus. Today, when signs and wonders (with various miracles) and gifts of the Holy Spirit are witnessed, they are proof of Jesus' saving work. When they are not seen, then Jesus is not being allowed to be Lord.

Prayer

Holy Spirit, keep pointing us to Jesus with signs, wonders, miracles and gifts so we can see Him crowned with glory and honour.

Notes: _____

_____

_____

The Spirit Who Sanctifies

"For He who sanctifies and those who are sanctified have all one origin..." (Hebrews 2:10–3:6).

*J*esus, the *"pioneer"* of our salvation, was made perfect through suffering. The Greek word for "perfect" means to accomplish the goal or purpose for which a person exists. Jesus accomplished the full payment for our salvation through the Cross and resurrection. He is the One who sanctifies us and sets us apart for holy use. He makes us one with Him through the Holy Spirit who dwells both in Him and in us.

We are holy, not because we haven't sinned, but because we have been forgiven and filled with the Holy Spirit who works a continuous process of sanctification through us every day. The Holy Spirit's work is not a once-in-a-lifetime experience, but a daily process of renewal. He makes it possible for us, like Jesus, to say, *"I will proclaim Thy Name to My brethren, in the midst of the congregation I will praise Thee...I will put my trust in Him."* Because Jesus has destroyed the devil and the power of death, He has become our High Priest who made the offering that was necessary to save us. We have been given the Holy Spirit to worship God.

Prayer

Holy Spirit, please do the work necessary to sanctify me for worship.

Notes: _____

_____

_____

The Warning Spirit

"Therefore, as the Holy Spirit says..." (Hebrews 3:7–19).

The Holy Spirit still warns us not to harden our hearts when we hear His Voice – because many of us do. The Israelites did not want to hear God's voice, so they told Moses to speak to them. They were afraid to open themselves up to actually hearing from God themselves – but God's desire was to know His people personally. Many people today are like the Israelites.

Like Pharaoh, they harden their hearts against what God wants. It is astounding to read about how determined Pharaoh was to ignore God, before he finally relented. In the same way, many today really don't want to hear what the Holy Spirit has to say to them, and so they stay away from church services and prayer meetings. No matter how "user friendly" a church may appear, people held in the grip of rebellion will not respond.

When the Gospel is preached and people are saved and filled with the Holy Spirit, their hearts are softened towards God. They want to hear from Him and know His plan for their lives. God wants to equip us with the Holy Spirit and the gifts of the Holy Spirit so that we can enjoy a wonderful relationship with Him and with His family, the Church.

Prayer

Holy Spirit, please speak to me every day, so that as a partaker of Christ, I can enjoy a personal relationship with God.

Notes: _____

_____

_____

The Spirit Who is in the Body

"For the Word of God...piercing to the division of soul and spirit..." (Hebrews 4:11–16).

Here we see just how powerful is *"the Word of God."* John identifies *"the Word"* as Jesus. We are cautioned not to be disobedient like the Israelites in the desert because *"the Word of God"* sees everything. Nothing escapes His eyes. He sees into the furthest corners of our hearts and has no need for anyone to tell Him about any man or woman.

Jesus is alive, and is so powerful that He can see right into the place where the human spirit (soul) and the Holy Spirit come together in our hearts. He can discern, or read, our inmost thoughts and intentions. Like it or not, every living person will stand totally revealed before Him when He comes back because He will be our Judge. At that time, we will be required to give an account of what we did with our precious lives to Him.

The exciting thing about Jesus being our High Priest is that He can empathize with our weaknesses because He was tempted as we are – yet He did not sin. Because He truly understands, we can go boldly to Him and find mercy and help.

Prayer
Holy Spirit, please fill me so that my heart will reflect Jesus.

Notes: _____

_____

_____

The Spirit Who Makes Partakers

"For it is impossible to restore again to repentance those who have once been enlightened...and have become partakers of the Holy Spirit...if they then commit apostasy..." (Hebrews 6:1–12).

Now this is something we don't want to hear. But, there is a line of sin over which a person can cross and lose their salvation. Many of us are shocked when we read this because many believe in the doctrine of "eternal security" which tells us that "once saved, we're always saved." But it does appear that even those who have been saved and become partakers of the Holy Spirit and tasted the Good Word of God can fall away. Jesus warned us about the one unforgivable sin: *"Truly, I say to you, all sins will be forgiven the sons of men, and whatever blasphemies they utter; but whoever blasphemes against the Holy Spirit never has forgiveness, but is guilty of an eternal sin"* (Mark 3:28,29). Now obviously, it is not a common occurrence but the danger is there. Our eternal security is connected to obedience to Jesus Christ and cooperation with the Holy Spirit so that *"signs will accompany"* (Mark 16:17,18) and will be evident in our witnessing. We must always be aware that we have not yet reached Heaven, and although we don't follow Jesus perfectly, we must serve Him prayerfully and carefully.

Prayer

Holy Spirit, please guard my heart and help me to know You so intimately that I would never blaspheme against You.

Notes: _____

_____

_____

The Spirit of the New Covenant

"...how much more shall the blood of Christ, who through the Eternal Spirit offered Himself without blemish to God, purify your conscience from dead works to serve the living God"

(Hebrews 9:1–15).

The first covenant, with its sacrifices and the earthly Tabernacle, could not "perfect the conscience of the worshippers." Forgiveness was temporary. But when Jesus came as our High Priest, His sacrifice was made in a *"holy place"* not made by human hands. His sacrifice was not made with the blood of animals, but with the blood of His own body. Jesus made the one and only – and final – sacrifice for sins on the Cross of Calvary. *"But when Christ had offered for all time a single sacrifice for sins, He sat down at the right hand of God"* (Hebrews 10:12). The "time of reformation" had come!

When we accept Jesus as our Saviour and receive the baptism of the Holy Spirit, it is the Holy Spirit who cleanses our consciences, so that whenever we remember our past sin, we no longer need to feel condemned. Our memories of the past are not cues to pick up the old guilt again, but are reminders to say, "Thank You, Jesus, for forgiving me for all of my past sin and washing me whiter than snow." The Holy Spirit reminds us that Jesus is the Mediator of the New Covenant.

Prayer

Holy Spirit, remind me to pray, "Thank You, Jesus, for Your blood which gives me a clean conscience and faith by which to live."

Notes: _____

_____

_____

The Spirit of the High Priest

"...how much more shall the blood of Christ, who through the eternal Spirit offered Himself..." (Hebrews 9:11–28).

The Second Covenant replaced the First. Jesus Christ became our High Priest and went into the real Holy of Holies in Heaven (of which the earthly one was a copy) to present His sacrifice, not with the blood of animals – but with His own blood – which secured eternal redemption for us. It is amazing, because Jesus, through the Holy Spirit, offered Himself without spot to God so that His blood might cleanse our consciences and free us from Satan's grasp, enabling us to serve the living God. The blood of Jesus is transferred into the Heavenly Temple by the Holy Spirit. Therefore, Jesus' blood becomes a symbol for the Holy Spirit as well. Thus, Jesus is the Mediator of the New Covenant which, in fact, becomes His legal "will," giving an inheritance to all who become heirs by faith.

And so, our High Priest, Jesus, following His resurrection, entered into the Heavenly sanctuary where He continues to represent us before God. He no longer makes yearly sacrifices because he was *"offered once to bear the sins of many..."* Jesus will *"appear a second time, not to deal with sin, but to save those who are eagerly waiting for Him."*

Prayer

Holy Spirit, please keep my conscience clean until Jesus returns.

Notes: _____

_____

The Spirit Who Bears Witness

"And the Holy Spirit also bears witness to us..."
(Hebrews 10:10–25).

The New Covenant is really amazing! Jesus, unlike every other priest who ever made daily sacrifices, offered for all time a single sacrifice for sins and then sat down at the right hand of God. By offering Himself, He made perfect those who are being sanctified (made holy). Under the New Covenant, the Lord said, *"I will put My laws on their hearts, and write them on their minds."* He does this through the Holy Spirit after we have been baptized with the Holy Spirit. The Spirit of God will speak to us if we will listen. Even many of those who can't read or write have discovered this. The Holy Spirit is our Heavenly Lawyer and knows all of God's laws which He imprints upon our hearts. All we have to do is to talk to Him and He will tell us about *"sin and righteousness and judgement"* and guide us *"into all the truth."* He will tell us *"the things that are to come"* and *"glorify"* Jesus. Listening to Him is crucial to serving God. He encourages us to *"not forsake the assembling of ourselves together"* so He can guide us and we can encourage each other in fellowship.

Prayer
Holy Spirit, thank You for bringing God's law into my heart and encouraging me to serve Him.

Notes: _____

_____

_____

The Spirit Who Gets Insulted

"How much worse punishment will be deserved by the man who has spurned the Son of God...and outraged the Spirit of grace?" (Hebrews 10:26–39).

Here is a frightening warning! Anybody who thinks that he or she can go on willfully sinning continuously, after receiving Jesus as Saviour and Lord and after receiving the knowledge of the truth, has no way left to find forgiveness. We have too many "jailhouse lawyers" in our churches these days who like to quote one Scripture verse against another to justify their sinning, and claim that they can't lose their salvation. If anyone who rejected Moses' law died without mercy, how much worse a punishment will the person receive who tramples the Son of God under foot, counts Jesus' blood as a common thing, and insults the Holy Spirit? God will repay such sin. It certainly is *"a fearful thing to fall into the hands of the living God."*

Certainly we will all have hard times of affliction and persecution and people taking advantage of us – but this calls for *"endurance"* so that we can receive God's promise. *"Blessed is the man who endures trial, for when he has stood the test, he will receive the crown of life..."*

Prayer

Holy Spirit, help me to endure my temptation so that I can receive the crown of life.

Notes: _____

_____

_____

The Spirit of the Lord's Supper

"This cup is the new covenant in My blood"
(1 Corinthians 11:23–26).

We celebrate the Lord's Supper in order to remember that Jesus died on the Cross of Calvary to pay for our sin. We celebrate it because He told us to do it. Jesus said, *"This is My body which is* (broken) *for you. Do this in remembrance of Me."* His body, of course, was amazingly given as a sacrifice for our sins. In teaching the church at Corinth how to partake of the Lord's Supper, Paul reminded them *"In the same way also the cup, after supper, saying, 'This cup is the New Covenant in My blood. Do this, as often as you drink it, in remembrance of Me.'"*

But participation in Communion is more than just a matter of remembering. We are called to serve God: *"...how much more shall the blood of Christ, who through the eternal Spirit offered Himself without blemish to God, purify your conscience from dead works to serve the living God?"* (Hebrews 9:14).

The wine represents Jesus' blood. Jesus' blood represents the Holy Spirit. The Holy Spirit, as evidence of the living presence of Jesus, cleanses our consciences and renews us when we drink from the cup of the New Covenant.

Prayer

Holy Spirit, please feed me at the Lord's Supper, that I may be renewed to serve Jesus.

Notes: _____

_____

The Spirit Who Discerns

"For anyone who eats and drinks in an unworthy manner eats and drinks judgment to himself, not discerning the Lord's body" (1 Corinthians 11:27–34).

There is blessing in coming to the Lord's Supper. But, there is also judgment for those who eat at the Lord's table in an unworthy manner. In the beginning, the Lord's Supper was a full meal, like a "pot-blessing" supper (as opposed to a "pot-luck," as luck has no place in God's plan), to which everybody brought food and it was supposed to be shared in a smorgasbord fashion. However, there were those who placed themselves in danger because they wouldn't share their food with other believers and got drunk. These people knew that the bread and wine represented Jesus' physical body, but they didn't recognize His spiritual Body which consists of all Christians who make up the Church. The result was that they wouldn't share their food but would just go ahead individually and eat and drink. This was a disgrace to Jesus. They, like anybody who does not recognize fellow Christians to be part of the Body of Christ and will not share the Lord's supper, were judged and became weak and sick.

Paul warns that we need the Holy Spirit's gift of discernment to recognize the Lord's Body.

Prayer

Holy Spirit, please help me to examine myself so that I can discern the Lord's Body and be blessed at His table.

Notes: _____

_____

_____

The Spirit Who Gives Us Our Own Gift

"But each has his own special gift from God, one of one kind and one of another" (1 Corinthians 7:1–17).

In discussing marriage, divorce and celibacy, Paul gives important instructions for Christians who have been baptized with the Holy Spirit: *"use your own spiritual gift* (charisma)." We are to use whichever of the 15 spiritual gifts (Romans 12:6–8; 1 Corinthians 12:8–10) of the Holy Spirit we have, regardless of our marital status. That way, we can remain faithful to Jesus. If married to an unbeliever, we can try to lead our spouse to Jesus. If divorced, we can minister to our ex-spouse and family as well as to other divorced people. If single, we can minister to other singles. By using our gifts, we will be giving *"a demonstration of the Spirit and of power,"* so the people we care for can have a *"faith"* which rests *"in the power of God"* (1 Corinthians 2:4,5), and we can find peace and fulfillment in ministry as we remain faithful to Jesus Christ. Through Him, we can resist the temptation to marry someone not of God's choice. Daily use of the spiritual gifts strengthens us to witness effectively to family, church, strangers and acquaintances.

Prayer

Holy Spirit, help me to use Your spiritual gifts, regardless of my marital state, so I can be an effective witness for Jesus Christ.

Notes: _____

_____

_____

The Spirit Who Baptized Jesus

"...He saw the Heavens opened and the Spirit descending upon him like a dove" (Mark 1:1–11).

John was sent to prepare the way for Jesus. They were a team ministry. John baptized people with water for repentance. Jesus would baptize people with the Holy Spirit.

No church would call such an unlikely looking pair to head up their ministry. John was a wild looking man dressed in camel's hair clothes with a leather belt around his waist. He ate locusts (grasshoppers) and honey. Jesus, on the other hand, dressed well in a remarkable seamless robe, and ate any kind of food He wished. People said of John, *"He has a demon."* Of Jesus, they said, *"Behold, a glutton and a drunkard, a friend of tax collectors and sinners!"* (Matthew 11:19). John preached, *"After me comes He who is mightier than I, the thong of whose sandals I am not worthy to stoop down and untie. I have baptized you with water; but He will baptize you with the Holy Spirit."* As Jesus came up out of the water after John baptized Him, the Heavens opened and the Spirit descended upon Him like a dove. A voice from Heaven said, *"Thou art my beloved Son; with Thee I am well pleased."*

We all need to be baptized by Jesus with the Holy Spirit so that we can hear God call us "beloved – with whom He is pleased."

Prayer
Holy Spirit, please fill me afresh so that I can serve effectively on Jesus' ministry team.

Notes: _____

_____

_____

The Spirit Who Helps us in Temptation

"And Jesus, full of the Holy Spirit, returned from the Jordan, and was led by the Spirit..." (Luke 4:1–13).

Like Jesus, preliminary to entering into our ministry, we must first be tempted and tested by the devil. Immediately after His baptism, the Holy Spirit led Jesus to the wilderness of temptation. Before any of us can face the devil, we must be saved and baptized in the Holy Spirit because we need His help to strengthen us for the confrontation.

The devil uses the same approach with us that he did with Jesus. First, he gets us questioning who we really are. Second, he asks us to somehow prove ourselves. Third, he holds out an enticing bribe to get us to worship him. Fourth, he leads us into circumstances of crisis and whispers suicide in our ear. With each temptation, we must consult the Holy Spirit who knows the whole Bible and counter the devil with Scripture. With the Holy Spirit's help, we can defeat him every time, and go on with God's plan for our lives. Without the Holy Spirit, the devil can easily tempt us to sin. But – *"God is faithful, and He will not let you be tempted beyond your strength, but with the temptation He will also provide the way of escape, that you may be able to endure it"* (1 Corinthians 10:13).

Prayer

Holy Spirit, please be my guide so I can endure temptation.

Notes: _____

_____

_____

The Spirit Who Gives the Body Life

"For as the body apart from the Spirit is dead, so faith apart from works is dead also" (James 2:14–26).

James is not talking about the human spirit (psyche) here. Rather, he is talking about the Holy Spirit (pneuma). He is saying that just as the human body without the Holy Spirit is spiritually dead and won't respond to Jesus, faith that doesn't look after people's needs is spiritually dead and can't please God. You can tell who has the Holy Spirit dwelling in them by their works, because He gives believers the same desire to minister to people as Jesus had. As the Holy Spirit gives life to the body, so faith that is alive is seen through works. Real faith grows through the baptism of the Holy Spirit and results in good works. Faith and works go hand in hand. Jesus tests our faith by sending people to us who are in need: the hungry, the thirsty, the stranger, the naked, the sick, and those in prison. How we treat them becomes our judgment (Matthew 25:40,44).

The Holy Spirit directs us to look after other people's needs. If we ignore them, we place our own spiritual life in jeopardy.

Prayer

Holy Spirit, give me Jesus' compassion for those in need so I can serve Him as I help others.

Notes: _____

_____

_____

The Spirit Who Dwells in Us

" He yearns jealously over the Spirit which He has made to dwell in us" (James 4:1–10).

$\mathcal{T}$he question we must answer is whether our goal in life is to submit to the will of God, or to gratify our own desires for the pleasures of this world. James warns us that if pleasure is our main goal, nothing but strife, hatred and division will result. The bottom line is a choice between pleasing ourselves and pleasing God.

The picture in this passage is one of "spiritual adultery," based on the Old Testament parallel of God as the husband of Israel and Israel as the bride of God (Isaiah 54:5; Jeremiah 3:20; Exodus 34:14–16). To disobey God is like breaking marriage vows. Sin is infidelity to God. The result is that the Spirit, which God made to dwell within us, jealously yearns for the full devotion of our hearts. God is a jealous lover who will not share our human hearts with any other god. He gave us the Holy Spirit so that we can share a love which is far beyond all earthly devotion (Luke 10:27). The result of knowing we are loved so deeply is a humility that draws us ever closer to God.

Prayer

Holy Spirit, show me how to love God with all of my heart, soul, strength and mind – first, before anything in this world.

Notes: _____

_____

_____

The Spirit Who Sanctifies

"To the exiles...sanctified by the Spirit for obedience to Jesus Christ..." (1 Peter 1:1–9).

When we become Christians, we become citizens of Heaven, which makes us exiles from the world system, strangers in a land not of our second birth, pilgrims on our way to our real home. We are scattered around the world according to God's plan. Jesus commanded us to *"Go into all the world and preach the Gospel to every creature"* (Mark 16:15). So, we shouldn't be surprised that He has dispersed us. We are chosen, destined, sanctified, ready for obedience, sprinkled, born anew to a living hope, with an inheritance in Heaven reserved for us. We can rejoice, even when grieved by various trials along the way.

This means that when we suffer trials, it is to prove the genuineness of our faith. When we are tested, instead of being destroyed, we'll break out into praise, honour and glory, because we know our heartaches are temporary hardships on our way to our promised reward. As Jesus pointed out, *"Blessed are you when men revile you and persecute you and utter all kinds of evil against you falsely on my account. Rejoice and be glad..."* (Matthew 5:10,11). Rejoicing is the key that witnesses to people and draws them to Jesus Christ. When we rejoice, our love and faith grows, and we demonstrate the assurance of our salvation.

Prayer

  Holy Spirit, teach me to rejoice when I suffer for Jesus.

Notes: _____

_____

_____

The Spirit of Good News

"...those who preached the Good News to you through the Holy Spirit..." (1 Peter 1:10–21).

The prophets searched and inquired of God as to when Jesus would come. It was the Spirit of God in them who predicted the sufferings of Christ and His subsequent glory. Isaiah said, *"He was despised and rejected by men; a Man of sorrows, and acquainted with grief; and as One from whom men hid their faces he was despised, and we esteemed Him not. Surely He has borne our griefs, and carried our sorrows; yet we esteemed Him stricken, smitten by God, and afflicted. But He was wounded for our transgressions, He was bruised for our iniquities; upon Him was the chastisement that made us whole, and with His stripes we are healed"* (Isaiah 53:3–5).

Because the prophecies were for us and we, like the prophets, can speak through the power of the Holy Spirit, we can preach the Gospel – the "Good News" – to all who need it so desperately. In order to speak it most effectively, we must prepare our minds, be self-controlled, set our hope on Jesus and be obedient. But, most of all, we must be "holy" as God is holy. The result will be that those who hear us will have Jesus revealed to them and they too will receive Jesus as their Saviour.

Prayer

Holy Spirit, show me how to preach the Gospel so that others may be saved and healed.

Notes: _____

_____

_____

The Spirit of Sincere Love

"...obedience to the truth for a sincere love of the brethren..." (1 Peter 1:22–2:3).

We are called, in this passage, to do something *humanly* impossible – that is to love one another fervently with pure hearts. It is only after we have purified our souls by being born again and filled with the Holy Spirit that we can love (agape) our fellow Christians this way. Only after the incorruptible seed of the Word of God comes into our hearts, do we have the capacity to love the unlovable amongst our brethren – seventy times seven every day (Matthew 18:23). Only by the power of the Holy Spirit can we love each other with pure hearts.

Paul defines pure agape love. *"Love is patient and kind; love is not jealous or boastful, it is not arrogant or rude. It does not insist on its own way; it is not irritable or resentful; it does not rejoice at wrong, but rejoices in the right. Love bears all things, believes all things, hopes all things, endures all things. Love never ends..."* (1 Corinthians 13:4–8). This "Holy Spirit love" flows from sincere hearts which have developed a thirst for the milk of the Word. Having tasted this milk, they know that *"the Lord is gracious."*

Prayer

Holy Spirit, teach me to consciously love my brethren so that they will taste and see that the Lord is good.

Notes: _____

_____

_____

The Spirit Who Builds

"...and like living stones, be yourselves built into a spiritual house..." (1 Peter 2:4–12).

In this passage, the Holy Spirit takes on the highly skilled work of a master builder or construction supervisor. He is building a "spiritual house" or a house of the Spirit. This is no ordinary house. The stones are carefully chosen. They are "living stones" or born-again, Spirit-filled Christians. Jesus is the "chief Cornerstone" who supports the whole structure. Each of us is carefully put into place around the Cornerstone – who is also a stumbling block that causes people to trip over Him if they won't obey His Word. The spiritual house has one purpose, that being to offer "spiritual sacrifices" or sacrifices of the Holy Spirit which are acceptable to God. Our lives become sacrifices of praise, as we *"worship the Father in Spirit and in Truth"* (John 4:24).

More than that, we are *"a chosen race, a royal priesthood, a holy nation, God's own people,"* so that we can proclaim the praises of Jesus. We were a bunch of nobodies who have been made into a family of God's somebodies. Isn't it wonderful?

Prayer

Holy Spirit, please use me as a living stone so I can proclaim the praises of Him who called me into God's marvellous light.

Notes: _____

_____

_____

The Spirit Who Made Jesus Alive

"...being put to death in the flesh but made alive in the Spirit..." (1 Peter 3:14–20).

When Jesus was dying on the Cross, He shouted, *"It is finished!"* which meant that He had paid in full for all the sin of the world. He died in the flesh but was made alive in the Spirit...the Holy Spirit (Romans 8:9,11). From that point, for three days after He died, He went on the most fascinating preaching mission recorded in the Bible. First, He went to preach to *"the spirits in prison"* (including the unredeemed prior to the Cross and all the angels who sinned and are *"kept by Him in eternal chains"*) (2 Peter 2:4, Jude 6). He preached the Gospel to the dead (1 Peter 4:6), proclaiming His victory over sin, death and the devil; and establishing His Lordship and authority over death and the dead. There is no place where we can escape from Him (Psalm 139:7–12). Because Jesus said, *"I am the resurrection and the life"* (John 11:25), we know that He always had *"the keys of Hades and of Death"* (Revelation 1:18). During the three days He was dead, He also went to *"paradise"* (Luke 23:43; 16:19–31), where the saved are kept until the day of resurrection. Jesus was then raised from the dead, and because He lives, we shall live also!

Prayer

Holy Spirit, please help me to preach the Gospel so that many can be saved for Heaven.

Notes: _____

_____

_____

Spirit-Led Days

The Spirit of a Clear Conscience

"that though judged in the flesh like men, they might live in the Spirit like God" (1 Peter 3:20–4:6).

God loved the world so much that, during the three days between Jesus' death and resurrection, Jesus went and preached the Gospel to the dead (who were already judged in the flesh) so that they might be saved and live in the power of the Holy Spirit like God. This was a "one time" part of His work of salvation, but it shows us how God's patience extends His goodness that leads to salvation.

Equally interesting, is that water baptism corresponds to people being saved through the flood and Jesus preaching to the spirits of the dead so they could be saved. Taking the step of water baptism is a sign to the world that we are saved, not because our bodies are cleaned by water, but because we have repented and God has forgiven us, cleansing our consciences from any guilt of sin. Water can't go inside of us and touch our consciences – but the Holy Spirit can. Water is a symbol of the Holy Spirit, the living water, who goes inside our hearts and, in accordance with God's forgiveness, gives us a guilt-free, clean conscience (Hebrews 9:14). Thus, water baptism and a clean conscience go hand in hand, that we *"might live in the Spirit like God."*

Prayer (For those not yet water-baptized.)

Holy Spirit, please lead me through water baptism so I can have a clean conscience and live according to the will of God.

Notes: _____

_____

_____

The Spirit of Good Stewards

"As each has received a gift, employ it for one another, as good stewards of God's varied grace..." (1 Peter 4:7–11).

It takes serious prayer to be ready for Jesus' return, to love one another, and to use the charismatic gifts of the Holy Spirit that we have received. These have been given to us in order that we may minister to each other with the varied forms of grace (Romans 12:6–8; 1 Corinthians 12:4–11). Everybody who has been baptized with the Holy Spirit receives at least one gift and it is important that we learn to use these publicly in ministry. We are "stewards" (household managers or administrators) of God's good grace. That means we are responsible to use whatever gifts we have in order to glorify Jesus. Like "the faithful and wise servant," we must be faithful to use our gifts, because they give fellow servants their (spiritual) food in due season (Matthew 24:45–51). Peter encourages us to speak words, messages or oracles (utterance gifts) whenever God gives them to us (1 Peter 4:7–11). He also encourages us to use the power or might gifts (gifts of healing, miracles, service, giving, administration and mercy) so that in all things God may be glorified. Being good stewards proves to other people that we belong to Jesus Christ.

Prayer

Holy Spirit, teach me to be a good steward of Your grace, and to bring glory to God by ministering the gifts You have given me.

Notes: _____

_____

The Spirit of Glory

"...you are blessed, because the Spirit of glory and of God rests upon you." (1 Peter 4:12–19).

Peter tells us not to be surprised when fiery trials start happening to us. It is not strange or unusual. It is not a matter of "if" but rather "when" we are going to be persecuted or suffer as Christians. Most people who react against us don't even understand why they don't like us – or even hate us. The reason is that after we have been born again and baptized with the Holy Spirit, the presence of the Holy Spirit in us affects those people who have never allowed Jesus to be their Saviour and Lord. Without us trying to make people feel bad about their sin and lack of relationship with God, the Holy Spirit Himself will convict them of their sin. Trying to deflect their own guilt, they attack us.

Peter encourages us not to break our country's civil and criminal laws. If we are reproached for the Name of Jesus Christ, we must try not to take it personally; it's "the Spirit of Glory" and of God that the people will be reacting to. We will be blessed (Matthew 5:10). And so, *"if one suffers as a Christian, let him not be ashamed, but under that name let him glorify God."*

Prayer

Holy Spirit, when I suffer for the sake of Jesus please remind me to pray; and praise, worship, honour, exalt and glorify Jesus.

Notes: _____

_____

_____

The Spirit Who Adds

"...make every effort to supplement your faith..." (2 Peter 1:1–11).

After we have received God's "divine power" (Acts1:8) (the Holy Spirit), we need to cooperate with Him to assure our growth to maturity. This process of becoming mature Christians does not happen our way – but His.

In this passage, Peter gives us a spiritual mathematics lesson. The "product" is the choice we make about how fast or slow we grow. First of all, we have the platform of faith on which to add. We begin with a personal relationship with Jesus. To this we apply the formula for spiritual addition: faith, plus virtue, plus knowledge, plus self-control, plus perseverance, plus godliness, plus brotherly kindness, plus love (agape). The sum of it all is an exciting, fruitful Christian life.

As we subtract the elements of our old lives, these eight "plusses" open the door for everything we need to be multiplied to us – along with the huge dividend of eternal life. Those who do not wish to learn this math lesson are not forced to. But, those who don't won't make the grade. Those who do will be fruitful, have their needs met, and see many people added to the Kingdom.

Prayer

Holy Spirit, please help me to add the "plusses" to my life so that it will be of great benefit for Jesus.

Notes: _____

_____

_____

The Spirit Who Gives Prophecy

"...men moved by the Holy Spirit spoke from God"
(2 Peter 1:16–2:11).

Prophecy is one of God's tools for preparing us for His future plans. Through it, He gives direction and guidance to both churches and individuals. God likes to plan His surprises. *"Surely the Lord God does nothing without revealing His secret to His servants the prophets"* (Amos 3:7–8). Today, under the New Covenant, the prophets are those who have *"the gift of prophesy"* (Romans 12:6; 1 Corinthians 12:10). All prophecies should be written down to check their Scriptural accuracy (see August 11).

The rule of thumb, when examining prophecy, is that *"no prophecy of Scripture is a matter of one's own private interpretation"* (2 Peter 1:20,21). This means that any so-called prophet who humanly attempts to interpret or explain his or her prophecy will be wrong in the interpretation. The Holy Spirit will give *His own* interpretation to the person for whom the prophecy is meant. He gave it – and He will explain it. The second rule is that the prophecy must agree with the Scriptures. If it doesn't, it is not from God. Because there are many false prophets and false teachers today, Peter gave these instructions for our protection.

Prayer

Holy Spirit, please empower, remind and show us how to check out all prophecies to make certain they are from You.

Notes: _____

_____

_____

The Spirit of the Holy Life

"...what sort of person ought you to be in lives of holiness and godliness..." (2 Peter 3:8–18).

$\mathcal{T}$he Lord is not in a hurry to return because He wants to save as many people as possible. He is *"not wishing that any should perish but that all should reach repentance."* If we had God's attitude, we would be saying, "Please wait a little longer Jesus. My mother, father, brother, sister, relatives and neighbours are not yet saved." When Jesus returns, the world as we know it will be destroyed by fire and be replaced with new Heavens and a new Earth. When this happens, the only things that will be of any value are lives of holiness and godliness, which are products of the Holy Spirit being allowed to change us. We become holy, not by doing good works and observing religious rituals; but through forgiveness, and walking with God in the power of the Holy Spirit. On *"the day of the Lord,"* the only thing that will matter is whether we are living righteous lives. Because the Lord is not in a hurry, we have time to learn to be comfortable with Jesus, develop intimacy with the Holy Spirit, and enjoy our Heavenly Father. That is living in righteousness. To enjoy spending eternity with Him, we need to spend time enjoying Him now.

Prayer

Holy Spirit, please teach me how to walk in righteousness with God.

Notes: _____

_____

The Spirit Who Anoints Us

"...that it might be plain that they all are not of us. But you have been anointed by the Holy One, and you all know"
(1 John 2:18–23).

We know that we are in the last hour, because as we look around there is not only one "anti-Christ" person, but many. These are people who were once involved in the body of Christ and were thought to be fellow believers, but who did not stay in sincere fellowship, and thus showed that they were not real Christians. John ran into some of these people, and we have many more today. These "anti-Christ" people are liars because they deny that "Jesus is the Christ," our Saviour, Lord, and God and think they can believe in God without Jesus. They have listened to the god of this world, the devil.

Our protection is the *"anointing"* of the Holy Spirit. Anointing was first done with oil in order to identify someone who God was going to use in leadership. The oil was poured over the person from head to feet. Today, the Holy Spirit not only pours Himself over us from head to feet, but also fills us to overflowing. Today's anointing oil, the Holy Spirit, is our protection against "anti-Christs" and their false teaching. Those who have the anointing not only believe the truth about who Jesus is, but have an intimate relationship with Him.

Prayer

Holy Spirit, please guide me into all the truth about Jesus.

Notes: _____

_____

_____

The Spirit Who Abides

"But the anointing which you have received from Him abides in you..." (1 John 2:24–3:9).

The "anointing" is the oil of the Holy Spirit. He sets God's promise of eternal life in our hearts like concrete. Because the Holy Spirit abides (lives) in us, He will teach us about all things: whatever is true and whatever is a lie. The more attention we focus on developing dependence upon the Holy Spirit, the greater will be our confidence in looking forward to Jesus' coming. Everyone who lives a righteous life (one in right relationship with God) belongs to Him.

The proof of being born from above is that we are called "children of God." The world doesn't know or understand us. We are *"peculiar"* to them. The early Christians used the sign of the fish to identify fellow Christians. Unbelievers didn't know the sign. The anointing of the Holy Spirit is also a sign of recognition between believers. Those who do *not* have the anointing will get annoyed with talk about Jesus, the Holy Spirit and our Heavenly Father. Another sign is that believers stop sinning continuously. Other signs of recognition are the Jesus "signs" (Mark 16:17,18). If there are no signs of the Holy Spirit abiding within, there is no Christian.

Prayer

Holy Spirit, as You abide in me, please help me to develop a righteous life and honour Jesus Christ.

Notes: _____

_____

_____

The Spirit He Gave Us

"...we know that He abides in us, by the Spirit which He has given us" (1 John 3:10–24).

It's really amazing the difference the Holy Spirit makes in us. He makes it possible for us to love (agape) one another. The children of the devil follow a different road: *"They were filled with all manner of wickedness, evil, covetousness, malice. Full of envy, murder, strife, deceit, malignity, they are gossips, slanderers, haters of God, insolent, haughty, boastful, inventors of evil, disobedient to parents, foolish, faithless, heartless, ruthless"* (Romans 1:29–31). Righteousness expresses itself in love. Unrighteousness expresses itself in hatred and murder.

So, we shouldn't be surprised that the world hates us. It's not because we are doing anything wrong; it's because we are doing something right – following Jesus. When we know Jesus' love, we don't kill our brothers as Cain did, but are willing to die for our brethren. Love looks after those in need. When we keep God's commandments and have the mind of Christ, we can confidently go to Him, because He will give us whatever we need.

God's primary desire of us is that we believe in His Son and love one another. We know He abides in us because He has given us the Holy Spirit.

Prayer

Holy Spirit, as You abide in me, please help me to know Jesus better and to love my brethren more.

Notes: _____

_____

_____

The Spirit Who Tests Spirits

"By this we know the Spirit of truth and the spirit of error"
(1 John 4:1–6).

Today, many Christians are afraid to test the spirits in order to see whether they are from God. Just as in John's day, we have many false prophets. These so-called prophets threaten and try to intimidate us by telling us that to criticize them and their prophecies is to blaspheme the Holy Spirit. Any true prophets welcome being tested because they know that their prophecies will stand any Scriptural testing and God will honour them. The big test (with John and with us today) to determine whether someone is of God is whether or not they will confess that Jesus Christ (God) has come in the flesh. Most "religious" people do not believe this. We have many in our churches today who have the spirit of the antichrist. They are acceptable to the world. Because we believe in Jesus, those who are of the world will not listen to us, which proves that they aren't from God.

The big thing that we have going for us is that after we have been baptized with the Holy Spirit, *"He who is in you is greater than he who is in the world."* Because we know God, we know the difference between the Spirit of Truth and the spirit of error.

Prayer

Holy Spirit of Truth, please show me how to minister effectively to those who have the spirit of error.

Notes: _____

_____

_____

The Spirit Who Loves Endlessly

"...because He has given us of His own Spirit" (1 John 4:7–21).

The Holy Spirit and love are synonymous. Where the Holy Spirit is, there is agape love. It is His most powerful characteristic. When He fills a person's life with His baptism, the recipient is filled with love – God's unconditional love for the unloveable (we are all unloveable in our depths before being redeemed). If God had waited for us to come to Him it would not have happened. *"In this is love, not that we loved God, but that He loved us and sent His Son to be the expiation for our sins"* (v. 10). Imagine that! Jesus died for us as the sacrifice for our sins while we were still God's enemies!

This depth of love is no ordinary love. This is *agape love* (1 Corinthians 13). No one on Earth has it within them until it is received from the Holy Spirit (Romans 5:5). It is this love that makes us perfectly acceptable to God. It flows out of us to testify about Jesus and drives out all tormenting fear. Agape love is a fruit of the Spirit (Galatians 5:22) that is increasingly developed in us as we submit more and more to the Lordship of Jesus Christ. It is this love that enables us to obey the command that *"he who loves God should love his brother also"* (v. 21).

Prayer

Holy Spirit, please help me to love endlessly, as You do.

Notes: _____

_____

_____

The Spirit of the Three

"...the Spirit, the water, and the blood; and these three agree" (1 John 5:1–13).

God always requires two or three witnesses to give evidence. Thus, He offers us three witnesses in Heaven: the Father, the Son and the Holy Spirit. The amazing thing is that they are One. This is what the Church has called "the Trinity" or the "triune God." Fully explaining it is impossible, no matter how illustrative many have tried to be with eggs, oranges, et cetera. Anyway, we would quickly lose faith in a God we could explain. We need a God who can explain *us*, love us, save us, empower us and lead us. We have all of that in the Father who rules over us, the Son who walks alongside of us, and the Holy Spirit who lives inside of us. We are three-dimensional people who can't save ourselves. It takes blood, water and love – the blood of Jesus, the living water of the Holy Spirit, and the love of the Father.

We know that we are children of God when we love God and keep His commandments. Through the power of the Holy Spirit, we can overcome the world, introducing its people to Jesus as their Saviour (John 3:16). Through sharing our testimonies, they see evidence of Jesus' reality, leading them to have faith in God.

Prayer

Holy Spirit, show me how to love the world into faith in God through Jesus. Give me boldness to share my testimony.

Notes:

_____

_____

_____

The Spirit Who Builds Us Up

"But you beloved, build yourselves up in your most holy faith; pray in the Holy Spirit" (Jude 1–19).

No matter how bad a church may be, we, as born-again, Spirit-filled Christians, can protect ourselves and build ourselves up. Prayer is the key. Jude paints a grim view of the Church in his day; but it is no different today. Many ungodly people have secretly slipped into our churches and stepped into positions of leadership. These are highly immoral people who use their twisted interpretation of the Gospel as a license for immorality and sin. Unfortunately, many of us have turned a blind eye and a deaf ear to them because they love to quote: *"Judge not, that you be not judged"* (Matthew 7:1). With today's overbalanced approach to tolerance of all beliefs, they have no end of support in the community. As Jude reminds us, they sin shamelessly; but God will execute judgment on them when the angels come to carry them off to their reward – which will not be Heaven.

The best way to deal with these people, in whom there is no evidence of the Holy Spirit, is to pray for them "in the Spirit" and we shall be *"built up in our faith"* (1 Corinthians 14:2–4), keeping ourselves in God's love. As we do this, many ungodly people will be saved as trophies of God's grace.

Prayer

Holy Spirit, please help me to pray in You, strengthening me in God's love from now throughout eternity.

Notes: _____

_____

_____

The Spirit with the Small Voice

"...and after the fire a still small voice" (1 Kings 19:1–18).

Under Elijah's leadership, Israel chose to worship God over Baal, and had the 450 prophets of Baal killed. But, despite the awesome display of God's power and presence, he ran and hid in a cave, afraid for his life, when he received a message that the king's wife wanted him dead! And that is where God found him – having a pity party, whining that God and the people of Israel had forsaken him.

God asked, *"What are you doing here, Elijah?"*

He replied, *"I, even I only, am left; and they seek my life, to take it away."* He had forgotten that God could protect him.

This is what happens when even the greatest of God's leaders gets out of fellowship. They start thinking that everyone has failed them, including God. God had Elijah stand on the top of the mountain so that he could see who He really was. After an impressive display of wind, earthquake and fire, Elijah finally heard the *"still small voice"* of the Holy Spirit speak to him. With the news that he was not the only faithful person in Israel but that there were 7,000 others, Elijah obeyed God's instructions, went to anoint the new king of Israel, and choose Elisha as his own successor.

Prayer

Holy Spirit, speak to me in Your still small voice so I won't get out of fellowship and lose sight of who God really is.

Notes: _____

_____

_____

The Spirit Who Gives Eyes of Faith

"Then Elisha prayed, and said, 'O Lord, I pray Thee, open his eyes that he may see'" (2 Kings 6:8–23).

When the King of Syria went to war, he couldn't attack Israel without God telling Elisha so that he could warn Israel. Having discovered this, the King sent his army to capture Elisha. When Elisha's servant looked out in the morning and saw Syria's huge army surrounding the city, he was frightened. Elisha asked the Lord to open the young man's eyes spiritually so that he could see what was really going on. When God did, the servant saw God's army of horses and chariots of fire surrounding the Syrian army! As the Syrian army attacked, Elisha prayed and asked the Lord to strike them all blind – and He did! Then, Elisha led them away, right into Samaria, where the King of Israel gave them something to eat and drink and then sent them home. Having seen there was no point battling the God of Israel, the Syrians ceased their raids on Israel.

This is a great lesson in spiritual warfare (Ephesians 6:10–18). We need to ask Jesus to give us the "eyes of faith" (Matthew 5:8), so we can see the enemy with the "gift of discerning of spirits" (1 Corinthians 12:10) and know that God's army is greater. We need to learn to *"love* (our) *enemies and pray for those who persecute* (us)."

Prayer

Holy Spirit, keep my eyes on Jesus so I can win God's way.

Notes: _____

_____

_____

The Spirit in the Whirlwind

"Then the Lord answered Job out of the whirlwind..."
(Job 38:1–7).

No matter how bad life might seem to be going, it's a good idea to find out who is responsible before throwing the blame at God. Job's life was in shambles. His ten children had died in one day and he was bankrupt. His wife was in full nag, suggesting that he should curse God and die. His so-called friends tried to fix the blame for his condition on his sin. Nobody – except God – knew that Satan was trying to prove a point about Job to God. It was in the midst of Job's faith-mixed-with-despair that God spoke to him out of a whirlwind (the way the Holy Spirit came – like a rushing, mighty wind on the Day of Pentecost [Acts 2:2]).

There are some lessons here to be learned from Job. First, *"in everything God works for good with those who love Him, who are called according to His purpose"* (Romans 8:28). Second, we need to be aware that when Satan comes, God *"will not let you be tempted beyond your strength,"* but *"will provide the way of escape, that you may be able to endure it"* (1 Corinthians 10:13). Third, God the Creator is omnipotent and in total control, so we'll win in the end (John 19:30).

Prayer

Holy Spirit, speak often to me so I can endure my temptation and win the battle.

Notes: _____

_____

_____

The Spirit Who Flows Out

"On that day living waters shall flow out from Jerusalem..."
(Zechariah 14:1–21).

*H*ere is a prophecy about "the Day of the Lord" on which Jesus will come. It will happen after Jerusalem has been captured, houses have been plundered, women have been ravished, and people have been sent into exile. Then, the Lord will rise up and fight against the nations, destroying them in the battle of Harmageddon (Revelation 16:16). **Note: The "H" has mistakenly been dropped from Harmageddon in translation from the Greek, leading people to believe the final battle will be fought on the *plains* of Megiddo, when it will actually be in the *mountains* of Megiddo (as yet an unknown location).**

When He puts His feet on the Mount of Olives, it will split in two. There will be *"neither cold nor frost."* There will be no sun or moon but there will be light from the *"glory of God"* (Revelation 21:23).

"On that day, living waters shall flow out from Jerusalem," just as John described in the New Jerusalem (Revelation 22:1). The *"living waters"* refer to the Holy Spirit who will flow out to the east and to the west from Jerusalem. The Holy Spirit will sustain us in fellowship, and *"the Lord will be King over all the Earth; on that day the Lord will be One and His Name One."* Judgment will come to all who have made war against Jerusalem. God's signature will be written on everything: *"Holy to the Lord."*

Prayer

Holy Spirit, please remind me that we are "Holy to the Lord."

Notes: _____

_____

_____

The Spirit Who Catches Bread

"As you do not know how the Spirit comes..."

(Ecclesiastes 11:1–10).

The preacher in this passage is trying to educate us in the ways of God. He tells us to *"Cast your bread upon the waters: for you will find it after many days."* This sounds crazy. Everybody knows that if a person throws bread upon water, it will sink to the bottom. But the old preacher isn't talking about ordinary bread we eat, or ordinary water we drink. He says that we may know how to read people and even know the laws of nature; but when it comes to the ways of the Holy Spirit, people are totally ignorant. When it comes to God, people do not know the works of Him who made us all. Whatever people *think* they know is just *"vanity,"* – worthless pride.

After we have found Jesus as our Saviour and are baptized with the Holy Spirit – as we really get to know the way of the Spirit – we discover that when we cast our "bread" (our whole life's existence) upon "the living water" (the Holy Spirit), we really find ourselves. Then, we can "spiritually discern" the works of God and our vanity is replaced with humility.

Prayer

Holy Spirit, help me to throw myself fully into Your living waters so I can recognize the workings of God.

Notes: _____

_____

_____

The Spirit of the Beloved

"A garden fountain, a well of living water, and flowing streams from Lebanon" (Song of Solomon 4:1–16).

What a beautiful description of Jesus Christ's Bride, the Church, the pure and spotless Bride He awaits (Ephesians 5:21–27). Everything about the Church is beautiful. It is no wonder that He would lay down His life for her. *"You are all fair, my love."* Her nine fruits, like the fruit of the Holy Spirit, are incomparable. With the character of Jesus, she is His "beloved" for whom He came to seek and to save because she was lost (Luke 19:10). She has been made a "new creation" (2 Corinthians 5:17). Dressed in white (Revelation 7:13,14), she is beautiful beyond description, too marvellous for words. Jesus is utterly *"infatuated"* (Proverbs 5:19) with her.

What makes Jesus' Bride even more attractive is that she is a well of living waters who ministers salvation and the Holy Spirit. She is aglow with the Spirit and produces so *"much fruit"* (John 15:1–5) that it cannot be counted (Revelation 7:9). She is being prepared for the Bridegroom along with the ten bridesmaids (Matthew 25:1–13) who do not know when He will come.

Prayer

Holy Spirit, please prepare me as part of Jesus' Bride so I shall be ready.

Notes: _____

_____

_____

The Spirit Who Gives a Drink

"...I give water in the wilderness, rivers in the desert, to give drink to my chosen people..." (Isaiah 43:10–21).

A promise of hope right from the mouth of the Lord! He has chosen us to be His people – witnesses who know Him, believe Him, and understand that He is the only God. There is no other authentic God in existence; only spirits who pretend to be gods (Galatians 4:3). He promises to do a new thing. *"Remember not the former things, nor consider the things of old."* In other words, don't look back, look forward. *"Behold, I make all things new"* (Revelation 21:5).

God promises to make a road through the wilderness of life. John the Baptist went out into the wilderness to preach "repentance" and baptism with water. Jesus Christ came to save us and baptize us with the Holy Spirit, giving us a "drink" of the Holy Spirit in the desert of life. Jesus came to make us, *"a chosen race, a royal priesthood, a holy nation, God's own people"* (1 Peter 2:9). He is preparing a people whom He has formed to declare His praise. We know God personally in Jesus Christ, who said, *"He who has seen Me has seen the Father"* (John 14:9). We can not only praise Him for who He is, but thank Him for quenching our thirst.

Prayer

Holy Spirit, quench my thirst, that I may freely praise God my Father for who His is, and what He has done.

Notes: _____

_____

_____

The Spirit Who Gives Freely

"Ho, every one who thirsts, come to the waters; and he who has no money, come, buy and eat!" (Isaiah 55:1–13).

There are some things money can't buy. There is a thirst that ordinary water, wine, milk, coffee or tea can't quench. There is a hunger that meat and bread can't satisfy. That hunger and thirst is for righteousness. It is the innate desire for a right relationship with God. *"Blessed are those who hunger and thirst for righteousness, for they shall be satisfied"* (Matthew 5:6).

We can be satisfied only after we have had our hunger filled by Jesus who said, *"I am the bread of life; he who comes to Me shall not hunger, and he who believes in Me shall never thirst"* (John 6:35).

We cannot buy our way into eternal life with either money or good works. We receive salvation (bread) as a gift when we ask Jesus to forgive us for our sins, and living water when He baptizes us with the Holy Spirit. Then, our soul delights in abundance. We have an everlasting covenant with God, and we will glorify Him. We begin to see that when God's Word goes out, as He said, *"It shall not return to Me empty...and it shall prosper in the thing for which I sent it."* At the end of the day, we shall live in joy and peace.

Prayer

Holy Spirit, please give me Your living waters that alone can satisfy.

Notes: _____

_____

_____

The Spirit Who is a Fountain

"They have forsaken Me, the fountain of living waters..."
(Jeremiah 2:4–19).

"God has no grandchildren." That oft-heard warning means that God has only first-generation believers; His children who He adopts into the Family of God. He wants people who know Him first-hand – personally. Our society mirrors Israel in this passage: many people have gone away from God; have become idolaters worshiping other gods; have defiled the land; have forgotten our heritage; our clergy do not seek the Lord; government officials don't know God; the pastors break God's law; and the prophets prophesy by occult spirits. No wonder Israel was in trouble, and no wonder our world is in trouble!

Those who have forsaken God, *"the fountain of living waters,"* know something is missing, but, being spiritually blind, can't see that their hearts are spiritually dehydrated. Jesus alone can give us *"the living water"* so we will never thirst again. *"He who believes in Me, as the Scripture has said, 'out of his heart shall flow rivers of living water.' Now this He said about the Spirit, which those who believed in Him were to receive"* (John 7:37–38). Sadly, people who cringe at the Name of Jesus, chase after false gods and teachers who are broken cisterns, *"wells without water."*

Prayer

Holy Spirit, please be my fountain of living waters so I will always love God.

Notes: _____

_____

_____

The Spirit Who Flows

"He makes His wind to blow, and the waters to flow"
(Psalm 147:1–20).

God is really quite unpredictable. He builds up Jerusalem in a very unusual way by gathering together the outcasts and the broken-hearted, healing their wounds and calling them (us) by name. Paul reminds us that *"God chose what is low and despised in the world, even things that are not, to bring to nothing things that are, so that no human being might boast in the presence of God"* (1 Corinthians 1:28). No matter what our station in life, we are all allowed to feel lowly of heart at some time – usually the place where we find God. As God told Hosea: *"I say to Not my people, 'You are My people'; and he shall say, 'Thou art my God'"* (Hosea 2:23).

There is nothing greater than to belong to the family of God. In order to gather His children into His family, *"He sends forth His Word and melts them"* (Psalm 147:18). This means that God sent out Jesus, the Word made flesh, who melted our frozen hearts with His salvation. He then caused His wind of the Holy Spirit to blow and the living waters to flow. In discovering how God woos us to Himself, and the unimaginable cost of His method, we find the depth and beauty of praise. It surges up from our inmost being, the place of His habitation, and flows forth as the river of life.

Prayer
   Holy Spirit, please flow in me, so I can truly praise God for His goodness.

Notes: _____

_____

_____

The Spirit Who Shakes Reeds

"A reed shaken by the wind?" (Matthew 11:7–15).

*B*eing great in God's eyes is not the same as being considered great by the world's standards. God chooses some very strange people, like John the Baptist, to serve Him. The Holy Spirit was with John even in his mother's womb! With his preaching of baptism for repentance, he ended the Old Covenant and prepared the way for the New Covenant with Jesus (Luke 3:16). As far as Jesus was concerned, no one born of a woman was greater than John, and yet *"whoever is least in the Kingdom of Heaven is greater than he"* (Matthew 11:11).

Here is another of Jesus' apparently contradictory statements: *"He who is greatest among you shall be your servant"* (Matthew 23:11).

John said of Jesus, *"He must increase, but I must decrease"* (John 3:30).

Jesus taught, *"the Kingdom of Heaven has suffered violence, and men of violence take it by force"* (Matthew 11:12). People think that by killing God's people, like Jesus and John, they can control the Kingdom of Heaven with violence. *"A reed shaken by the wind,"* – a totally committed man of God (like John) – will stand and be faithful unto death even when shaken to his depths by the wind of the Holy Spirit.

Prayer

Holy Spirit, let me be a reed, so rooted in Jesus, that as I am shaken by Your wind, I will draw people to Him.

Notes: _____

_____

_____

The Spirit Who Gives New Wine

"and they say, 'Behold, a glutton and a drunkard'"
(Matthew 11:16–30).

*I*t is amazing that we still do not understand the way that God operates! John and Jesus were God's ministry team for salvation, each representing extreme ministries, yet complementing each other. Here is an example of God's *"wisdom"* being *"justified by her deeds"* (v. 19). John drank only water and was on a God-given diet. People claimed that he had a demon. On the other hand, Jesus drank wine and was free to eat whatever He wanted. People complained about them both. John drank no "old wine" but only water, representing the Holy Spirit who guided his life – but people couldn't see that he was drinking "new wine" in the form of water. Jesus drank the "new wine" of the Holy Spirit which people mistook for old wine and so they called Him a drunk. On the Day of Pentecost, the first believers to be baptized in the Holy Spirit were mistaken for being drunk. Peter had to explain that they weren't drunk *"as you suppose"* (Acts 2:15).

God's plan for each of us might look very different for each person, but we are all *"fellow workers."* As long as we have the Holy Spirit, "new wine" or "living waters," we must work together like John and Jesus.

Prayer

Holy Spirit, help me to appreciate Your wisdom and serve Jesus faithfully in the particular ministry ordained for me.

Notes: _____

_____

_____

The Spirit of the Eagles

"Where the body is, there the eagles will be gathered"
(Luke 17:22–37).

*E*very generation keeps asking, "When will the Kingdom of God come?" There will always be people who like to make us think they know when Jesus is coming back, as though God has given them a special peek into the future. Interestingly, God is not going to tell anyone, not even Jesus (Matthew 24:36). Anyone who says they know when He is coming back is wrong – period. When Jesus comes back it will happen like a flash of lightning – the twinkling of an eye – so fast that nobody will be able to think fast enough to try to repent.

It will happen just like the way God dealt with Noah. Life was going on as usual. People gradually lost interest in Noah and his ark over the 100 years it took to build the ark. So, when the flood came, everybody was taken by complete surprise except Noah and his family.

The same thing happened with Jesus. Jesus is telling us that anyone who wants to know when He is coming back, should watch the Body, His Church. When the eagles (symbols of the Holy Spirit) start flying, then you'll know. *"They that wait upon the Lord shall renew their strength; they shall mount up with wings like eagles"* (Isaiah 40:31), and gather together to meet Jesus in the air.

Prayer

Holy Spirit, prepare me as one of Your eagles in the Church, ready to fly for Jesus.

Notes:

_____

_____

The Spirit Who Gives Good Things

"...how much more will your Father who is in Heaven give good things to those who ask Him!" (Matthew 7:7–12).

Here is a guarantee we all need to hear. Jesus brings us the wonderful reassurance that we don't have to be afraid that our Heavenly Father will withhold those things most important to us. He loves us and has no intentions of hurting us. He desires a prayer relationship with us. *"Ask,"* and keep on asking, just the way a child in a normal household would pester his father for something – repeatedly – over and over again, indicating its importance to him. Children don't give up with the first request. We might call this prayer principle "the law of the children." Be persistent and keep on asking, knocking and seeking. Let your Heavenly Father know how important your request is and He won't disappoint you. If you ask for bread (Jesus), you won't get a stone. If you ask for a fish (Jesus), you won't get a serpent (devil). If we know how to give good gifts to our children, *"how much more our Heavenly Father will give good things to those who ask Him"* (v. 11).

Luke identifies the *"good things"* (Luke 11:1–13) as the Holy Spirit. *"All his benefits"* (Psalm 103) include salvation, the gifts and fruit of the Holy Spirit, healing and much more.

Prayer

Holy Spirit, help me to go to the Father for His good things.

Notes: _____

_____

_____

The Spirit of the Shepherd

"Thou anointest my head with oil; my cup overflows"
(Psalm 23:1–6).

We all need a shepherd to look after us because *"all we like sheep have gone astray; we have turned every one to his own way"* (Isaiah 53:6). Jesus came to be our *"good Shepherd"* (John 10:11). Psalm 23 describes exactly how He looks after us. He restores our souls, meaning that He makes our lives fresh again as He saves us from evil, and gives us the right to go to Heaven. He leads us in paths of righteousness: He establishes a right relationship between God and us. He walks with us through the valley of the shadow of death: He protects us when our lives are in danger. His companionship gives us comfort. He feeds us at His table with the bread of life. He anoints our heads with oil and our cups run over, meaning that He baptizes us with the Holy Spirit and gives us an endless flow of living waters which can't be contained!

Our Good Shepherd (John 10:14) supplies all of our needs *"according to His riches in glory in Christ Jesus"* (Philippians 4:19). He blesses us with goodness and mercy publicly, even in front of our enemies. And, finally, our Shepherd leads us Home, where we shall live in the Lord's house forever (John 14:2,3).

Prayer

Holy Spirit, thank You for being my proof that I belong to the Good Shepherd.

Notes: _____

_____

_____

The Spirit Who Compels

"...like new wineskins, it is ready to burst" (Job 32:10–22).

$\mathcal{J}$ob's friends showed up to try to comfort him in the midst of his temptation. Elihu arrived to share something that we all need to know about how God deals with us. He says that *"But it is the Spirit in a man, the breath of the Almighty, that makes him understand."* When the Holy Spirit comes into our hearts, He gives us God's understanding about life and about what God is doing. Paul points out clearly that spiritual matters are *"spiritually discerned"* (1 Corinthians 2:14), or explained by the Holy Spirit. Without the Holy Spirit telling us what God is doing, we can only play a guessing game, like Job's first three friends who were wrong in their explanations.

When the Holy Spirit does speak to us, we shall have no peace until we pass it on to whomever the Lord intended. Elihu said, *"For I am full of words; the Spirit within me constrains me. Indeed my heart is like wine that has no vent; like new wineskins, it is ready to burst...I must speak, that I may find relief."* And the same thing is true for us today. When the Holy Spirit compels us to speak, speak we must.

Prayer

Holy Spirit, please help me to hear You clearly, so that as I seek Your peace, I shall tell others correctly.

Notes: _____

_____

_____

The Spirit Who Speaks in Dreams

"The Spirit of God has made me, and the breath of the Almighty gives me life" (Job 33:1–18).

*M*any of us close our ears so that we won't hear what God wants to tell us about His plans for us. We are constantly "contending with Him" which means that we are in opposition, fighting, struggling against what He wants us to do. Job was no different than we are. If God can't catch our attention when we are awake, He'll catch it when we are asleep. *"For God speaks in one way, and in two, though man does not perceive it. In a dream, in a vision of the night...then He opens the ears of men, and terrifies them with warnings"* (v. 14–16). We can be in a "saved rebellion" against God that keeps us running away from Him – from Christians, the Bible, Christian books, church, or anything through which He might communicate with us. But He always finds a way, even if it has to be when we are asleep. One of my brothers ran all the way to Taiwan in order to escape God while he was investigating another religion. But God went with him and spoke to him in a dream, which resulted in his salvation and a call to full-time ministry. Peter explained on the Day of Pentecost that we would dream God's dreams (Acts 2:17).

Prayer

Holy Spirit, open my ears to hear the instructions God may give to me in dreams so I can know His will.

Notes: _____

_____

_____

The Spirit Who Disrupts Funerals

"And He said, 'Young man, I say to you, arise'"
(Luke 7:11–17).

As Jesus was entering the city of Nain, he came across the funeral of a young man, the only son of a widow. Jesus had compassion on the mother. *"Do not weep,"* He comforted her. Stopping the pall bearers, He commanded the dead man, *"Young man, I say to you arise."* The dead man immediately sat up and began to talk. Jesus has a shocking way of disrupting funerals! Some of the people who saw this were terrified, but they glorified God because some believed that, *"A great prophet has arisen among us,"* and others said, *"God has visited His people."* Indeed He did.

Jesus had the power to raise the dead. He said, *"It is the Spirit that gives life; the flesh is of no avail. The words that I have spoken to you are Spirit, and life"* (John 6:63). His words are not human spirit; they are the Holy Spirit and resurrection life. Jesus said, *"I am the resurrection and the life"* (John 11:25). He will raise the dead on the last day. His power to heal and raise the dead resides in us, after we have been baptized by the Holy Spirit (Mark 16:17,18).

Prayer

Holy Spirit, teach me how to minister with words that are Spirit and life.

Notes: _____

_____

_____

The Spirit Who Uses Oil

"...and let them pray over him, anointing him with oil in the Name of the Lord" (James 5:13–15).

*H*ealing has always been a part of God's Covenant with us. James encourages those who are sick to be anointed with oil by the elders of the church so they will be healed. It is an act of obedience. James makes it very clear that *"the Lord will raise him up."* The oil is not some kind of a medicinal remedy. It is a symbol of the Holy Spirit who is present to glorify Jesus in healing the sick person (John 16:14,15). Many use olive oil, although it isn't prescribed. I remember the first time a new elder (an automobile mechanic not familiar with accepted practices with regard to healing oil) was called on by a sick church member to go and pray for healing. He took along a quart of 10W30 motor oil, poured it all over the man's head – and he was healed! Unfortunately, most people don't call on the elders or other Christians to pray for them when they are sick (Mark 16:18).

Divine healing has always been an integral part of the Church's ministry. It is important to call on other Christians to pray for us when we are sick so that we can be healed and give thanks to Jesus.

Prayer
Holy Spirit, please remind me to call on the elders to pray and anoint me with oil in Jesus' Name when I need to be healed.

Notes: _____

_____

_____

The Spirit Who Gives Visions

"And the Lord said to Paul one night in a vision..."
(Acts 18:5–17).

*W*hen we are willing to serve Jesus as Paul did, we will be expected to receive direction and guidance from Jesus at any time, in a variety of ways, including visions. Paul had been preaching and testifying to the Jews about Jesus. Their reaction was so negative that Paul decided to leave and take the message to the Gentiles. In a vision, God told him not to leave town. He stayed on for one and a half years teaching the Word of God with great success.

Most of us Christians misread people's reactions to our preaching and witnessing for Jesus Christ. When people react negatively against what we are saying, we usually take it personally and walk away, sometimes angrily – before thoroughly seeking God to make sure that we see things through His eyes. Disappointed, we vow not to let it happen again and wall ourselves off from vulnerability. This happens often in a church situation where people may have tried going to various churches, but leave at the first hint of conflict, and claim never to have found God. It takes patience to stay and develop relationships and continue to seek God. We need to learn to see through God's eyes and discern what He is really doing.

Prayer

Holy Spirit, please give me a vision of what is really happening in my ministry so I won't give up, but will stay to complete it.

Notes: _____

_____

The Spirit of Heavenly Visions

"I was not disobedient to the Heavenly vision..."
(Acts 26:19–32).

Paul was on trial for his life because he refused to stop preaching the Gospel. As a Roman citizen, he exercised his right of appeal to the Roman emperor for justice. But before he was moved to Rome, he was taken before King Agrippa, who was curious about the man who had caused such an uproar in Jerusalem. Standing before the king, Paul did not hesitate to share his personal testimony, starting with his persecution of believers until his own meeting with Jesus, who had risen from the dead.

Most people admire Paul's boldness. It was the fulfillment of Jesus' promise: *"When they bring you to trial and deliver you up, do not be anxious beforehand what you are to say; but say whatever is given you in that hour, for it is not you who speak, but the Holy Spirit"* (Mark 13:11). The king was under conviction and he said, *"In a short time you think to make me a Christian?"*

"Whether short or long," Paul answered, *"I would to God that not only you, but also all who hear me this day..."* Many of us have been on trial for our faith, whether before governments or church councils, and have experienced the Holy Spirit telling us what to say – just as Jesus promised He would.

Prayer

Holy Spirit, please give me the words to say so that others will become Christians.

Notes: _____

_____

_____

The Spirit of Heavenly Boasting

"...But I will go on to visions and revelations of the Lord"
(2 Corinthians 12:1–10).

Having visions and revelations from the Lord doesn't make one Christian more spiritual, or closer to God, than any other Christian. These are given by the Holy Spirit for various reasons: for repentance, direction, teaching, correction, encouragement, assurance, and as tools God uses to call us into ministry. They are no basis for trying to impress others with our so-called spiritual maturity. Paul talked about another man's experience of being caught up into Paradise. He wasn't certain of all the facts, because the experience was so remarkable that it was impossible for the man to put it fully into words. Paul reminds us that visions and revelations are nothing to boast about, because they are not earned by good works. He boasted only about his so-called weaknesses. He had a thorn in the flesh, a messenger of Satan, that harassed him to keep him from becoming conceited. Three times he asked the Lord to take it away. But Jesus told him, *"My grace is sufficient for you, for My power is made perfect in weakness."* Like Paul, we need to boast about the grace of Jesus and be content regardless of our circumstances. When we are weak in ourselves, we are strong in Jesus.

Prayer

Holy Spirit, help me to boast only about Jesus, whose power is perfect in my weakness.

Notes: _____

_____

_____

The Spirit of True Apostles

"Did we not act in the same spirit?" (2 Corinthians 12:11–21).

There will always be fleshly so-called "super-apostles" or as the Greek word says, "outstanding, special, extra-special" apostles who promote themselves as being far superior to the authentic ones, like Paul. They are legends in their own minds who deceive gullible believers into thinking that the real, Holy Spirit-anointed apostles are not really as good as they are. Paul reminds the Corinthians (and us) that when he was with them, *"the signs of a true apostle were performed among you in all patience, with signs and wonders and mighty works."* A true apostle has had a visible encounter with the risen Jesus, has planted churches, and has a ministry of signs, wonders and miracles.

This passage contains a warning to all of us. There are many so-called "super-apostles" on the loose today, who are constantly building themselves up at the expense of other Christians and ministries instead of for the benefit of others. True apostles work together in the Holy Spirit as Paul and Titus did. They never go beyond Scripture (1 Corinthians 2:4,5). They build up the Church with true Biblical signs, wonders and miracles.

Prayer

Holy Spirit, please help me to recognize, honour, support, encourage, and pray for Jesus' true apostles.

Notes: _____

_____

_____

The Spirit Who Sees the Fool

"So is he who lays up treasure for himself, and is not rich toward God" (Luke 12:13–21).

*I*t can be dangerous to ask Jesus a question. In this passage, a greedy man asked Jesus to order his brother to divide his inheritance with him. The question he should have asked was, *"Good Teacher, what must I do to inherit eternal life?"* He betrayed his heart.

Jesus warned us to guard against all kinds of greed. He told a parable about a rich man who was proud of his business success and decided to *"take...ease, eat, drink, and be merry."* God called him a *"Fool,"* because, *"This night your soul is required of you; and the things you have prepared, whose will they be?"*

The rich man had misunderstood his real needs and how to fulfill them. Yes, he needed to eat, drink, and be merry – but only in God. He had tried to satisfy a hunger and thirst for righteousness with earthly possessions. He needed to eat salvation, drink the new Wine of the Holy Spirit, and be merry with the joy of the Lord. While rich with the wealth of the world, this man was not rich toward God. He would be eternally spiritually bankrupt. We all need to *"lay up for yourselves treasures in Heaven. For where your treasure is, there will be your heart also"* (Matthew 6:20,21).

Prayer
  Holy Spirit, help me make rich investments in Heaven.

Notes: _____

_____

_____

The Spirit of Servanthood

"We are unworthy servants; we have only done what was our duty" (Luke 17:5–10).

"Increase our faith," the apostles beseeched Jesus. They (like us) would have liked to ask Jesus to give them enormous volumes of faith, thinking that the more they had, the more signs and wonders they would be able to do.

Such a request indicates a total misunderstanding of faith and servanthood. Faith stems from time spent with Jesus, developing a relationship with Him in the presence of the Holy Spirit. Only after salvation and baptism in the Holy Spirit, can we confidently order mountains of problems to be cast into the sea.

Jesus shared a parable about a man who had a servant who was working his fields and looking after his animals. When the servant would return from the fields, it was his duty to prepare supper and serve it to his master, before he himself could eat. In speaking of the master, Jesus asked, *"Would he thank the servant because he did what he was commanded?"* No. We increase our faith by doing everything Jesus tells us to do as He speaks to us through the Holy Spirit (John 16:13–15). In order to be attuned to His voice, we need to have been baptized by the Holy Spirit. Then we can do "our duty" in the Spirit of Godly servanthood.

Prayer

Holy Spirit, tell me whatever Jesus wants me to do so I can be a faithful servant and increase my faith.

Notes: _____

_____

_____

The Spirit of the Sower

"Hear then the parable of the sower" (Matthew 13:3–9; 18–23).

Jesus spoke in parables so that only those who were supposed *"to know the secrets of the Kingdom of Heaven"* would understand. In the parable of the sower, Jesus describes four kinds of soil, of which only one produces fruit. Only the *"good soil"* produces one hundred, sixty, and thirty-fold yield.

I once talked with a Mennonite missionary who had spent 30 years in South America. He had built a church of 1,500 members with a staff of 7 pastors. He said that he was proud of his achievements until he heard that 2 Pentecostal missionaries, who had started their missionary work in the same country, in the same year as he did, had started 1,500 churches with over 3,000,000 members. He was troubled. How could 2 farmers using the same seed in the same field have such different yields? After comparing the 2 ministries, he realized that the difference was "the baptism of the Holy Spirit." He determined that if that was what he needed, he wouldn't be satisfied until he got it. And he did. His ministry in retirement yielded more fruit than before. The Holy Spirit makes good soil!

Prayer

Holy Spirit, make me into *"good soil"* so I can have a yield of one hundred, sixty, and thirty-fold fruit.

Notes: _____

_____

_____

The Spirit of Meeting Needs

"Truly, I say to you, as you did it to one of the least of these My brethren, you did it to Me" (Matthew 25:31–46).

Here we have a preview of Judgment Day. There will be many surprises when we see who are the real sheep and who are the real goats. The sheep, Jesus warns, will be recognizable as those who have looked after the hungry, the thirsty, the stranger, the naked, the sick and the prisoner – because each one in need was Jesus in disguise.

In the same manner that Jesus looks after our needs – as a privilege and without complaint – He expects us to care for the physical needs of others. However, there is more here than meets the eye. We must not forget the *spiritual* needs which must be *spiritually* discerned. Yes, we must give food to the hungry but we must also give salvation, *"the bread of life."* The physically thirsty need water; but we must also give *"living water,"* the Holy Spirit. We must give clothes to the naked, but we must also offer new white *"robes of righteousness."* In caring for the sick, we must pray for their healing. We must not only visit the prisoner, but set him free from sin (John 8:36) with the Gospel message. Welcoming the stranger into the Family of God is an awesome privilege. Sheep look after both physical and spiritual needs.

Prayer

Holy Spirit, please show me how to meet both the physical and spiritual needs of those you send to me.

Notes: _____

_____

_____

The Spirit of Paradise

"Father Abraham...send Lazarus to dip the end of his finger in water and cool my tongue" (Luke 16:19–31).

Here is a "Rich Man–Poor Man" story that should make everyone of us take inventory of our lives. Wealth and privilege that don't look after the needs of hungry people is called *"unrighteous mammon"* because of its selfishness. God does not help us make a lot of money just to spend on ourselves, but so that we can invest it in the Kingdom of God – or, as Jesus says, *"store up for yourselves treasures in Heaven"* (Matthew 6:20). James warns that our wealth *"will be evidence against you"* (James 5:3).

This story tells of a generous rich man who let poor Lazarus eat his garbage and die of starvation and sickness at his door. When they both died, the rich man went to Hell, and the poor man went to Paradise where he had more than enough to eat and drink. The tormented rich man begged for a drop of water to cool his tongue – but couldn't have it. The only water that satisfies and can keep us out of Hell is the living water of the Holy Spirit. As the rich of the world, how we treat the poor of the world has a lot to do with our final destination. Seeing that he had no hope, the rich man begged that someone warn his five brothers. Abraham replied that if they wouldn't heed Moses and the prophets, they wouldn't be convinced *"if someone would rise from the dead."*

Prayer

Holy Spirit, show me how to look after the poor of my world.

Notes: _____

_____

_____

The Spirit of Spiritual Gifting

"For I long to see you, that I may impart to you some spiritual gift to strengthen you..." (Romans 1:8–17).

The church in Rome had a good reputation, and so Paul wanted to go and visit those believers and have fellowship with them. He prayed for them, *"without ceasing,"* that God might let him visit them. It was his desire to impart some spiritual gifts to them. This is a ministry that many of us have. We pray with people not only for salvation and the baptism of the Holy Spirit, but for the *"spiritual gifts"* (charismatic gifts) that Paul mentions later (Romans 12:6–8; 1 Corinthians 12:8–10). This "ministry of gifting" equips the saints to do ministry for each other and for other people. The gifts of the Holy Spirit strengthen and encourage faith among the believers.

The gifts also have an evangelistic function, which is to draw people to believe in Jesus Christ as Saviour, Lord, Healer and Deliverer. As Paul told the Corinthians, *"My speech and message were not in plausible words of wisdom, but in demonstration of the Spirit and of power"* (1 Corinthians 2:4,5). The gifts are necessary as a sign to unbelievers that the Gospel is true and they can "live by faith."

Prayer

Holy Spirit, please give me the ministry of gifting other believers, so I can equip them to live by faith.

Notes: _____

_____

_____

The Spirit of Spiritual Fruit

"If we live by the Spirit, let us also walk by the Spirit"
(Galatians 5:22–6:10).

Both the fruit and gifts of the Holy Spirit are necessary in order for us to have a "normal Christian life" so we can minister to the needs of other people. Without both, we end up with faith without works or works without faith.

The fruit of the Spirit is absolutely necessary so that the gifts of the Holy Spirit can be accepted and received by people without fear. Love is foundational in using all of the gifts so that people can trust the Holy Spirit. Joy is needed so that people can understand that the gifts bring happiness into our lives. Peace is required so that people will know that the gifts of the Holy Spirit can give us serenity in the midst of life's storms. Patience is important so that people will take the necessary time to receive the gifts. Kindness is crucial in demonstrating that the gifts flow through nice people. Goodness is required so people will know that only moral people can be trusted with the gifts. Faithfulness demonstrates that the gifts are always available. Gentleness shows that the gifts are used under the guidance of the Holy Spirit. Self-control reassures people that the Holy Spirit doesn't cause people to do crazy, embarrassing things.

Prayer

Holy Spirit, please teach me to use Your gifts with Your fruit that I may honour Jesus.

Notes: _____

_____

_____

The Spirit of Endless Supply

"The jar of meal was not spent, neither did the cruse of oil fail..." (1 Kings 17:8–16).

It is not always easy to trust the Lord God, especially when we have run out of money and almost out of food. This was the situation in which the widow of Zarephath found herself. Elijah asked her for something to eat, but she barely had enough flour and oil to feed her son and herself, let alone Elijah. They were going to eat the little they had left and die; but Elijah asked her to trust God and give *him* the last of her food. He sounded selfish but he wasn't. He was teaching her the lesson that we all need to learn; do what God says and you will never run out. *"Give, and it will be given to you; good measure, pressed down, shaken together, running over, will be put into your lap. For the measure you give will be the measure you get back"* (Luke 6:38). Elijah told the widow that God said, *"The jar of meal shall not be spent, and the cruse of oil shall not fail, until the day that the Lord sends rain upon the earth."* In faith, she fed the prophet.

The flour and oil are symbols of Jesus and the Holy Spirit. They never run out. God is still Jehovah-Jireh, our Provider. When we do what Jesus tells us, He will meet all of our needs until He comes again.

Prayer

Holy Spirit, please always remind me that God's flour and Your oil will never run out.

Notes: _____

_____

_____

Spirit-Led Days

The Spirit of Fresh Oil

"...thou hast poured over me fresh oil" (Psalm 92:1–15).

What a wonderful experience of worship! Look at how this psalm progresses:

"It is good to give thanks to the Lord, to sing praises to Thy Name, O Most High; to declare Thy steadfast love in the morning, and Thy faithfulness by night, to the music of the lute and the harp..."

We all need to learn to worship God this way. When we do, we can see clearly what God is doing to expose the fools, the wicked, and the workers of iniquity. He causes them to grow just like in the parable of the wheat and the tares (Matthew 13:36–43). He lets them grow until the harvest so that the wheat, His people, will not be destroyed. Weeds always grow faster than the wheat; so, like the wicked, they expose themselves to everyone.

The exciting thing about worshiping God *"in Spirit and in truth"* is that we are anointed with His fresh oil and are *"filled with the Spirit"* (Ephesians 5:18) in the midst of worship. We are treated like kings, prophets and priests (they were the only ones that God anointed with oil) because that's who we are in Jesus Christ. The new oil of the Holy Spirit refreshes and renews us so we can flourish and bear fruit. We can declare that Jesus *"is my rock."*

Prayer

Holy Spirit, pour Your anointing oil over me so I can be refreshed in Jesus.

Notes: _____

_____

_____

The Spirit of Precious Oil

"It is like the precious oil upon the head..." (Psalm 133:1–3).

The writer of Hebrews encouraged people not to get in the habit of missing worship. In this psalm, David tells us what we miss when we stay away. The New Testament word is "fellowship"; getting together to stir up one another to love and to do good works. Fellowship is the work of the Holy Spirit in creating a partnership (a bond) binding us to each other, to other Christians, to Christ and to God. We can't have it when we are alone. That is why Jesus created a "Church" which means "called-out people" or people who are invited by Jesus to come together to meet with Him to worship.

David describes what happens – and happens only – in worship. *"Behold how good and pleasant it is for brethren to dwell together in unity."* The Holy Spirit causes *"unity"* in worship, in serving Jesus Christ and in ministry. This *"unity"* is like *"precious oil upon the head."* That's what the anointing of the Holy Spirit is like; He covers us from the top of our heads to the tips of our toes. There is no shortage of the Holy Spirit in worship. We mustn't miss Him by isolating ourselves from fellowship and worship.

Prayer

Holy Spirit, please pour Your oil over me because it feels so good.

Notes: _____

_____

_____

The Spirit of Excellent Oil

"It shall be an excellent oil..." (Psalm 141:1–10 KJV).

*L*ike David, we call on the Lord to hurry up and pay attention to us when we have a problem. When we are in trouble, we'll promise to do anything for God – like pray or (Heaven forbid) lift up our hands in a sacrifice of praise.

"God, if You'll answer my prayer the way I want, I'll do anything for you!" How many times has God heard that waiting-to-be-broken promise of a prayer?

David was a man willing to take correction. *"Set a guard over my mouth, O Lord, keep watch over the door of my lips!"*

Here we have a problem. James tells us that *"the tongue is a fire, a world of iniquity"* (James 3:6). It's the most uncontrollable organ in the body. To correct it takes the *"excellent oil"* of the Holy Spirit who alone can take control of the stubborn rudder. That is why, on the Day of Pentecost, the believers all began to speak in tongues *"as the Spirit gave them utterance"* (Acts 2:4). With the Holy Spirit in control, 3,000 people were saved that day. With the Holy Spirit's guard, we are free to be "witnesses" who go into all the world to preach the Gospel. If we are ready for correction, it's right there waiting for us in the Scriptures (2 Timothy 3:16). With it, we can escape safely from our problems.

*P*rayer

Holy Spirit, please correct me and be the guard over my mouth.

*N*otes: _____

_____

_____

The Spirit of the Apostles

"For you are the seal of my apostleship in the Lord"
(1 Corinthians 9:1–27).

*A*postles are created by God. Not everyone who claims to be an apostle is one. It's not something we can decide to be. To be an apostle, a person must have seen and talked with Jesus after He was physically raised from the dead; be sent by Jesus to plant or build up churches; and have a ministry of signs, wonders and miracles.

In this passage, Paul was reminding the Corinthians (and us) that they were his *"seal"* or the trademark of his *"work in the Lord."* Therefore, he and Barnabas had the right to receive their meals, have their wives accompany them, and receive financial support – just as the other apostles did. As apostles, they had the right to make a living from their ministry in the same way that any other professional worker had the right to be paid for his work. Since they had sown spiritual things (works of the Holy Spirit), including salvation, the baptism of the Holy Spirit, healing, deliverance, signs, wonders, and miracles, they, and all those in full-time ministry, had a right to receive material things in order to carry on their ministry (1 Corinthians 9:11). The necessity to preach the Gospel is laid on all apostles so that others can be saved.

Prayer

Holy Spirit, I trust You to meet my material needs as I spread the Gospel.

Notes: _____

_____

_____

The Spirit Who Gives Food

"...all ate the same supernatural food, and all drank the same supernatural drink" (1 Corinthians 10:1–33).

$\mathcal{P}$aul is cautioning, in this passage, not to make the mistake of thinking that because we eat spiritual food (salvation) and drink spiritual drink (the living water of the Holy Spirit), we are free to do anything we like – even to sin according to our own pleasure.

In the desert, the Israelites learned this the hard way. People may be saved – but that does not give them license to sin. It gives them freedom to be faithful and overcome temptations.

What happened to the Israelites is a warning for us not to desire evil as they did. Like them, we who eat and drink at the Lord's Table will be tempted by the devil to see if we will be faithful to Jesus. Fortunately, we will not be tempted beyond our strength. Because Jesus is the rock of our salvation, He gives us the spiritual bread (Jesus Himself) and the spiritual wine (the Holy Spirit). The word "spiritual" refers to anything that comes from the Holy Spirit. So, Jesus gives us Holy Spirit food so that we can have power to say "no" to every temptation to sin. We must have the liberty to minister to everybody, regardless of who they are, to the glory of God, so that many can be saved.

Prayer

Holy Spirit, please feed me spiritual food so I can always be faithful to Jesus and help many to be saved.

Notes: _____

_____

_____

The Spirit of Thanks

"You did not anoint My head with oil, but she has anointed My feet with ointment" (Luke 7:36–50).

*E*ven Jesus notices bad manners. It did not escape Him that his host, Simon the Pharisee, had neglected to welcome Him with the customary courtesies. Meanwhile, a sobbing woman came in and stood behind Jesus. She had heard that He was eating at the Pharisee's house. As her tears began to wet Jesus' feet, she wiped them with her hair. Kissing His feet, she anointed them with her precious perfume. Simon was shocked that Jesus would let this woman, obviously a prostitute (with the telltale evidence of an alabaster flask), touch Him.

Jesus led Simon to understand that those who are forgiven the most will love the most. The woman's great love proved that she had been forgiven her many sins. Jesus then reminded His host of his bad manners. He had given Jesus no water – but the woman had washed His feet with her tears. Simon had given Jesus no kiss – but she had not stopped kissing His feet since His arrival. Simon had given Jesus no oil – but she had poured it on His feet. Water represents salvation, the forgiveness of sin. Oil, or ointment, represents the Holy Spirit. A kiss represents a "thank you." Like Simon, no one can give what they don't have.

Prayer

Holy Spirit, I give thanks because Jesus forgave me. I am so grateful for His salvation.

Notes: _____

_____

_____

The Spirit of God's Glory

"...so that the priests could not stand to minister because of the cloud; for the glory of the Lord filled the house of God"
(2 Chronicles 5:1–14).

*W*hat an impressive worship service for the opening of the Temple in Jerusalem! Everyone was there: King Solomon, the elders of Israel, the priests, the Levites, all of the congregation of Israel. The Ark of the Covenant was brought into the Holy of Holies. Then, the musicians began to lead in praise and thanksgiving. The 120 priests played their trumpets, their cymbals and other instruments. As they praised God, a cloud filled the house of the Lord. It was the *Shekinah Glory* – God's presence; the presence of His Holy Spirit – that filled the whole Temple. The 120 priests could not stand up in the presence of God. It was an awesome sight as the Glory caused them all to fall down!

This can still be our experience in worship today. When the Holy Spirit fills God's temple (1 Corinthians 3:16,17), His believers and "royal priesthood" often fall down. It is a physical reaction to the Holy Spirit called "falling under the power" or "being slain in the Spirit." We shouldn't be surprised if it happens to us because, *"Who can stand before this holy Lord God?"* It occurs so we can be *"snared and caught"* (Isaiah 28:13).

Prayer

Holy Spirit, fill us who are Your temple with the Lord's Shekinah Glory.

Notes: _____

_____

_____

The Spirit Who Defends Us

"When He said to them, "I am He," they drew back and fell to the ground" (John 18:1–11).

The Pharisees and the Temple guards ran into a problem they had not counted on when they went to arrest Jesus. The soldiers found themselves being thrown backward onto the ground. They didn't know it, but this was the Holy Spirit causing them to fall (Isaiah 28:13). With Jesus' permission, the soldiers arrested Him in order to fulfill prophecy. Jesus attempted to go peacefully, but Peter, the fisherman, drew a sword and tried to defend Him, succeeding only in cutting off the ear of the high priest's servant. Peter misunderstood when Jesus told his disciples, *"And let him who has no sword sell his mantle and buy one"* (Luke 22:36). He didn't understand that *"the weapons of our warfare are not worldly but have divine power to destroy strong-holds"* (2 Corinthians 10:4). The sword to which Jesus was referring, was *"the sword of the Spirit"* (Ephesians 6:17), which is the Word of God. We must not make the same mistake.

The Holy Spirit often comes to our defense when people attempt to harm us. *"Touch not mine anointed, and do my prophets no harm"* (Psalm 105:15) is God's warning. There are terrible consequences to pay when anyone harms God's people.

Prayer
Holy Spirit, please show me how to use Your sword in order to win people for Jesus Christ.

Notes: _____

_____

_____

Spirit-Led Days

The Spirit of the Mount of Transfiguration

"He was still speaking when lo, a bright cloud overshadowed them..." (Matthew 17:1–9; Mark 9:1–9).

The trouble with us is that whenever we have an experience with God, we try to build some sort of a monument. Jesus took Peter, James and John high up on a mountain and was transfigured before their eyes. His face shone with bright light the way Moses' did after he met with God, and His clothes reflected the same light. Suddenly, Moses and Elijah appeared and began to talk with Him.

Peter was more than impressed! Not knowing what to do, but wanting to do something, he suggested building three little booths (chapels) right there. As he was talking, a bright cloud, the Shekinah Glory of God's presence, came upon them. God said, *"This is my beloved Son, with whom I am well pleased; listen to Him."* The message was to stop talking and start listening to Jesus. The disciples fell on their faces. It was an awesome experience. We all need to show the same respect for Jesus that God demanded of the disciples, and have this experience of the Holy Spirit daily, as we spend time with Jesus. *"Blessed are the pure in heart, for they shall see God"* (Matthew 5:8).

Prayer

Holy Spirit, please help me to see Jesus transfigured and to listen only to Him.

Notes: _____

_____

_____

The Spirit of the Faithful Steward

"Who then is the faithful and wise steward, whom his master will set over his household, to give them their portion of food at the proper time?" (Luke 12:41–48).

£very Christian who has been baptized with the Holy Spirit has been given at least one spiritual or charismatic gift to use until Jesus returns. This makes everyone a *"steward"* with a household duty to look after our fellow servants in Jesus' household. *"As each one has received a gift, minister it to one another, as good stewards of the manifold grace of God"* (1 Peter 4:19). The portions of food that we are to distribute are portions of spiritual food or "Holy Spirit food" (1 Corinthians 10:1–22). The unfaithful steward distributes unspiritual food by abusing fellow servants and eating and getting drunk. He does not give them the bread of life (Jesus), nor the wine of eternal life (the Holy Spirit). Neither sharing nor living the Gospel, he thinks he can get away with any kind of bad behaviour. Unfortunately, there are numbers of people in our churches who abuse fellow Christians in a variety of ways; but they will not get away with it, because Jesus is coming at a time when they least expect Him. He will punish them. Let us be the servants who do what our Master tells us to do.

Prayer

Holy Spirit, please show me how to be a good steward, looking forward to the Master's return.

Notes: _____

_____

_____

The Spirit Who Casts Fire

"I came to cast fire upon the earth..." (Luke 12:49–56).

John the Baptist said, *"I baptize you with water; but He who is mightier than I is coming...He will baptize you with the Holy Spirit and with fire"* (Luke 3–16). Jesus *"cast fire upon the Earth"* on the Day of Pentecost when 120 believers were all filled with the Holy Spirit and began to speak in tongues. The fire raged on that day until there were 3,000 people saved, baptized with the Holy Spirit and speaking in tongues. By the end of the week, there were 5,000. The infilling of the Holy Spirit then moved from Jews to Gentiles, of whom Peter said, *"And God who knows the heart bore witness to them, giving them the Holy Spirit just as He did to us."*

The fire continues to burn today, and can be identified by the *"signs following"* (Mark 16:17,18). Jesus warned us that He came, not to bring peace, but division. This is the division that comes when people have to make a choice between God and sin, between Jesus and the devil, between the Holy Spirit and evil spirits. It's the choice of whether or not to allow Jesus to be Saviour and Lord. It's the choice that causes whole families to divide against each other. Jesus advises us to learn to interpret the times "spiritually."

Prayer

Holy Spirit, keep Your fire burning in me, so I can stand with Jesus.

Notes: _____

_____

The Spirit Who Heals the Blind

"...he spat on the ground and made clay of the spittle and anointed the man's eyes with the clay..." (John 9:1–41).

*W*e have to stop putting blame for their misfortunes on those (or their relatives) who are sick, handicapped or physically challenged. In the case described in this passage, Jesus said nobody was to blame. He made some clay by spitting on the ground, anointed the blind man's eyes and told him to, *"Go, wash in the pool of Siloam."* The fellow did as he was told and came back with his eyesight restored.

It's a wonder that somebody hasn't developed a doctrine of spittle-made clay for healing blind eyes. Believe it or not, many have argued over so-called healing properties of the spit, or the earth, or both. I don't believe it was any of those combinations that healed the man's eyes. Since Jesus was sinless, his spit was without bacteria and is a symbol of the Holy Spirit who not only has power to raise the dead, but to heal the sick. Jesus used His authority over sickness in a very unusual manner, activating the man's faith and releasing healing power into the once sightless eyes. The man said, *"One thing I know: that though I was blind, now I see."* We too must be willing to pray for the blind and obey the leading of the Holy Spirit.

Prayer

Holy Spirit, let me be Your instrument of healing so that others can see.

Notes: _____

_____

_____

The Spirit Who Heals Infirmities

"And he laid his hands upon her, and immediately she was made straight and she praised God" (Luke 13:10–17).

*I*t is interesting how differently Jesus demonstrates His healing ministry. In this passage, He encountered a woman who was physically bent out of shape so badly that she couldn't stand up straight. She had suffered from *"a spirit of infirmity"* for eighteen years. The Greek word here means "sickness, disease, weakness." Despite her years of pain, discomfort and total inability to live life normally, Jesus dealt with her problem very easily. He simply laid His hand upon her and said, *"Woman, you are freed from your infirmity."* Immediately, she straightened up and praised God! Imagine what that must have been like for her!

It is always interesting to see the reactions of people when Jesus heals someone, either sovereignly, or by using someone like you or me. Some try to ignore the healing. Some deny that the sickness was as serious as it was. Some accuse the person of pretending sickness. Others, like the synagogue ruler, don't think people should be healed on the Sabbath or in their church. Instead of getting excited and praising God, he got angry. We have to learn to cooperate with the Holy Spirit and do as Jesus did – lay our hands on the sick so they can be healed.

Prayer

Holy Spirit, give me the courage to cooperate with You so that I can be instrumental in healing people as Jesus did.

Notes: _____

_____

_____

The Spirit Who Heals the Deaf

"And his ears were opened, his tongue was released, and he spoke plainly" (Mark 7:31–37).

*J*esus ministered healing in another unusual manner in this passage. The man who was brought to Him was deaf and had a speech impediment. Jesus took him aside, away from the crowd, so He could deal with the man privately. First of all, He put His fingers in the man's ears. Second, He spit and touched the man's tongue with the spit on his finger. Third, He commanded the ears, *"Be opened."* Fourth, the man's ears were healed so he could hear, and his speech impediment was healed so he could speak plainly. The people were astonished at Jesus' healing ministry.

There have been many attempted explanations of what the dynamics might have been to bring about the man's healing; but I believe that natural explanations are out of the question. It was a deliberate demonstration to us of how we can cooperate with the Holy Spirit in order to bring about healing. Jesus' spit (not normal spit but sin and germ free) is a symbol of the Holy Spirit. Jesus, through the power of His Holy Spirit touched the man, as we are called to do (Mark 16:17,18), and the healing power of the Holy Spirit brought about the man's healing.

Prayer

Holy Spirit, give me the boldness to cooperate with You so that others can be healed and Jesus thanked.

Notes: _____

_____

_____

The Spirit Who Raises Dead Children

"...He went in and took her by the hand, and the girl arose" (Matthew 9:18,19; 23–26).

Nothing can break the heart of parents more than to look on helplessly as their child dies before their eyes. This passage tells the story of a father who did more than watch; he ran to Jesus for help. Frantically he explained, *"My daughter has just died; but come and lay Your hand on her, and she will live."* He had faith that reached right into death. Jesus went to his house, where He found the mourners weeping and the musicians playing, in an attempt to deal with their grief. Jesus cleared the house, saying, *"Depart; for the girl is not dead but sleeping."* Everybody laughed at Him. She was clearly dead. But Jesus took the girl by the hand and she stood up. So much for that funeral!

We must learn to use our faith by cooperating with *"the Spirit of Him who raised Jesus from the dead"* (Romans 8:11). Jesus showed us that He, Himself, *"is the Resurrection and the Life"* (John 11:25) with the power to raise the dead. Death is the most challenging opponent that we have to face. We must be willing to exercise our authority and lay hands on both the living and the dead to bring healing and resurrection as the Spirit leads us.

Prayer

Holy Spirit, please prepare me to deal with the last enemy so that those who should be raised from death will be raised.

Notes: _____

_____

_____

The Spirit of Healing Waters

"And at once the man was healed, and took up his pallet and walked" (John 5:1–17).

There are many people who run around looking for healing and miracles in the wrong places. They will go anywhere – except to the God of the Bible. Jesus went to the man who had been paralyzed and who sat, hoping he would get healed, by a pool of water for 38 years. Jesus asked him, *"Do you want to be healed?"* A strange question, one might think, but not everyone *does* want to be healed. Some enjoy their sickness and the attention it attracts. However, the man said, "Yes." Jesus said simply, *"Rise, take up your pallet and walk."* The man did – after 38 years of waiting!

Predictably, the man got a reaction from the religious people for carrying his bed on a Sabbath. When asked, he didn't even know who Jesus was; he just knew that a man had healed him. When Jesus saw the fellow later, He warned, *"Sin no more, that nothing worse shall befall you."* In this case, obviously sin had had something to do with the paralysis. We too must be willing to offer healing and share the Gospel with those who are sick, despite however we may *feel*. It is simple obedience to Jesus to carry the living waters of the Holy Spirit to people for healing.

Prayer

Holy Spirit, give me boldness to offer people healing with Your power.

Notes:

_____

_____

_____

The Spirit of Resurrection and Life

"...Jesus called out in a loud voice, 'Lazarus, come out'"
(John 11:17–44,53).

Jesus was intentionally late going to see His sick friend in order that He might demonstrate the "glory of God." Mary and Martha were upset because He had not arrived in time to heal their brother. Jesus reassured them, *"I am the resurrection and the life. He who believes in Me, though he die, yet shall he live, and whoever lives and believes in Me shall never die."* He then had Lazarus' tomb opened, and He shouted, *"Lazarus, come out."* To everyone's astonishment, out came Lazarus, stinking and wrapped in his burial cloths! The religious authorities then decided that they would have Jesus put to death.

This was Jesus' last miracle. Whenever we do ministry in the power of the Holy Spirit, using the miracle working *"gifts of the Holy Spirit"* (Mark 16:17,18; Romans 12:6–8; 1 Corinthians 12:8–10), there will be religious people who react because of God's power challenging their unbelief. It is the Father (Galatians 1:1), and the Son (John 5:21) and the Holy Spirit (Romans 8:11) who work through us to heal the sick and raise the dead when we cooperate. What a reunion it must have been for Lazarus with his sisters!

Prayer

Holy Spirit, show me how to work with Jesus, my resurrection and my life, to minister to others.

Notes: _____

_____

_____

The Spirit Who is Seven

"...and from the seven Spirits who are before His throne..."
(Revelation 1:1–6).

*T*his is a unique picture of the Holy Spirit who is referred to as *"seven Spirits."* It underscores His "omnipresence" – His ability to be in all places at the same time. Since John is writing to seven actual churches in Asia, and each had the Holy Spirit guiding them, it seems appropriate to picture the one Holy Spirit as "seven Spirits" distributed amongst the seven churches. Therefore, the Holy Spirit is often depicted as a fire with seven flames. Since seven is a perfect number, He is the *"perfect Spirit"* or *"the Spirit of the living God"* (2 Corinthians 3:3).

On the Day of Pentecost, the Holy Spirit is pictured as 120 tongues of fire distributed and resting on each of the believers, or "120 spirits"– but He was still only *"one Holy Spirit"* with many flames. In the same way, as He takes up residence in the hearts of believers baptized in the Holy Spirit, He could be pictured as millions of Spirits – but is only the one Holy Spirit.

We all need to be baptized with the Holy Spirit so that we can have the kind of intimate fellowship experience with Him that John had. Then, wherever we are, He will be with us.

Prayer

Holy Spirit, I need Your fellowship. Help me to worship freely, as You bring God's throne into my heart.

Notes: _____

_____

_____

The Spirit of Revelation

"I was in the Spirit on the Lord's Day, and I heard behind me a loud voice..." (Revelation 1:7–11).

*J*ohn was praying and experienced the presence of the Holy Spirit as this passage unfolds. He was not in any ecstatic state in which he was not in control of himself. He was clear-minded – as any person must be in order to receive a revelation from God. He heard a trumpet-like voice telling him to *"Write what you see in a book and send it to the seven churches."* God knows that our memories are short, even when it comes to having experiences with Him. Revelations and communications from Him have a tendency to get lost, distorted or exaggerated. Even the most sincere Christian needs to learn from John by keeping a book and pen close at hand whenever we take time to pray.

John, like Paul, had learned the importance of praying *"in the Spirit"* or in the prayer language of tongues that each of us receive if we are baptized in the Holy Spirit. It is as we exercise our gift of tongues that we *"speak mysteries"* (1 Corinthians 14:2). Jesus will talk to us about spiritual needs, or reveal things about the future as we pray in the Spirit. Any of the gifts of the Holy Spirit can be activated when we begin to pray, speaking mysteries to God that we neither understand nor intellectually direct.

Prayer
Holy Spirit, reveal the mysteries of God to me when I pray.

Notes: _____

_____

_____

The Spirit of the Sword

"...from His mouth issued a sharp two-edged sword..."
(Revelation 1:12–20).

*W*hen John turned to see who was speaking to him, he saw, *"the Son of Man."* The figure before him was unbelievably awesome. With hair as white as snow, He wore a long robe with a golden band around His chest, and his eyes were like blazing fire. With feet like bronze glowing in a furnace and His voice sounding like rushing water, He had a sharp two-edged sword coming out of his mouth. His face shone like the sun at noonday, and in His hand, He held seven stars. This was Jesus as He walked amidst His churches – Jesus, in the power of the Holy Spirit, which caused Him to glow and speak with the Sword of the Spirit (Hebrews 4:12,13). He is the "Sword," the Word of God.

The presence of the Lord was so strong that John fell to the ground, like a dead man. This is what many people call "falling down under the power," or "being slain in the Spirit" (2 Chronicles 5:14; Isaiah 28:13). John couldn't move, but his mind was clear and he could hear and see what was going on. Jesus again told him to *"write what you see, what is and what is to take place hereafter."* This was a "prophetic vision" for the whole Church.

Prayer

Holy Spirit, as I spend time with You, please show me what my local church needs to know.

Notes: _____

_____

_____

The Spirit Who Speaks to Ephesus

"He who has an ear, let him hear what the Spirit says to the churches" (Revelation 2:1–7).

The Holy Spirit has something to say to all of our churches. He can tell us what Jesus wants us to know about our specific congregation. He knows of our works, our patience, our perseverance, and of our tireless efforts. He also sees our failure to serve Jesus as our first priority. Like the church in Ephesus, it can be said of many of us, *"...you have abandoned the love you had at first. Remember then, from what you have fallen, repent and do the works you did at first. If not, I will come to you and remove your lampstand from its place, unless you repent."*

Along with the warning to us, there is also a promise: *"To him who conquers I will grant to eat of the tree of life, which is in the paradise of God."* Every church is like an "endangered species," threatened with extinction if the people will not listen to the Holy Spirit. Our worst nightmare is having Jesus close our churches – not the devil. Unfortunately, the Christians in Ephesus did not listen to the Holy Spirit and there is no church there today. Let us spend time listening to Him and following His advice – or our church could be next!

Prayer

Holy Spirit, please speak to me so I can help my church back to its first love.

Notes: _____

_____

_____

The Spirit Who Speaks to Smyrna

"He who has an ear, let him hear what the Spirit says to the churches" (Revelation 2:8–11).

Smyrna had a "good news / bad news" church. The "good news" was that they had done great works for Jesus Christ, suffered persecution, and, while they lived in physical poverty, they were spiritually rich. The "bad news" was that some of the members would be thrown into prison for ten days and some would be killed. The "good news" was that if they were faithful until death, they would receive the crown of Life. Those who overcome will not be hurt in the second death after the judgment.

Most of us have never faced the degree of persecution that could result in us being killed for being Christians. Our North American churches are usually "persecution resistant" in that, at the first sign of trouble, most people are gone. Overcomers we are usually *not*. The church at Smyrna was commended by Jesus for their willingness to be imprisoned, and even to die for Him. We need to understand the richness there is in denying ourselves, taking up our crosses, and following Jesus even to death. The Holy Spirit will provide His "way of escape" (1 Corinthians 10:13).

Prayer

Holy Spirit, help me to be an overcomer, willing to be faithful – even unto death.

Notes: _____

_____

_____

The Spirit Who Speaks to Pergamos

"He who has an ear, let him hear what the Spirit says to the churches" (Revelation 2:12–17).

Every church's ministry has to be evaluated, not by numbers, but in terms of its faithfulness to the living "Word of God," Jesus Christ, and the written "Word of God," the Scriptures. Jesus is very aware of those who have paid the highest price for faithfulness – their lives – through martyrdom.

In our age of tolerance, our efforts to accommodate everyone in our multicultural, multireligious society, put us at risk of falling to the temptation to compromise and include non-Christian worship and teaching in our churches. The church at Pergamos had fallen into this trap. They had forgotten that God said, *"You shall have no other gods before me."* He tolerates no rivals or cooperation in worshiping other gods (Exodus 20:3,4). The Pergamos church had allowed the worship of Baal along with its sexual immorality. This church was like many today who have accommodated the world to the exclusion of Jesus Christ as their only Saviour, Lord and God.

The only solution is repentance. Otherwise, Jesus Himself will come against this kind of church. He will tolerate no rivals.

Prayer

Holy Spirit, teach me to be an overcomer who will not compromise.

Notes:

_____

_____

_____

The Spirit Who Speaks to Thyatira

"He who has an ear, let him hear what the Spirit says to the churches" (Revelation 2:18–29).

There is nothing like a big, successful church for the ability of the corruption that lies hidden amongst its membership, to escape detection in the name of tolerance. The church at Thyatira was a lot like many of our churches today. The people there had become accustomed to turning a deaf ear to the Holy Spirit. Their foundation of works, love, service, faith and patience was commendable; and their ministry was growing by leaps and bounds – or, so it seemed. But, tolerating sin in order to grow numerically always catches Jesus' attention. The Thyatirans had allowed a so-called "prophetess" to teach and encourage sexual immorality, resulting in the sickness of many who would die if they didn't repent. God has not removed the penalty for sin. Nor has He removed the rewards of faithfulness. To the faithful, he promised power over the nations and *"the morning star."*

We must constantly examine our ministries by the Scriptures and not allow expediency to replace faithfulness to Jesus Christ.

Prayer

Holy Spirit, please show me any sin in my life, or in the life of my church, so I can repent, be an overcomer and hold fast to Jesus – my morning star.

Notes: _____

_____

_____

The Spirit Who Speaks to Sardis

"He who has an ear to hear, let him hear what the Spirit says to the churches" (Revelation 3:1–6).

The impression of success and faithfulness is easy to communicate in a big church building with a large church staff. However, these tell us nothing of what is really happening or not happening within the ministry and fellowship there. Sardis had such a church. It was like many today which, from the outside, look prosperous and successful – but whose reputation of being alive is false, because they are really dead. The shrinking memberships and low attendance in worship and church groups prove the lack of life through the Holy Spirit. Their works are less than perfect. Every church must evaluate itself Scripturally. How many people have been saved, baptized in the Holy Spirit, healed, restored, received deliverance, and worshiped in Spirit and in Truth?

Our churches do not need statistical reports on membership; they need spiritual reports that demonstrate the degree of faithfulness to Jesus Christ. The warning to Sardis is one that we all need to heed: *"He who conquers shall be clad thus in white garments, and I will not blot out his name from the Book of Life."* The seven Spirits refer to the Holy Spirit who sees everything in each of the seven churches.

Prayer

Holy Spirit, please nudge me to repent if I defile my spiritual garments.

Notes:

_____

_____

_____

The Spirit Who Speaks to Philadelphia

"He who has an ear, let him hear what the Spirit says to the churches" (Revelation 3:7–13).

To the church that keeps God's word and does not deny Him, there is an open door to do ministry. We may appear weak, but our strength is in the Lord (Psalm 27:1) who has told us, *"My grace is sufficient for you, for My power is made perfect in weakness"* (2 Corinthians 12:9). The church at Philadelphia had discovered the key to being faithful. These people didn't just listen to Jesus' command to persevere, they obeyed it. They had discovered that perseverance was rooted in the power of the Holy Spirit. Because of their faithfulness, Jesus told them, *"I will keep you from the hour of trial which is coming on the whole world, to try those who dwell on the earth."* Perseverance protects us from even worse trials and temptations.

When we are faithful, Jesus promises that we shall wear the victory crown and be made pillars *"in the temple of my God."* Jesus will write His address on us for special delivery on the Day of the Lord, including *"the Name of My God," "the name of the city of My God, the New Jerusalem"* and *"My new Name."*

Prayer

Holy Spirit, please help me to be an overcomer. I want to be among those who go to the New Jerusalem.

Notes: _____

_____

_____

The Spirit Who Speaks to Laodicea

"He who has an ear, let him hear what the Spirit says to the churches" (Revelation 3:14–22).

The most frightening thing about the church at Laodicea, is that it looks and sounds like too many of our churches today. It consisted of self-satisfied Christians resting on past successes. Having become lukewarm, they were no longer "on fire" for Jesus. They made Him so nauseous that He was about to vomit them out of His mouth. This was an affluent congregation who measured their success on the basis of their bank accounts and investments, instead of salvations and spiritual strength. Because they did not use their wealth for ministry, they were really wretched, miserable, poor, blind, and naked in Jesus' sight. They had forgotten that, in the end, their wealth would be evidence against them and would eat their flesh like fire (James 5:2,3).

True wealth is gained through being firey "hot" for Jesus and leading others to Him, thereby purchasing *"real gold,"* *"white garments,"* and *"eye salve"* so we can see reality. Jesus will come to us, visit with us and be Lord of our lives, if we invite Him in. Then He will invite us to sit with Him on His throne.

Prayer

Holy Spirit, help me to be a firey hot overcomer who purchases true wealth.

Notes: _____

_____

_____

The Spirit Who Speaks Continually

"He who has an ear, let him hear what the Spirit says to the churches" (Revelation 2:7,11,17,29; 3:6,13,22).

Through this passage, Jesus is trying to catch the attention of the whole Church – meaning the entire Body of Christ. While the seven specific churches addressed were actual local entities, they represent aspects of the whole of the Church of Jesus Christ. Every church is faced with any and all of the dangers that Jesus pointed out here. Every church that will not listen to what the Holy Spirit is saying is in danger of having its lampstand removed. Seven times, Jesus says the same thing: *"Let him hear what the Spirit says to the churches."* **Listen. Listen. Listen. Listen. Listen. Listen. Listen**. He repeats Himself, because we are not listening. The result is that we keep making the same mistakes over and over again and fail to correct our deficiencies.

Just look around at the churches today. All seven are there: the loveless church, the persecuted church, the compromising church, the corrupt church, the dead church, the faithful church,and the lukewarm church. We need to spend time learning to listen to the Holy Spirit who will guide us into all the truth.

Prayer

Holy Spirit, please speak to me and help me to hear what my church needs to do to bring glory to Jesus. Use me as You will.

Notes: _____

_____

_____

The Spirit Who Shows Heaven

"At once I was in the Spirit, and lo, a throne stood in Heaven..." (Revelation 4:1–11).

*A*mazing things happen when we spend time in prayer. When we start praying in the Spirit (1 Corinthians 14:2,15) we enter the realm of the Holy Spirit and He speaks to us, revealing what God wants us to know. John was shown God's throne with God sitting on it, just as it was shown to Isaiah (Isaiah 6:1–13). John saw the twenty-four elders and the seven lamps of fire which are the seven Spirits of God. He saw the crystal sea and the seraphim, the living creatures. The colors and pageantry amazed him.

The worship in Heaven goes on continuously night and day. The praise of *"Holy, Holy, Holy, Lord God Almighty, Who was and is and is to come"* rang in John's ears, as it should in ours, until he could go there permanently. He saw and heard the elders leading in worship, casting their thrones before Jesus and praising Him. This vision should give us a tremendous desire to submit to the urging of the Holy Spirit within us to engage in worship on Earth as much as possible so we shall be prepared for Heavenly worship. We need to go out of our way to be with others with whom we can worship freely.

Prayer

Holy Spirit, teach me to worship God continuously until I stand before Him in Heaven to continue worshipping there.

Notes: _____

_____

_____

The Spirit Who is Seven Lamps

"...and before the throne burn seven torches of fire, which are the seven Spirits of God" (Revelation 4:5).

It is very interesting that the seven torches of fire burned before the throne to symbolize the continuous and perfect working of the Holy Spirit who enlightens all who worship God. The seven torches of fire had their earthly counterparts in the Tabernacle which God instructed Moses to have constructed for worship (Exodus 25:31–40; 37:17–24). They represent the presence of the Holy Spirit. Whether in Heaven or on Earth, the Holy Spirit is absolutely central to the worship of God.

Jesus said, *"God is Spirit, and those who worship Him must worship Him in Spirit and in truth"* (John 4:24). The Greek word for "spirit" refers to the Holy Spirit, not the human spirit or soul. It is only when the Holy Spirit is indwelling us that we can offer acceptable worship to God, whether on Earth or in Heaven. The seven torches were connected at one end, through which the oil was supplied. The seven spirits are connected at one end also, to show that they are really one, emanating from the common base. The Holy Spirit connects all believers so we are one. Isn't that a wonderful picture?

Prayer

Holy Spirit, fill me with Your power, that I may worship God in Spirit and in truth.

Notes: _____

_____

_____

The Spirit Who Discerns

"...the great city which is allegorically called Sodom and Egypt..." (Revelation 11:1–14).

John was given a rod to measure God's Temple, which is God's people and their worship. Without Jesus, they do not measure up to God's standard because of their sin. God sent two witnesses. The two witnesses are called two olive trees and two lampstands standing before the God of the Earth. Both are symbols of the Holy Spirit. As witnesses, they will tell about all *"the wonderful works of God"* and call people to receive Jesus as their Saviour and Lord. They will also prophesy and do mighty works. Many people will react against them and become their enemies. Finally, they will be killed by *"the beast"* and their bodies will lie *"in the street of the great city,"* Jerusalem, which is identified spiritually with the help of the Holy Spirit.

But the two witnesses will be raised again by *"the breath of life from God,"* who is the Holy Spirit (Romans 8:11) and will ascend into Heaven. Following a devastating earthquake which will kill 7,000 people, the 90% of the city who survive will be terrified and give glory to God. We too need the Holy Spirit so we can be faithful witnesses (Acts 1:8).

Prayer

Holy Spirit, show me spiritually those things which are going to happen so I can give glory to the God of Heaven without terror.

Notes:

_____

_____

_____

The Spirit of the Saints

"'Blessed indeed,' says the Spirit, 'that they may rest from their labours, for their deeds follow them!'" (Revelation 14:9–13).

The time is coming when *"the beast"* will demand to be worshipped. It appears to be a political / religious power (Revelation 13) which will wage war against the saints. The beast will require everyone to have its mark on their right hand or forehead. This is an attempt to copy what God does to his saints when we are sealed (Revelation 7:4), which means that we have God's mark of ownership placed upon us. The *"signs following"* (Mark 16:17) are also trademarks; marks of authenticity, or "brands" by which Christians can be identified. Everything the beast tries to do is an attempt to copy God – a counterfeit of the real thing. But, as always, we have a choice about whether we will serve the devil or not, regardless of his threats or promises. Anyone who worships the beast will feel God's wrath and be tormented forever. Many others will die for Christ. Serving Jesus has always called for endurance, or the willingness to withstand pain or hardship for Him. When will this happen? In one sense, it's always happening! Everyone, in every generation, is tempted to worship the beast – regardless of the drama waiting to unfold.

Prayer

Holy Spirit, help me to endure by having faith in Jesus, keeping God's commands, and resting in Him.

Notes: _____

_____

_____

The Spirit Who Carries Us Away

"And he carried me away in the Spirit into the wilderness"
(Revelation 17:1–18).

*I*t is amazing what the Holy Spirit will show us about the spiritual warfare that is going on and will go on in the future. John was shown a woman who was dressed in purple and scarlet and identified as *"Babylon,"* the mother of all prostitutes. She was drunk on the blood of Christian martyrs. Babylon, along with the beast, will be defeated by the Lamb, Jesus, because *"He is the Lord of lords and King of kings and those who are with Him are called, chosen and faithful."* The beast, the woman, and all those whose names are not written in the Book of Life will be sent to everlasting Hell.

God's plan is to allow the leadership of sin, the devil, the beast, the scarlet woman and all who follow them, to work together with one mind until His plans are fulfilled. God wants us to know that He has everything under control as far as the "end times" are concerned. All we have to concern ourselves with is our willingness to serve Jesus in the power of the Holy Spirit – because with Jesus, we win in the end! By keeping our eyes on Him and listening to the Holy Spirit, we have no need of worry.

Prayer

Holy Spirit, thank You for reminding me that with Jesus we win in the end. Please help me to keep my eyes on Jesus and my ears open to You.

Notes: _____

_____

_____

The Spirit of Testimony

"For the testimony of Jesus is the spirit of prophecy"
(Revelation 19:1–10).

This passage depicts an awesome scene in Heaven! Everyone is rejoicing! *"Hallelujah!"* is on the lips of all assembled. Praise echoes throughout all of Heaven in celebration of God's victory. The marriage of the Lamb has come! The Bride, His Church, is ready. To John, an angel said, *"Blessed are those who are called to the marriage supper of the Lamb!"* John was so impressed with the angel that he fell down at his feet to worship him. The angel was embarrassed and ordered John to stop: *"I am your fellow servant, and of your brethren who have the testimony of Jesus. Worship God."* Angels are our co-workers, each with a testimony of Jesus. We are to worship God – never angels.

The angel continued, *"The testimony of Jesus is the spirit of prophecy,"* which means that all prophecy given by the Holy Spirit must point us to Jesus – what He has done, and is going to do for us as a Church and as individuals. Prophecy is for the building up of the Church (1 Corinthians 14:3). This is why Paul said, *"But earnestly desire the higher* (spiritual) *gifts"* (1 Corinthians 14:1), *"especially that you may prophesy"* (1 Corinthians 14:5).

Prayer

Holy Spirit, help me to fulfill prophecy by sharing my testimony of Jesus.

Notes:

_____

_____

_____

The Spirit Who Shows the Future

"And in the Spirit He carried me away to a great, high mountain and showed me the holy city Jerusalem..."
(Revelation 21:1–27).

The Holy Spirit allowed John to see the New Jerusalem coming down out of Heaven. It shone with the glory of God. We are given a tour of the awesome city in which those of us who are going to be saved will live. It is more than amazing. Standing 1,500 miles high, it measures 1,500 miles square. That's about the distance from New York city to Oklahoma City, squared, or from Toronto to Winnipeg, squared. There will be more than enough room in the New Jerusalem for all the saved who are *"a great multitude which no one can number,"* of all nations, tribes, peoples and tongues.

There was no temple in the city, because God and the Lamb *are* its Temple. This means that we shall have access to God and Jesus at all times. It is a reminder that, after we have been baptized with the Holy Spirit, even on Earth we have full access to God and Jesus at all times, through His indwelling presence. In Heaven, God's glory will illuminate the city since there will no longer be a sun or moon. The gates are always open to those whose names are written in the Lamb's Book of Life.

Prayer

Holy Spirit, help me to live for Jesus, as one whose name is written in the Lamb's Book of Life.

Notes: _____

_____

_____

The Spirit of Life

"Then he showed me the river of the water of life..."
(Revelation 22:1–5).

The water of life is crucial for every one of us. Jesus talked with the Samaritan woman at the well about the *"spring of water welling up to eternal life"* (John 4:14). Later, Jesus said, *"He who believes in Me, as the Scripture has said, 'Out of his heart shall flow rivers of living water.' Now this He said about the Spirit, which those who believed in Him were to receive; for as yet the Spirit had not been given, because Jesus had not yet been glorified"* (John 7:38,39). After Jesus was glorified, on the Day of Pentecost, He poured out His Holy Spirit upon all flesh.

The "water of life" is "the living water," who is the Holy Spirit. The water of life flows from the throne of God right down the "Main Street" of New Jerusalem, giving and sustaining eternal life. We shall always need Him to be our Counselor, guiding us to glorify God and Jesus. Through His example of being invisible and transparent, the Holy Spirit will continue to be our perfect example of how to best glorify our Heavenly Father and Jesus.

Prayer

Holy Spirit, thank You for the assurance that You will always pour Your water of life into us, even in the Holy City. Please remind me to be invisible and transparent as I seek to glorify Jesus.

Notes: _____

_____

_____

The Spirit of the Prophets

"And the Lord, the God of the spirits of the prophets, has sent His angel..." (Revelation 22:6–14).

The angel reassured John that everything that he had shown John was from God – the same God whose Holy Spirit spoke through and guided the prophets. Everything revealed in the Book of Revelation must take place. The angel said this because everything that God is going to do will line up with what He has already prophesied in the past. The whole Book of Revelation is a preview of what will happen, so that we shall know what to expect. The angel encourages us with Jesus' words: *"And behold, I am coming soon."*

John made the same mistake a second time; he fell down to worship the angel. Again, the angel told him, *"You must not do that! I am a fellow servant with you...Worship God."* I don't know what it is about people, even Christians, who are so quick to bow their knees to worship angels or any other spiritual being. It is no wonder Satan can attract worship when he comes as an *"angel of light"* (2 Corinthians 11:14). For those shallow individuals who worship today's body beautiful, they may find it difficult to worship the precious One who loved us and died for us. Jesus may not be as handsome as they demand (Isaiah 53:2)! But there has never been one more beautiful!

Prayer

Holy Spirit, please drill it into our heads to worship God and serve Him only.

Notes: _____

_____

_____

The Spirit Who Invites Us

"The Spirit and the Bride say, 'Come'"

(Revelation 22:16–21).

The book of Revelation ends with an invitation (an altar call) to come to Jesus for salvation, the baptism of the Holy Spirit and eternal life. The Holy Spirit and the Church invite us to "come," and keep coming, to receive Jesus as our Saviour and Lord. They invite us to come to receive the "water of life." It doesn't cost any money. Jesus paid for it all. All we have to do is to "come" and "take." *"O taste and see that the Lord is good."*

Non-Christians may ask, "How do I 'come' and 'take'?"

Christians must be prepared to lead them in a simple prayer. We just have to say, "Jesus, I would like to know You personally as my Saviour and Lord and have the right to go to Heaven, the New Jerusalem. Please forgive me for any sin I have committed. Please baptize me with the Holy Spirit, and fill me with *'the water of life.'* Amen." At this point, every sin or wrong the person has ever done is forgiven and his or her name is written in the Book of Life (Revelation 20:12). He or she will receive gifts of the Holy Spirit and the fruit of the Holy Spirit will begin to form within.

Prayer

Holy Spirit, thank You for coming into my heart so I can turn to You every moment of every day for help.

Notes: _____

_____

_____

The Spirit of Justice

"...and a Spirit of justice to Him who sits in judgment..."
(Isaiah 28:1–6).

We have to be very careful not to ask God for justice. Justice applies God's law to our lives. Justice says, "If you break a law, you have to pay the prescribed penalty for it." *"The wages of sin is death"* (Romans 6:23). Death is the reward for breaking God's law. The Holy Spirit is the "Spirit of justice" because He is our "legal Counselor" who knows God's whole law. He is the One who Jesus said would guide us into all truth.

Whether we want to believe it or not, there are spiritual laws that govern the universe, just as there are physical laws that govern it. Just as we can get hurt or killed by breaking a physical law, we will suffer when we break the spiritual laws of the universe.

The Spirit of justice will tell us that there is no hope in asking God for justice because we have sinned and the penalty is Hell. However, since Jesus paid for all our sin on the Cross, the Holy Spirit will tell us we can ask for mercy in Jesus' Name. He will give it and we shall find *"the gift of God is eternal life through Jesus Christ our Lord"* (Romans 6:23).

Prayer

Holy Spirit, show me the sins for which I still need to ask forgiveness, so I can be on solid footing with Jesus.

Notes: _____

_____

_____

The Spirit of Another Tongue

"...but by men of strange lips and with an alien tongue the Lord will speak to this people..." (Isaiah 28:6–12).

The mistake that most people who have drinking problems make, is that they don't connect their tremendous (though usually unrecognized) desire for a relationship with God with their thirst for alcoholic beverages. Because they don't make the connection, they go on drinking themselves to death. Isaiah saw that most people tried to satisfy this *"hunger and thirst for righteousness"* (Matthew 5:6) with drugs and other addictions that they thought would satisfy this desire. Everyone has this built-in need for God.

God saw that the solution was to clean us up through salvation and baptize us with the Holy Spirit to keep us clean. When a person is baptized in the Holy Spirit, a common "initial evidence" (Acts 2:4) is that he or she speaks in tongues or another language. This is what was prophesied in this passage. *"...but by men of strange lips and with an alien tongue the Lord will speak to this people..."* Paul sees this prophecy fulfilled in the Church. *"Thus, tongues are a sign not for believers but for unbelievers"* (1 Corinthians 14:22). Tongues is a supernatural sign to let people know that Jesus can fulfill their thirst and draw them to Him.

Prayer

Holy Spirit, please satisfy my thirst and give me another language as a sign.

Notes: _____

_____

_____

The Spirit Who Makes Us Fall

"...That they might go and fall backward, and be broken and snared and taken" (Isaiah 28:13–19).

This experience of people falling down under the power of God happens from time to time in worship services. In this passage, God tells us why He slays people in the spirit. After hearing the Word of God, we need more than an intellectual acceptance. It is *"a demonstration of the Spirit and of power, that your faith might not rest on the wisdom of men but in the power of God"* (1 Corinthians 2:4,5).

This phenomenon is often called "being slain in the Spirit" or "falling under the power." It is an involuntary physical reaction to the Holy Spirit, one of the manifestations of *"the gift of miracles"* (1 Corinthians 12:10). When it occurs, people are laid out on the floor by the Holy Spirit so that Jesus can perform a miracle. The Greek does not use the word "miracle" but rather "the gift of energizing power." Therefore, when a person with the gift of miracles prays for people, they often fall down on the floor because of the power of the Holy Spirit. Miracles such as salvation, the baptism of the Holy Spirit, healing or deliverance might occur. It could also be that the person might have a vision, or God might speak to them about His plan for their lives. No one gets hurt when the Holy Spirit places a person on the floor.

Prayer

Holy Spirit, please deal with me in whatever way necessary.

Notes:

_____

_____

The Spirit of Jesus Christ

"And His Name will be called Wonderful, Counselor, Mighty God, Everlasting Father, Prince of Peace" (Isaiah 9:6–7).

Today, we celebrate the birthday of Jesus. His name means "Jehovah is salvation." As God spoke through Isaiah, we learned some of His other names as well. These other names tell us exactly who Jesus is. They are other names of the God who *"became flesh and dwelt amongst us full of grace and glory."* He is called, *"Wonderful,"* and *"Counselor,"* in reference to the Holy Spirit who is, *"the Spirit of Christ."* The Holy Spirit is *"Wonderful,"* because of the amazing things He does as He pours God's love into our hearts, all the while keeping Himself invisible so that people will see only Jesus. He is also our Heavenly legal *"Counselor,"* who, when He enters our hearts through the baptism of the Holy Spirit, gives us gifts, develops fruit and guides us. Our God is *"Mighty God,"* who created this world and us in it. He is our *"Everlasting Father,"* who *"so loved the world that He gave His only Son, that whoever believes in Him should not perish but have eternal life"* (John 3:16). Jesus is all of these – God's "Christmas gift package" – sent special delivery for us.

Prayer

Holy Spirit, help me to know Jesus more, the One who came to show me the Father, the Son and the Holy Spirit.

Notes: _____

_____

_____

The Spirit of Myrrh

"Then, opening their treasures, they offered him gifts, gold and frankincense and myrrh" (Matthew 2:1–12).

We need to learn the lesson of the wise men who travelled for about two years, at great cost, to find Jesus. They followed His star to Jerusalem and then to Bethlehem. Overcoming great and unforeseen obstacles in the course of their journey, they allowed nothing to keep them from their destination. Anyone today with such a strong desire to find Jesus that they'll not let anything hold them back, will find Him too.

The wise men took gifts for Jesus. The first was gold, a gift for a king – the *"King of kings and Lord of lords"* (Revelation 19:16). The second was frankincense, a gift for a priest. Jesus is our *"high priest"* (Hebrews 5:15) who offered His body *"once for all"* (Hebrews 7:27) and who represents us in Heaven. The third gift, myrrh, was a gift for one who was to die. It was to prepare His body not only for death but for His resurrection from the dead. Myrrh is a sign of the Holy Spirit of whom Paul said, *"If the Spirit of Him who raised Jesus from the dead dwells in you, He who raised Christ Jesus from the dead will give life to your mortal bodies also through His Spirit which dwells in you"* (Romans 8:11). Myrrh represents Jesus who said, *"I am the resurrection and the life"* (John 11:25).

Prayer

Holy Spirit, show me how I can further give my life as a gift to Jesus: my King, Priest and Resurrection.

Notes: _____

_____

_____

The Spirit of Touch

"Someone touched Me; for I perceive that power has gone forth from Me" (Luke 8:43–48).

Faith can touch the power of God. This passage tells of a desperate woman who had tried everything she could to be healed of a flow of blood. She had exhausted her financial resources on unsuccessful doctors. Buried in the crowd that surrounded Jesus, she desperately extended her hand to simply touch the hem of His garment. Feeling the Holy Spirit's movement in response to her faith, Jesus asked, *"Who was it that touched me?"* as His power poured forth to heal her.

I once sat at my wife's hospital bedside, praying that Jesus would stop her postoperative hemorrhaging. Out of desperation, the doctor sent a nurse to get a pint of blood in order to give her a transfusion. We were alone in the room when suddenly, Ruth sat up in bed and reached across her bed to an unseen Visitor. "Jesus, I am reaching out to touch the hem of your garment," she said politely, then laid back in her bed. The nurse made one final examination and exclaimed, "It's stopped!"

The healing power of the Holy Spirit is available today when by faith we touch the hem of His garment.

Prayer
Holy Spirit, I am reaching out to touch Your hem of healing.

Notes: _____

_____

_____

The Spirit of Spit

"...and when He had spit on his eyes and laid His hands upon him, He asked him, 'Do you see anything?'" (Mark 8:22–26).

*W*hat an unusual way to heal blind eyes! Jesus spit on the man's eyes and laid His hands on him. Then, He laid his hands on the man a second time – and his eyesight was completely restored. As I mentioned previously, many people have tried to explain that there is healing ability in our saliva, a theory that I doubt. Our spit contains bacteria, carrying germs and disease. However, this was spit from Jesus, the one who was tempted in every way and yet did not sin. He was free from sin, sickness and death. His body fluids carried the *"living water"* of the Holy Spirit. When Jesus put his saliva in the man's eyes and laid his hands on him, the healing power of the Holy Spirit flowed into those blinded eyes with a miracle of healing.

The point today, is that Jesus had to lay hands on the man a second time before he was totally healed. This is exactly what Jesus tells us to do when He talks about the *"signs following"* believers (Mark 16:17,18). *"They will lay hands on the sick and they will recover."* The meaning of the original Greek here implies a continuous action. Thus, Jesus tells us to *keep laying hands on the sick continuously* until they are healed!

Prayer

Holy Spirit, please remind and encourage me to keep praying for the sick again and again, until they are healed.

Notes: _____

_____

_____

The Spirit of the Power of the Lord

"...and the power of the Lord was with Him to heal"
(Luke 5:17– 26).

We all need friends who have the faith to carry us to Jesus for healing. This paralyzed man had friends who not only carried him to the house where Jesus was teaching but, when they found the place crowded out; carried him up on the roof, cut a hole in it, and lowered the man, on his bed, down in front of Jesus. *"The power of the Lord was present,"* means that the power of the Holy Spirit was always there to heal. Jesus said, *"But you shall receive power when the Holy Spirit has come upon you; and you shall be my witnesses..."* (Acts 1:8). Jesus always had that power in Him.

Jesus said, *"Man, your sins are forgiven you."* Not all sickness or physical disabilities are the result of a specific sin, but apparently, this man's paralysis was. Jesus ministered healing in spite of his critics. *"But that you may know that the Son of Man has authority on earth to forgive sins...I say to you, rise, take up your bed, and go home."* The man was healed!

We too must minister healing in the power of the Holy Spirit regardless of what others might think.

Prayer

Holy Spirit, please give me boldness and show me how to minister healing in Your presence.

Notes: _____

_____

_____

The Spirit Who Forbids

"They were forbidden by the Holy Spirit to speak the Word in Asia" (Acts 16:1–6).

We should not be surprised when the Holy Spirit forbids, hinders, or prevents us from going to certain places to carry out our ministries. It is His responsibility to guide us according to God's specific plan and not ours. To ignore His warnings means to step outside of God's will. The Holy Spirit can give us detailed instructions from God, complete with the right timing. When we follow His leading, opportunities to share the Gospel will open up for us and people will be receptive to our ministry. This is a lesson we all need to learn. It saves a lot of frustration.

Jesus sent the Holy Spirit to be our Counselor. We need to ask His advice before we decide to go anywhere or do anything; regardless of whether it is a personal matter, a ministry concern, a business decision, travel plans, vacations, investments or family decisions. Paul and those travelling with him learned always to wait for direction from the Holy Spirit. This time He said, "Don't go there." Paul took His advice. We too need to learn to be obedient to His guidance.

Prayer

Holy Spirit, please speak to me so that I will go only where and when You send me.

Notes: _____

_____

_____

The Spirit of Visions

"And a vision appeared to Paul in the night: a man of Macedonia...calling...'Come over to Macedonia and help us'"
(Acts 16:9–15).

God still uses visions to give us direction and guidance. On the Day of Pentecost, Peter explained that after people were baptized with the Holy Spirit, as Joel prophesied, *"your young men shall see visions"* (Acts 2:17).

Since the Holy Spirit had prevented Paul and his companions from going to Asia and Bithynia, they were praying to find out where they should go. Then Paul had a vision of a Macedonian pleading with them to come and help them. They recognized this vision as God's call to preach the Gospel to the Macedonians.

We all need to have a "vision" for direction in ministry from God. His guidance can come through prayer, through reading the Bible, dreams, visions, revelations, and in any way that the Holy Spirit wants to communicate God's plans for our lives. It doesn't matter what method God uses to call us; we must be willing to follow it. *"Where there is no vision, the people perish"* (Proverbs 29:18). This is a good time to pray for a clear vision of what Jesus is calling us to do as we face the future.

Prayer

Holy Spirit, please use visions or any other means to guide me according to Jesus' plans for my life.

Notes: _____

_____

_____

BIBLIOGRAPHY

Bibles

Biblica Hebraica, Ed. Rud. Kittel, American Bible Society, New York, by Wurttembergische Bibelanstalt. Stuttgart: 1963.

The Greek New Testament, Third Edition (corrected), United Bible Societies. West Germany: 1983.

The Holy Bible, The Authorized King James Version, The World Publishing Company. Cleveland, Ohio: 1945.

The Holy Bible, Revised Standard Version, Zondervan Bible Publishers. Grand Rapids, Michigan: Fourteenth printing, 1981.

The Good News Bible, Today's English Version, New Testament, American Bible Society. New York: 1978.

The NIV Study Bible, New International Version, Zondervan Bible Publishers. Grand Rapids, Michigan, U.S.A.: 1984.

The Spirit Bible, Ed. Eugene S. Geissler, Ave Maria Press, Notre Dame. Indiana: 1973.

The Spirit-Filled Life Bible, New King James Version, Thomas Nelson Publishers. Nashville: 1991.

Bible Commentaries

The International Critical Commentary on the First Epistle of St. Paul to the Corinthians: Rev. S. R. Driver, A. Plummer, C. A. Briggs. T. & T. Clark. Edinburgh: 1967.

The Daily Study Bible, The New Testament Books: The Gospel of Matthew, The Gospel of John; The Letters of James and Peter; The Letters of John and Jude; The Revelation of John. William Barclay. The Saint Andrew Press. Edinburgh, Scotland: 1960.

The Daily Bible Series, Ezekiel. Peter C. Craigie. The Westminster Press. Philadelphia, Pennsylvania: 1983.

The Layman's Bible Commentaries, Ezekiel, Daniel. C. G. Howie. SCM Press Ltd. Bloomsbury Street, London: 1962.

An Analysis of the Greek New Testament. Max Zeerwick and Mary Grosvenor. Biblical Institute Press. Rome: 1981.

Concordances and Lexicons

A Concordance to the Greek New Testament, Ed. by Rev. W. F. Moulton, Rev. A. S. Geden, Rev. H. K. Moulton. T. & T. Clark. Edinburgh: 1963.

The Exhaustive Concordance of the Bible. James Strong. Abingdon Press. New York, Nashville, U.S.A.: 1965.

Hebrew and English Lexicon of the Old Testament. Francis Brown, S. R. Driver, Charles Briggs. Oxford University Press. London: 1962.

A Greek-English Lexicon of the New Testament. Wm. F. Arndt and F. Wilbur Gingrich. The University of Chicago Press. Chicago, Illinois: 1960.

Other Books

Meditations on the Holy Spirit. Toyohiko Kagawa. Cokesbury Press. Nashville: 1939.

New Testament Words, William Barclay, SCM Press Ltd., Bloomsbury Street, London, 1964.

The Miracles of Jesus. David A. Redding. First Harper & Row Paperback Edition, New York, 1977.

The Parables He Told, David A. Redding, First Harper & Row Paperback Edition. New York: 1976.

Quotations and or references, whether directly or indirectly, are from the above sources.

INDEX

Genesis

Page   15—Genesis 1:1-2:7
Page   16—Genesis 6:1-8
Page   16—Genesis 2:16,17
Page   17—Genesis 41:33-41
Page   59—Genesis 22:14

Exodus

Page   11—Exodus 20:5
Page   18—Exodus 31:1-5
Page   18—Exodus31:5
Page   47—Exodus 13:21
Page 283—Exodus 34:15-16
Page 362—Exodus 25:31-40
Page 362—Exodus 37:17-24

Leviticus

Page 226 —Leviticus 17:11

Numbers

Page   19—Numbers 11:16
Page   19—Numbers 17:24-25
Page   19—Numbers 11:14
Page   20—Numbers 11:26-30
Page   21—Numbers 24:1-13
Page   22—Numbers 27:15-23
Page   22—Numbers 26:65

Deuteronomy

Page   11—Deuteronomy 4:24
Page   23—Deuteronomy 34:9-12

Judges

Page   24—Judges 3:10,11
Page   25—Judges 6:34-7:9
Page   26—Judges 11:4-40
Page   27—Judges 13:24,25
Page   27—Judges 14:1-9
Page   27—Judges 15:14-16,20
Page   27—Judges 16-20

1 Samuel

Page   16 —1 Samuel 16:14
Page   28—1 Samuel 10:1-13
Page   29—1 Samuel 16:1-13
Page   30—1 Samuel 16:14-23
Page   30—1 Samuel 15:23

1 Kings

Page 219—1 Kings 22:5-28,37
Page 302—1 Kings 19:1-18
Page 332—1 Kings 17:8-16

2 Kings

Page   32—2 Kings 2:9-18
Page 303—2 Kings 6:8-23

1 Chronicles

Page   31—1 Chronicles 12:16-19

2 Chronicles

Page   51 —2 Chronicles 16:9
Page 339 —2 Chronicles 5:1-14
Page 352 —2 Chronicles 5:14

Nehemiah

Page   33—Nehemiah 9:20-25,
               29-31

Job

Page   17 —Job 33:14-18
Page   34—Job 32:1-8
Page   35—Job 34:10-20
Page   56—Job 33:15
Page 304—Job 38:1-7
Page 317—Job 32:10-22
Page 318—Job 33:1-8

Psalms

Page   29—Psalm 51:10
Page   36—Psalm 51:1-12

Page   37—Psalm 104:24-30
Page   37—Psalm 37:25
Page   37—Psalm 104:29 KJV
Page   38—Psalm 19:7-18
Page   38—Psalm 139:8,9
Page   62—Psalm 139:13
Page   74—Psalm 107:9
Page   195—Psalm 116:13
Page   195—Psalm 116:17
Page   288—Psalm 139:7-12
Page   311—Psalm 147:1-20
Page   316—Psalm 23:1-6
Page   333—Psalm 92:1-15
Page   334—Psalm 133:1-3
Page   335—Psalm 141:1-10 KJV
Page   340—Psalm 105:15
Page   358—Psalm 27:1

Proverbs

Page   39—Proverbs 1:20-33
Page   42—Proverbs14:12
Page   59—Proverbs 29:18
Page   177—Proverbs 29:18
Page   307—Proverbs 5:19
Page   380—Proverbs 29:18

Ecclesiastes

Page   26—Ecclesiastes 5:4-6
Page   306—Ecclesiastes 11:1-10

Song of Solomon

Page   307—Song of Solomon 4:1-16

Isaiah

Page   40—Isaiah 11:1-9
Page   41—Isaiah 32:14-18
Page   42—Isaiah 40:10-14
Page   43—Isaiah 42:1-9
Page   44—Isaiah 44:1-8
Page   45—Isaiah 59:16-21
Page   46—Isaiah 61:1-6
Page   75—Isaiah 42:1-4

Page   176—Isaiah 28:13
Page   283—Isaiah 54:5
Page   285—Isaiah 53:3-5
Page   308—Isaiah 43:10-21
Page   309—Isaiah 55:1-13
Page   339—Isaiah 28:13
Page   340—Isaiah 28:13
Page   352—Isaiah 28:13
Page   361—Isaiah 6:1-13
Page   369—Isaiah 53:2
Page   371—Isaiah 28:1-6
Page   372—Isaiah 28:6-12
Page   373—Isaiah 28:13-19
Page   374—Isaiah 9:6,7

Jeremiah

Page   283—Jeremiah 3:20
Page   310—Jeremiah 2:4-19

Ezekiel

Page   48—Ezekiel 1:28-2:8
Page   48—Ezekiel 2:4
Page   49—Ezekiel 3:12-17
Page   49—Ezekiel 3:17
Page   50—Ezekiel 3:22-27
Page   51—Ezekiel 11:1,5,16,
             17,19,20
Page   51—Ezekiel 11:19
Page   52—Ezekiel 36:22-32
Page   53—Ezekiel 37:1-14
Page   54—Ezekiel 39:21-29
Page   55—Ezekiel 43:1-13
Page   148—Ezekiel 3:17

Daniel

Page   56—Daniel 4:1-37

Hosea

Page   311—Hosea 2:23

Joel

Page   57—Joel 2:21-32

Amos

Page 293—Amos 3:7,8

Micah

Page 58—Micah 3:8-12

Haggai

Page 59—Haggai 1:13,14
Page 59—Haggai 2:1-9
Page 59—Haggai 1:2

Zechariah

Page 60—Zechariah 4:6-10
Page 61—Zechariah 12:10-13
Page 61—Zechariah 14:8,9
Page 305—Zechariah 14:1-21

Matthew

Page 7—Matthew 3:11
Page 22—Matthew 14:30
Page 26—Matthew 5:37
Page 46—Matthew 3:11
Page 47—Matthew 12:31
Page 49—Matthew 16:24
Page 53—Matthew 24:29
Page 63—Matthew 19:26
Page 65—Matthew 19:26
Page 66—Matthew 1:18-25
Page 68—Matthew 3:1-12
Page 69—Matthew 3:13-17
Page 70—Matthew 4:1-11
Page 72—Matthew 16:24
Page 74—Matthew 6:6-13
Page 74—Matthew 7:7-12
Page 75—Matthew 12:9-21
Page 76—Matthew 12:22-32
Page 78—Matthew 10:16-20
Page 81—Matthew 22:41-46
Page 83—Matthew 5:1-13
Page 84—Matthew 3:11
Page 85—Matthew 7:11

Page 88—Matthew 7:14
Page 96—Matthew 28:16-20
Page 99—Matthew 18:21-35
Page 100—Matthew 11:18,19
Page 110—Matthew 9:17
Page 112—Matthew 25:21,23
Page 114—Matthew 24:9
Page 116—Matthew 7:21
Page 126—Matthew 5:11-12
Page 132—Matthew 7:15,16
Page 132—Matthew 25:31-46
Page 135—Matthew 25:1-13
Page 154—Matthew 18:22
Page 155—Matthew 15:10-20
Page 158—Matthew 25:21,23
Page 167—Matthew 5:27
Page 167—Matthew 19:8-9
Page 168—Matthew 25:14-30
Page 169—Matthew 25:14-30
Page 170—Matthew 12:34
Page 174—Matthew 17:20
Page 178—Matthew 24:24
Page 197—Matthew 16:24
Page 204—Matthew 5:12
Page 209—Matthew 25:21
Page 154—Matthew 25:40
Page 211—Matthew 18:22
Page 212—Matthew 11:28,29
Page 213—Matthew 21:13
Page 216—Matthew 25:40,45
Page 218—Matthew 13:1-9
Page 218—Matthew 18:23
Page 222—Matthew 13:33
Page 222—Matthew 16:6,11
Page 225—Matthew 27:45-54
Page 229—Matthew 5:6
Page 229—Matthew 3:11
Page 248—Matthew 16:24
Page 257—Matthew 24:36
Page 280—Matthew 11:19
Page 282—Matthew 25:40,44

Page 284—Matthew 5:10,11
Page 286—Matthew 18:23
Page 290—Matthew 24:45-51
Page 291—Matthew 5:10
Page 301—Matthew 7:1
Page 303—Matthew 5:8
Page 307—Matthew 25:1-13
Page 309—Matthew 5:6
Page 312—Matthew 11:7-15
Page 312—Matthew 11:11
Page 312—Matthew 23:11
Page 312—Matthew 11:12
Page 313—Matthew 11:16-30
Page 314—Matthew 24:36
Page 315—Matthew 7:7-12
Page 325—Matthew 6:20,21
Page 327—Matthew 13:3-9
Page 327—Matthew 13:18-23
Page 328—Matthew 25:31-46
Page 329—Matthew 6:20
Page 333—Matthew 13:36-43
Page 341—Matthew 17:1-9
Page 341—Matthew 5:8
Page 347—Matthew 9:18,19
Page 347—Matthew 9:23-26
Page 372—Matthew 5:6
Page 375—Matthew 2:1-12

Mark

Page   20—Mark 9:39
Page   27—Mark 3:29
Page   43—Mark 16:17,18
Page   44—Mark 10:14
Page   44—Mark 16:17
Page   45—Mark 16:17
Page   68—Mark 1:1-8
Page   69—Mark 1:9-11
Page   70—Mark 1:12,13
Page   76—Mark 16:17
Page   77—Mark 3:20-30
Page   79—Mark 13:9-13

Page   82—Mark12:35-40
Page   89—Mark 7:21-23
Page   97—Mark 16:15-20
Page 103—Mark 16:17
Page 110—Mark 2:22
Page 130—Mark 16:17,18
Page 158—Mark16:17,18
Page 159—Mark 12:44
Page 161—Mark 16:17,18
Page 179—Mark 16:17
Page 210—Mark 4:39
Page 216—Mark 9:35
Page 224—Mark 16:17,18
Page 227—Mark 16:17
Page 243—Mark 11:17
Page 268—Mark 16:17,18
Page 272—Mark 16:17,18
Page 272—Mark 3:28,29
Page 280—Mark 1:1-11
Page 284—Mark 16:15
Page 296—Mark 16:17,18
Page 319—Mark 16:17,18
Page 322—Mark 13:11
Page 341—Mark 9:1-9
Page 343—Mark 16:17,18
Page 346—Mark 7:31-37
Page 346—Mark 16:17,18
Page 349—Mark 16:17,18
Page 364—Mark 16:17
Page 377—Mark 8:22-26
Page 377—Mark 16:17,18

Luke

Page   21—Luke 6:28
Page   23—Luke 7:7-8
Page   40—Luke 2:40
Page   62—Luke 1:5-17
Page   63—Luke 1:26-38
Page   64—Luke 1:39-56
Page   65—Luke 1:18-23
Page   65—Luke 1:57-80

Page   67—Luke 2:22-35
Page   68—Luke 3:15-18
Page   69—Luke 3:21,22
Page   70—Luke 4:1-13
Page   71—Luke 4:14,15
Page   72—Luke 4:16-28
Page   73—Luke 10:21-24
Page   73—Luke 10:18
Page   74—Luke 11:1-13
Page   76—Luke 9:1
Page   76—Luke 10:17
Page   80—Luke 12:8-12
Page   95—Luke 23:44-49
Page   98—Luke 24:36-49
Page   110—Luke 5:37-39
Page   126—Luke 10:10,11
Page   126—Luke 21:12
Page   138—Luke 16:16
Page   155—Luke16:16
Page   214—Luke 17:10
Page   220—Luke10:25-37
Page   221—Luke 11:33-36
Page   221—Luke 11:13
Page   222—Luke 17:21
Page   223—Luke 16:1-13
Page   224—Luke 17:20,21
Page   227—Luke 11:14-28
Page   227—Luke 11:13
Page   281—Luke 4:1-13
Page   283—Luke 10:27
Page   288—Luke 23:43
Page   288—Luke 16:19-31
Page   312—Luke 3:16
Page   314—Luke 17:22-37
Page   315—Luke 11:1-13
Page   319—Luke 7:11-17
Page   325—Luke 12:13-21
Page   326—Luke 17:5-10
Page   329—Luke 16:19-31
Page   332—Luke 6:38
Page   338—Luke 7:36-50

Page   340—Luke 22:36
Page   342—Luke 12:41-48
Page   343—Luke 12:49-56
Page   345—Luke 13:10-17
Page   376—Luke 8:43-48
Page   378—Luke 5:17-26

John

Page   7—John 3:16
Page   8—John 14:26
Page   9—John 3:3
Page   9—John 4:23
Page   12—John 3:30
Page   24—John 7:24
Page   15—John1:1-3
Page   32—John 3:34
Page   32—John 7:38
Page   34—John 3:5
Page   37—John 14:9
Page   43—John3:16
Page   43—John 14:12
Page   48—John 16:13
Page   52—John 3:5
Page   54—John 14:9
Page   61—John 19:37
Page   61—John 7:38
Page   66—John 1:14
Page   69—John 1:29-34
Page   84—John 3:1-8
Page   85—John 3:31-36
Page   86—John 4:4-15
Page   87—John 4:16-26
Page   88—John 6:52-69
Page   88—John 6:56
Page   89—John 7:37-52
Page   89—John 7:37
Page   90—John 14:12-24
Page   91—John 14:25-31
Page   92—John 15:26-16:4
Page   93—John 16:4-11
Page   94—John 16:5-15

Spirit-Led Days

Page   99—John 20:19-23
Page   99—John 19:30
Page 132—John 10:11
Page 137—John 15:17
Page 154—John 8:10,11
Page 161—John 14:12
Page 193—John 5:39
Page 208—John 15:7
Page 212—John 8:2-11
Page 214—John 2:5
Page 216—John 13:5
Page 219—John 16:13-15
Page 224—John 3:7-8
Page 226—John 19:31-37
Page 226—John 19:36
Page 226—John 7:38,39
Page 228—John 13:1-17
Page 229—John 2:1-11
Page 245—John 14:27
Page 245—John 14:6
Page 246—John 10:10
Page 288—John 11:25
Page 300—John 3:16
Page 304—John 19:30
Page 307—John 15:1-5
Page 308—John 14:9
Page 309—John 6:35
Page 310—John 7:37,38
Page 312—John 3:30
Page 316—John 10:11
Page 316—John 10:14
Page 316—John 14:2,3
Page 319—John 6:63
Page 319—John 11:25
Page 320—John 16:14,15
Page 326—John 16:13-15
Page 340—John 18:1-11
Page 344—John 9:1-41
Page 347—John 11:25
Page 349—John 5:1-17
Page 349—John 11:17-44,53

Page 349—John 5:21
Page 362—John 4:24
Page 368—John 4:14
Page 375—John 11:25

Acts

Page   9 —Acts 1:8
Page 12—Acts 19:2
Page 24—Acts 2:38
Page 34—Acts1:8
Page 40—Acts 1:8
Page 44—Acts 2:38
Page 45—Acts 2:4
Page 54—Acts 2:4
Page 56—Acts 2:17
Page 57—Acts 2:16-21
Page 100—Acts 1:1-5
Page 101—Acts 1:6-11
Page 102—Acts 1:15-26
Page 103—Acts 2:1-13
Page 103—Acts 11:16
Page 103—Acts 15:8
Page 104—Acts 2:14-37
Page 105—Acts 2:14-47
Page 106—Acts 3:6-8
Page 106—Acts 4:1-22
Page 107—Acts 4:23-35
Page 107—Acts 4:25
Page 108—Acts 5:1-15
Page 109—Acts 5:27-42
Page 111—Acts 6:1-7
Page 112—Acts 6:1-15
Page 113—Acts 7:1-3
Page 113—Acts 7:42-53
Page 114—Acts 7:54-8:3
Page 115—Acts 8:4-8
Page 115—Acts 8:14-17
Page 116—Acts 8:9-13
Page 116—Acts 8:18-24
Page 116—Acts 8:23

Page 117—Acts 8:26-40
Page 118—Acts 9:1-19
Page 119—Acts 9:26-31
Page 120—Acts 10:9-23
Page 121—Acts 10:24-48
Page 122—Acts 11:1-18
Page 123—Acts 11:19-30
Page 124—Acts 13:1-5
Page 125—Acts 13:4-13
Page 126—Acts 13:44-52
Page 127—Acts 15:1-12
Page 127—Acts 2:4
Page 128—Acts 15:22-29
Page 129—Acts 16:6-10
Page 130—Acts 19:1-10
Page 131—Acts 20:16-27
Page 131—Acts 9:15-16
Page 132—Acts 20:28-38
Page 132—Acts 20:35
Page 133—Acts 21:1-14
Page 134—Acts 28:16-31
Page 141—Acts 2
Page 141—Acts 8:16
Page 141—Acts 19
Page 155—Acts 15:29
Page 159—Acts 10
Page 167—Acts 9:17
Page 197—Acts 17:6
Page 202—Acts 2:4
Page 217—Acts 4:33
Page 224—Acts 1:8
Page 238—Acts 21:11-14
Page 241—Acts 5:20
Page 261—Acts 2:4
Page 261—Acts 15:8
Page 263—Acts 1:8
Page 266—Acts 1:16
Page 292—Acts 1:8
Page 304—Acts 2:2
Page 313—Acts 2:15
Page 318—Acts 2:17

Page 321—Acts 18:5-17
Page 322—Acts 26:19-32
Page 335—Acts 2:4
Page 363—Acts 1:8
Page 372—Acts 2:4
Page 378—Acts 1:8
Page 379—Acts 16:1-6
Page 380—Acts 16:9-15
Page 380—Acts 2:17

Romans

Page   8 —Romans 8:29
Page   9 —Romans 12:1,2
Page   9 —Romans 12:6-8
Page   16—Romans 6:23
Page   29—Romans 3:23
Page   30—Romans 11:29
Page   42—Romans 8:28
Page 110—Romans 12:6-8
Page 112—Romans 12:11
Page 136—Romans 2:23-29
Page 137—Romans 5:1-11
Page 138—Romans 7:1-6
Page 138—Romans 3:10
Page 139—Romans 7:13-25
Page 140—Romans 8:1-8
Page 141—Romans 8:9-11
Page 142—Romans 8:12-17
Page 143—Romans 8:18-25
Page 144—Romans 8:26-30
Page 144—Romans 8:28
Page 145—Romans 9:1-2
Page 145—Romans 9:19-32
Page 146—Romans 11:16-36
Page 146—Romans 11:26
Page 147—Romans 12:1-8
Page 148—Romans 12:1-8
Page 149—Romans 12:1-8
Page 150—Romans 12:1-8
Page 151—Romans 12:1-8
Page 152—Romans 12:1-8

Page 153—Romans 12:1-8
Page 154—Romans 12:1-8
Page 155—Romans 14:4-23
Page 156—Romans 15:1-13
Page 157—Romans 15:14-17
Page 158—Romans 15:17-21
Page 159—Romans 15:22-29
Page 160—Romans 15:30-32
Page 169—Romans 12:6-8
Page 177—Romans 12
Page 181—Romans 11:29
Page 200—Romans 10:17
Page 208—Romans 5:5
Page 209—Romans 14:17
Page 211—Romans 2:4
Page 213—Romans 15:14
Page 225—Romans 8:11
Page 236—Romans 12:6-8
Page 242—Romans 12:2
Page 247—Romans 8:28
Page 249—Romans 12:2
Page 250—Romans 2:29
Page 261—Romans 12:6-8
Page 264—Romans 8:9
Page 279—Romans 12:6-8
Page 288—Romans 8:9,11
Page 290—Romans 12:6-8
Page 293—Romans 12:6
Page 297—Romans 1:29-31
Page 299—Romans 5:5
Page 304—Romans 8:28
Page 330—Romans 1:8-17
Page 330—Romans 12:6-8
Page 347—Romans 8:11
Page 349—Romans 8:11
Page 349—Romans 12:6-8
Page 363—Romans 8:11
Page 371—Romans 6:23
Page 375—Romans 8:11

1 Corinthians

Page   9—1 Corinthians 12:1-11
Page 10—1 Corinthians 13:4-8
Page 15—1 Corinthians 2:14
Page 34—1 Corinthians 12:14
Page 39—1 Corinthians 12:8
Page 44—1 Corinthians 12:10
Page 53—1 Corinthians 15:51-54
Page 55—1 Corinthians 3:16-17
Page 58—1 Corinthians 12:10
Page 81—1 Corinthians 2:14
Page 100—1 Corinthians 1:25
Page 103—1 Corinthians 12:10
Page 110—1 Corinthians 12:8-11
Page 118—1 Corinthians 14:18
Page 147—1 Corinthians 12:11
Page 147—1 Corinthians 12:11
Page 158—1 Corinthians 2:4,5
Page 161—1 Corinthians 2:1-5
Page 162—1 Corinthians 2:6-12
Page 163—1 Corinthians 2:14-16
Page 163—1 Corinthians 12:4-11
Page 164—1 Corinthians 3:1-15
Page 165—1 Corinthians 3:16-23
Page 166—1 Corinthians 6:9-20
Page 167—1 Corinthians 7:1-40
Page 167—1 Corinthians 9:5
Page 167—1 Corinthians 7:24-26
Page 169—1 Corinthians 12:4-10
Page 169—1 Corinthians 13:10
Page 170—1 Corinthians 12:1-4
Page 171—1 Corinthians 12:4-7
Page 172—1 Corinthians 12:7
Page 173—1 Corinthians 12:8
Page 174—1 Corinthians 12:9
Page 175—1 Corinthians 12:9
Page 176—1 Corinthians 12:10
Page 177—1 Corinthians 12:10
Page 177—1 Corinthians 12
Page 177—1 Corinthians 14:3

Page 177—1 Corinthians 4:6
Page 178—1 Corinthians 12:10
Page 179—1 Corinthians 12:10
Page 180—1 Corinthians 12:10
Page 181—1 Corinthians 12:4-11
Page 182—1 Corinthians 12:12-26
Page 183—1 Corinthians 12:27-31
Page 184—1 Corinthians 12:31-
13:13
Page 184—1 Corinthians 14:1-5
Page 185—1 Corinthians 14:1-25
Page 186—1 Corinthians 14:1-25
Page 186—1 Corinthians 4:6
Page 187—1 Corinthians 14:13-19
Page 188—1 Corinthians 14:26-40
Page 189—1 Corinthians 14:37-40
Page 189—1 Corinthians 4:6
Page 190—1 Corinthians 15:35-49
Page 192—1 Corinthians 2:4,5
Page 202—1 Corinthians 14:21
Page 208—1 Corinthians 13:4-7
Page 216—1 Corinthians 7:9
Page 216—1 Corinthians 9:25
Page 236—1 Corinthians 12:4-11
Page 245—1 Corinthians 1:30
Page 261—1 Corinthians 14:18
Page 261—1 Corinthians 12:8-10
Page 268—1 Corinthians 12:8-11
Page 277—1 Corinthians 11:23-26
Page 278—1 Corinthians 11:27-34
Page 279—1 Corinthians 7:1-17
Page 279—1 Corinthians 12:8-10
Page 279—1 Corinthians 2:4,5
Page 281—1 Corinthians 10-13
Page 286—1 Corinthians 13:4-8
Page 290—1 Corinthians 12:4-11
Page 293—1 Corinthians 12:10
Page 301—1 Corinthians 14:2-4
Page 303—1 Corinthians 12:10
Page 304—1 Corinthians 10:13

Page 311—1 Corinthians 1:27,28
Page 317—1 Corinthians 2:14
Page 324—1 Corinthians 2:4,5
Page 330—1 Corinthians 12:8-10
Page 330—1 Corinthians 2:4,5
Page 336—1 Corinthians 9:1-27
Page 336—1 Corinthians 9:11
Page 337—1 Corinthians 10:1-33
Page 339—1 Corinthians 3:16,17
Page 342—1 Corinthians 10:1-22
Page 349—1 Corinthians 12:8-10
Page 351—1 Corinthians 14:2
Page 354—1 Corinthians 10:13
Page 361—1 Corinthians 14:2,15
Page 366—1 Corinthians 14:5
Page 366—1 Corinthians 14:1
Page 366—1 Corinthians 14:3
Page 372—1 Corinthians 14:22
Page 373—1 Corinthians 12:10
Page 373—1 Corinthians 2:4,5

2 Corinthians

Page 3—2 Corinthians 5:8
Page 31—2 Corinthians 10:4
Page 69—2 Corinthians 5:21
Page 184—2 Corinthians 11:5
Page 191—2 Corinthians 1:15-24
Page 192—2 Corinthians 3:1-6
Page 193—2 Corinthians 3:4-6
Page 194—2 Corinthians 3:7-18
Page 195—2 Corinthians 4:13-18
Page 195—2 Timothy 1:12
Page 198—2 Corinthians 11:1-15
Page 199—2 Corinthians 13:5-14
Page 245—2 Corinthians 10:3,4
Page 260—2 Corinthians 11:14
Page 307—2 Corinthians 5:17
Page 323—2 Corinthians 12:1-10
Page 324—2 Corinthians 12:11-21
Page 340—2 Corinthians 10:4

Page 350—2 Corinthians 3:3
Page 358—2 Corinthians 12:9
Page 369—2 Corinthians 11:14

Galatians

Page 110—Galatians 5:22,23
Page 138—Galatians 6:2
Page 142—Galatians 4:5
Page 167—Galatians 5:23
Page 200—Galatians 3:1,2
Page 201—Galatians 3:3,4
Page 202—Galatians 3:5-9
Page 203—Galatians 4:1-11
Page 204—Galatians 4:21-31
Page 205—Galatians 5:1-12
Page 206—Galatians 5:13-21
Page 207—Galatians 5:22-26
Page 208—Galatians 5:22,23
Page 209—Galatians 5:22,23
Page 210—Galatians 5:22,23
Page 211—Galatians 5:22,23
Page 212—Galatians 5:22,23
Page 213—Galatians 5:22,23
Page 214—Galatians 5:22,23
Page 215—Galatians 5:22,23
Page 216—Galatians 5:22,23
Page 217—Galatians 5:25-6:6
Page 217—Galatians 6:2
Page 218—Galatians 6:7-18
Page 245—Galatians 2:16
Page 299—Galatians 5:22
Page 308—Galatians 4:3
Page 331—Galatians 5:22-6:10
Page 349—Galatians 1:1

Ephesians

Page 130—Ephesians 1:13
Page 230—Ephesians 1:1-14
Page 231—Ephesians 1:15-23
Page 232—Ephesians 2:11-22
Page 233—Ephesians 3:1-13

Page 234—Ephesians 3:14-21
Page 235—Ephesians 4:1-7
Page 236—Ephesians 4:8-16
Page 237—Ephesians 4:11-16
Page 238—Ephesians 4:11-16
Page 239—Ephesians 4:11-16
Page 240—Ephesians 4:11-16
Page 241—Ephesians 4:11-16
Page 242—Ephesians 4:17-24
Page 243—Ephesians 4:25-5:1
Page 244—Ephesians 5:3-20
Page 245—Ephesians 6:10-17
Page 246—Ephesians 6:18-24
Page 303—Ephesians 6:10-18
Page 333—Ephesians 5:18

Philippians

Page 17—Philippians 4:11
Page 38—Philippians 4:7
Page 59—Philippians 4:19
Page 234—Philippians 3:10
Page 245—Philippians 4:13
Page 247—Philippians 1:12-21
Page 248—Philippians 1:27-30
Page 249—Philippians 2:1-11
Page 250—Philippians 3:1-16

Colossians

Page 37—Colossians 1:15
Page 41—Colossians 3:15
Page 54—Colossians 1:15
Page 210—Colossians 3:15
Page 251—Colossians 1:3-13
Page 252—Colossians 2:1-19

1 Thessalonians

Page 187—1 Thessalonians 5:17
Page 245—1 Thessalonians 5:8
Page 253—1 Thessalonians 1:1-5
Page 254—1 Thessalonians 1:6-10
Page 255—1 Thessalonians 4:1-12
Page 256—1 Thessalonians 5:12-28

2 Thessalonians

Page 257—2 Thessalonians 2:1-13
Page 258—2 Thessalonians 2:13-17

1 Timothy

Page 259—1 Timothy 3:1-16
Page 260—1 Timothy 4:1-10
Page 261—1 Timothy 4:11-13

2 Timothy

Page   86—2 Timothy 1:7
Page   91—2 Timothy 2:15-21
Page 150—2 Timothy 2:15
Page 214—2 Timothy 1:12
Page 241—2 Timothy 2:15
Page 262—2 Timothy 1:1-6
Page 263—2 Timothy 1:7-10
Page 264—2 Timothy 1:12-18
Page 265—2 Timothy 3:1-13
Page 266—2 Timothy 3:14-4:5
Page 335—2 Timothy 3:16

Titus

Page 267—Titus 3:1-11

Hebrews

Page   3—Hebrews 13:5
Page   10—Hebrews 13:5
Page   16—Hebrews 13:5
Page   27—Hebrews 6:4-6
Page   36—Hebrews 13:4
Page   45—Hebrews 13:5
Page 157—Hebrews 5:5
Page 157—Hebrews 10:12
Page 193—Hebrews 8:7,13
Page 213—Hebrews 12:6
Page 225—Hebrews 9:15
Page 245—Hebrews 4:12,13
Page 268—Hebrews 2:1-9
Page 269—Hebrews 2:10-3:6
Page 270—Hebrews 3:7-19
Page 271—Hebrews 4:11-16
Page 272—Hebrews 6:1-12
Page 273—Hebrews 9:1-15
Page 273—Hebrews 10:12
Page 274—Hebrews 9:11-28
Page 275—Hebrews 10:10-25
Page 276—Hebrews 10:26-39
Page 352—Hebrews 4:12,13
Page 375—Hebrews 7-27
Page 375—Hebrews 5:15

James

Page   39—James 1:5
Page 172—James 1:5
Page 282—James 2:14-26
Page 283—James 4:1-10
Page 320—James 5:13-15
Page 329—James 5:3
Page 335—James 3:6
Page 359—James 5:2,3

1 Peter

Page   9 —1 Peter 1:2
Page   95—1 Peter 3:18-20
Page 157—1 Peter 2:9
Page 209—1 Peter 1:6-8
Page 260—1 Peter5:8
Page 284—1 Peter 1:1-9
Page 285—1 Peter 1:10-21
Page 286—1 Peter 1:22-2:3
Page 287—1 Peter 2:4-12
Page 288—1 Peter 3:14-20
Page 288—1 Peter 4:6
Page 289—1 Peter 3:20-4:6
Page 290—1 Peter 4:7-11
Page 291—1 Peter 4:12-19
Page 342—1 Peter 4:19

2 Peter

Page   58—2 Peter 1:20
Page   133—2 Peter 1:20
Page   186—2 Peter 1:20
Page   238—2 Peter 1:20,21
Page   288—2 Peter 2:4
Page   292—2 Peter 1:1-11
Page   293—2 Peter 1:16-2:11
Page   293—2 Peter 1:20,21
Page   294—2 Peter 3:8-18

1 John

Page   295—1 John 2:18-23
Page   296—1 John 2:24-3:9
Page   297—1 John 3:10-24
Page   298—1 John 4:1-6
Page   299—1 John 4:7-21
Page   300—1 John 5:1-13

Jude

Page   288—Jude 6
Page   301—Jude 1-19

Revelation

Page   8—Revelation 2:7,11,17,
              26, 29
Page   8—Revelation 3:5,12,21
Page   8—Revelation 3:6,13,22
Page   10—Revelation 2-3
Page   55—Revelation 21:22
Page   66—Revelation 12:11
Page   92—Revelation 12:11
Page   156—Revelation 21:2
Page   156—Revelation 7:9
Page   197—Revelation 2:10
Page   221—Revelation 2:4,5
Page   229—Revelation 19:9
Page   234—Revelation 2:4
Page   242—Revelation 7:14

Page   307—Revelation 7:13,14
Page   307—Revelation 7:9
Page   308—Revelation 21:5
Page   350—Revelation 1:1-6
Page   351—Revelation 1:7-11
Page   352—Revelation 1:12-20
Page   353—Revelation 2:1-7
Page   354—Revelation 2:8-11
Page   355—Revelation 2:12-17
Page   356—Revelation 2:18-29
Page   357—Revelation 3:1-6
Page   358—Revelation 3:7-13
Page   359—Revelation 3:14-22
Page   360—Revelation 2:7,11,29
Page   360—Revelation 3:6,13,22
Page   361—Revelation 4:1-11
Page   362—Revelation 4:5
Page   363—Revelation 11:1-14
Page   364—Revelation 14:9-13
Page   364—Revelation 13
Page   364—Revelation 7:4
Page   365—Revelation 17:1-18
Page   366—Revelation 19:1-10
Page   367—Revelation 21:1-27
Page   368—Revelation 22:1-5
Page   369—Revelation 22:6-14
Page   370—Revelation 22:16-21
Page   370—Revelation 20:12
Page   288—Revelation 1:18
Page   305—Revelation 21:23
Page   305—Revelation 22:10
Page   305—Revelation 16:16

Books, Audio Cassettes, and Videos
by Rev. Gordon Williams

Prices include taxes, shipping and handling.

"Like a Rushing, Mighty Wind"
by Rev. Gordon Williams with Diane Roblin Lee
Book: $20.00   Quantity _____ Total _____

"The Testimony of Gordon Williams"
Making Yourself Available to Jesus Christ
Video: $20.00   Quantity _____ Total _____
Audio Cassette: $10.00   Quantity _____ Total _____

"The Baptism & Gifts of the Holy Spirit"
Using the Spiritual Gifts Skillfully
Video: $20.00   Quantity _____ Total _____
Audio Cassette: $10.00   Quantity _____ Total _____

"From Caterpillar to Butterfly"
The Key to Christian Maturity
Video: $20.00   Quantity _____ Total _____
Audio Cassette: $10.00   Quantity _____ Total _____

"Clock Watchers Incorporated"
Ministry for End Times
Book: $5.00   Quantity _____ Total _____

"The Answer" by Lifeline Music Ministry
featuring Margaret Williams
Music Cassette: $15.00   Quantity _____ Total _____
Music CD: $10.00   Quantity _____ Total _____

"Spirit-led Days" Daily Devotional
by Rev. Gordon Williams with Diane Roblin Lee
Book: $23.95   Quantity _____ Total _____

Please send to: **TOTAL** _____

Gordon Williams Evangelistic Association or G.W.E.A.
11 Bayberry Rd., Orangeville, ON, Canada L9V 1A1

Name	E-mail
Address	Phone
City	Prov./State
Country	Postal/ZIP

To book evangelistic meetings and crusades,
please phone, fax or e-mail:

The Gordon Williams Evangelistic Association Office:

Phone 519-940-9197
Fax   519-940-8365

11 Bayberry Road
Orangeville, Ontario
Canada L9V 1A1

website gordwilliams.com

e-mail gordwea@rogers.com